POWER WHERE IS IT?

with best wishes

[signature]

Sept 23, 2011

October 27, 2011

Diana —

My good friend Donald
Savoie (maybe you met him
at the BMO dinner) wrote this.
He is a Fellow of the RSC.

Thanks for the power you
put into your work at BMO.

Sandra Irving

DONALD J. SAVOIE

POWER WHERE IS IT?

McGill-Queen's University Press
Montreal & Kingston | London | Ithaca

Legal deposit third quarter 2010
Bibliothèque nationale du Québec

Printed in Canada on acid-free paper that is 100% ancient
forest free (100% post-consumer recycled), processed
chlorine free

This book has been published with the help of a grant
from the Université de Moncton.

McGill-Queen's University Press acknowledges the
support of the Canada Council for the Arts for our
publishing program. We also acknowledge the financial
support of the Government of Canada through the Book
Publishing Industry Development Program (BPIDP) for
our publishing activities.

Library and Archives Canada Cataloguing in Publication

Savoie, Donald J., 1947–
Power : where is it? / Donald J. Savoie.

Includes bibliographical references and index.
ISBN 978-0-7735-3726-2 (bnd)
ISBN 978-0-7735-3758-3 (pbk)

1. Power (Social sciences) – Canada.   2. Canada – Politics
and government – 21st century. I. Title.

HN49.P6P698 2010   303.3'30971   C2010-900646-1

Set in 10/13 Sabon with Frutiger
Book design & typesetting by Garet Markvoort

To all my students, past and present

CONTENTS

PREFACE

This book was born of a strong desire to understand why our political and administrative institutions are in a state of disrepair. It seems clear to me that they, along with the values governing political and economic life in Canada – and, indeed, in much of the Anglo-American world – have lost their vitality. I decided to seek answers by looking at those who hold or aspire to power and influence, whether political, bureaucratic, or economic. As a result, this study examines institutions, organizations, globalization, relations between the public and private sectors, the media, the public service, and a multitude of other policy actors. We need to understand their various roles if we are to see where power is located today.

The result is a book that is longer than I initially envisaged. Readers may become impatient with the material, but I hope that they will persevere. The state of representative democracy matters to all of us, and citizens need to be aware that it is in danger of being seriously eroded. Those with power see no problem: they are well served by the way things are.

My hope is that this book will shed some light on how the current situation came about and why. More particularly, I hope that it will prompt citizens to take a strong and informed interest in the state of their political and administrative institutions and organizations.

All authors are greatly in debt to colleagues, friends, and those who have travelled the territory before them. I acknowledge many such intellectual debts in the endnotes. Others, however, are not so formally acknowledged.

I have always benefited greatly from conversations with current and former senior government officials, at both the elected and appointed levels. This work is not different from my earlier books in that it would not have been possible without their assistance and insights. I also want to thank the two referees who reviewed the study for McGill-Queen's University Press, when it was in manuscript form, for their observations and suggestions.

I owe a special thank-you to my wife Linda for putting up with my insatiable appetite for work, to my longtime assistant Ginette Benoit for her continued support and good cheer in the face of my constant demands, to Joan Harcourt for her sharp mind and her ability to make my sentences read better, and to Carlotta Lemieux for her fine work in editing the manuscript. But all the defects of this book are mine.

Donald J. Savoie
Université de Moncton

POWER WHERE IS IT?

INTRODUCTION

Bertrand Russell once argued that power was the "fundamental concept" in social science in the same sense that "energy is the fundamental concept in physics." He added that much like energy, power takes various forms, including wealth, the military, civil authority, and influence on opinion.[1] But unlike energy, power can be created and destroyed. Like energy, however, it can move from place to place and take different forms. Indeed, political history is all about power – who held it and how it was employed. Cato, the Roman politician, referred to power having different forms when he observed, "When Cicero speaks, Romans marvel; when Caesar speaks, Romans march." Power in Cato's time was fairly straightforward, and one did not need to look very far to see where it was located. A handful of individuals, institutions, and organizations held power in politics, commerce, and the military.

Today, things are vastly different. How organizations go about acquiring power differs from how individuals go about it, and in this book we examine power and its corollary – responsibility – from different perspectives in an attempt to locate where it now resides. Thus, politics and politicians, bureaucrats, public administration, globalization, the business community, organizational models, centralization, decentralization, the role of the media, and the impact of new means of communications will all be invoked. When I told a colleague of my plans for this book, he responded, "You have my best wishes, but it is very unlikely that you will be able to pull it off."[2]

To be sure, there are significant risks and drawbacks in pursuing such a highly ambitious agenda. I cannot possibly satisfy the specialists of the many issues raised in this book. Power is not only one of the core concepts in political science, it is also one of the most controversial.[3] Even a lifetime is not long enough to read all that has been written about it. The topic is of strong interest to philosophers, historians, political scientists, sociologists, economists, and those pursuing many other disciplines. But the risk is worthwhile if we are to make progress in mapping out where power and responsibility now reside. I will consider it a success if I can interest more students in the social sciences and humanities to tackle the question. The purpose of this book, then, is to open the way to further empirical and theoretical work on what I now consider to be the single most important question confronting representative democracy.

Things have changed considerably since 1938 when Russell's book was first published. Power has become more fluid and considerably more difficult to locate. Its location – notably though not exclusively in political power – is now anything but clear. Elections do not always decide the question; the shaping of public policies and the delivery of public services are no longer just the product of democratically legitimized action by governments.[4] A good number of citizens in Western democracies understand this and, having little belief that they can have any influence, do not think it worthwhile to vote.[5] "Power to the people," citizens' participation, and the merits of e-democracy may make for fine political speeches, but they do not appear to have much traction when it comes to creating public policy, making government decisions, or convincing citizens that they can play a meaningful role in the process or even hold governments to account. If one is to judge by voter turnout, one might conclude that citizens throughout the Western world no longer believe that they have any real influence over their governments and that they are progressively losing interest in helping to decide who should be elected to political office. What they may not realize is that politicians also have increasingly limited control.[6]

Constitutions no longer decide where political power resides to the extent that they once did. Given the demands and complexities of modern government, it is no longer possible, for example, for either of the senior orders of government in a federation to operate in a hermetically sealed jurisdiction. Accordingly, for the last thirty years at least, governments have devised numerous administrative instruments and processes to sidestep constitutional provisions.[7] The need to respond to rapidly changing socio-economic circumstances and fast-emerging political developments has pushed them to search for flexibility in planning new initiatives and delivering public services. Most statutes are now broadly worded in order to provide greater flexibility for decision makers. To be sure, flexibility has its advantages, but it also makes it more difficult to locate precisely where political power and administrative authority lie.

Whether in North America or Europe, power and responsibility flow effortlessly between governments, between departments within governments, and, to a certain extent, between the public and private sectors. The European Community, the North American Free Trade Agreement (NAFTA), and collaborative federalism have mingled responsibilities to the point where it has become very difficult even for politicians to determine who is responsible for what in government. One can only imagine what it must be like for the voters. In addition, there is a wealth of analyses suggesting that political power has become highly dispersed and that non-state or non-government actors are increasingly competing with state actors as sources of power.[8]

We know that in recent times presidents and prime ministers have sought to concentrate political power in their own hands or their own offices;[9] former Canadian prime minister Jean Chrétien went to the heart of the matter when he wrote, "Politics is about wanting power, getting it, exercising it and keeping it."[10] There is no question that today considerable political power resides in the office of the Canadian or British prime minister or in the office of the president of the United States.[11] But this hardly tells the whole story. Indeed, presidents and prime ministers may well have decided to shift more power to their own offices precisely because of the amorphous nature of political power. Viewed from their perspective, power appears increasingly fragmented, hence the need to centralize whatever "loose" political power is available in their hands in order to get things done.

Max Weber had a straightforward way of establishing and locating power: by looking at "the probability that a command with a given specific content will be obeyed by a group of persons."[12] Caesar knew that his commands would be obeyed, but Cicero was much less certain about his. Caesar had power while Cicero, more often than not, had influence. Those with power can issue a command, make a decision, and expect that they will be obeyed. Influence, meanwhile, is the ability to change the behaviour or attitude of others without the exertion of force or hierarchical command and control. Put differently, power is the ability to make things happen, while influence is the ability to advise those who have power.[13] This book makes the case that institutions and organizations have lost power to individuals and that, as a result, citizens are less and less able to locate where power lies.

Power requires two parts to work: someone or some body to give a command and someone or some body with an obligation, a duty, or desire to obey. Many of us were brought up in the belief that governments operating within defined geographical borders (the nation-state, a province, or a municipality) provided the locus of authority. Borders and boundaries dividing the responsibilities of institutions and government departments, together with hierarchy, serve many purposes. They certainly make it easy to identify who has political and administrative power and who assigns responsibility. They establish who has legitimate access to certain decision-making arenas, who is responsible for what, who gives a command, and who obeys.

Borders and boundaries also enable those at senior levels to exercise control and to hold subordinates to account for their decisions and activities. Government agencies and departments have historically been organized in a defined hierarchy of offices with clear lines of authority. John Stuart Mill argued more than 125 years ago in his *Representative Government* that responsibility is best provided and the work best done if all the functions of a similar subject "be allocated to single departments."[14] This notion has guided the development of the machinery of government in Anglo-American democracies since the nineteenth century. It also informs Weber's claim that political authority requires the probability that a specific command will be obeyed.

Parts of the machinery of government, however, have witnessed far-reaching changes in recent years, and the traditional and fundamental aspects of the machinery are being challenged as never before. Public policy issues have become complex and interconnected, and it is now clear that no single government department has all the necessary policy tools and program instruments to deal with them. In short, the great majority of public policy issues no longer respect geographical borders, let alone organizational boundaries, and as a result both policy making and decision making in government have become horizontal, consultative, and porous. Accordingly, to have any chance of success, policy prescriptions need to be the product of many hands, which suggests that power should also now reside in many hands.

Governments everywhere have identified new policy processes and a new vocabulary: "horizontal" government in Canada, "joined-up" government in Britain, "whole-of-government" in Australia, and "collaborative" government in the United States. Yet government officials, at least those at the centre, still operate with the same machinery and with some of the same organizational principles that were in place forty years ago.[15] As a result, government officials have been left to try "this or that" to see what works; or, in the words of a former British cabinet secretary, "Actively promoting the philosophy of what matters is what works."[16] What works may hold considerable appeal for meeting the circumstances and demands of the day and producing timely decisions. However, it does very little to clarify who wields political or administrative power.

Looking to Globalization

Much has already been written about the impact of globalization on nation-states. Suffice it to note here that it has deeply affected our traditional understanding of power, authority, legitimacy, and sovereignty. There is now wide agreement that it has given rise to new power relationships.[17]

Susan Strange writes that the exercise of power is no longer limited to officials of the state and, further, that institutions other than those of the state now wield considerable power. She argues that political power is increasingly exercised by both the market and transnational institutions.[18] Pierre Pettigrew, Canada's former minister of foreign affairs, explains that globalization means that "corporations can decide to carry out a given industrial function in a given geographic region for economic reasons, notwithstanding any political considerations." He adds, "Globalization ignores political borders and merges economic spaces. And thus, on the margin of the state's areas of responsibility, there emerges a new anonymous and stateless power, a power that is at once intoxicating and fearsome. In this time of globalization, then, the vertical power of the state is gradually replaced with the horizontal power of the marketplace."[19] None of this, he says, springs from decisions that were made in Cabinet.[20] Peter Harder, a highly respected former senior official in the Government of Canada, maintains that today "economic space is greater than political space."[21] If this is so, how can one identify who has power or assigned responsibility?

Globalization, perhaps more than any other development, has muddied the location of power and, further, has allowed those with power to shift responsibility away from their decisions. Governments in many jurisdictions have been privatizing state enterprises, deregulating economic sectors, and lowering tariffs and taxes. Political leaders explain that the competitive nature of the global economy is forcing their hand. They argue that the United States, Britain, China, Brussels, or international competition – not domestic competition – made them do it; either they follow the lead, they insist, or their country will pay a steep economic price. Not only have nation-states withdrawn to some extent from managing national economies, but national governments have had to gear a good part of their machinery to an international policy agenda. New regional, cross-border, and international collaborative arrangements have been established. These, too, point to shared responsibility, if only because power and influence increasingly have to be shared among nation-states if national economies are to flourish.

Thomas Friedman's observation that in today's economy everyone is connected, but no one is in control, appears to resonate more and more.[22] National markets can no longer isolate themselves from developments outside their borders. Subprime mortgage losses in the United States in the summer of 2007 sent shock waves everywhere. The very survival of Northern Rock, a bank in northern England, came into question after it revealed that it had substantial exposure to subprime mortgages.[23] Soon other banks were encountering similar difficulties, including Bear Stearns, whose shares tumbled from $50 to $2 in little over one month, while Lehman Brothers went out of business.[24]

The Bank of England, the Bank of Canada, and the US Federal Reserve had little choice but to intervene to deal with difficulties in credit markets. In the process, the Bank of Canada may well have violated the Bank Act. In the middle of the credit crisis, it decided to expand the types of security it would purchase in open-market operations. Informed observers maintain that in doing so, the bank overstepped the Bank of Canada Act.[25] This is in line with the culture that maintains that "what matters is what works."[26] This culture may provide for timely and effective decisions, but it does little to clarify how those who wield power should be held responsible.

The point here is that globalization is changing our understanding of power and making it more difficult to locate. In brief, the exercise of power, including political and administrative power, is no longer limited to government officials or national borders to the extent that it was, say, thirty years ago. We now need to search where power actually lies rather than where it should lie or where it lay in the past.

Looking to the Private Sector

There have been major new developments in the business community that have also muddied the location of power and responsibility. As is well known, much of the Western world has in recent years embraced neoliberalism, albeit with less enthusiasm since the fall of 2008. Notwithstanding stock market meltdowns in the fall of 2008, the private sector is still widely regarded as being far more efficient than the public sector, and there is evidence everywhere that public servants have recently been borrowing management practices from the private sector.[27] To this day, there is a widespread belief in the Western world that the business community has shown greater flexibility and creativity than the public sector in expanding the economic pie and increasing productivity. Public-private partnerships established to deliver public services also remain in fashion throughout the Western world.[28] These partnerships may hold economic benefits, but they entail problems of accountability and inhibit our ability to locate power.

The belief that the private sector is superior to the public sector and that the latter should emulate the former is held particularly in Anglo-American democracies. Study after study reports that countries that have embraced the private sector have outperformed those that have not.[29] After all, Ireland became the "Celtic tiger" after it decided to promote a pro-business agenda, and China became an economic powerhouse virtually overnight once it unleashed market forces. The Celtic tiger later had a meltdown but it has not, it seems, shaken our faith in the private sector as the engine of economic growth. Gordon Brown, Britain's Labour prime minister, said as much at the 2009 Davos gathering. He called for a reform of international organizations and recommended the "building of an international early response system," but insisted that private initiatives remain the key to economic growth.[30]

Judith Maxwell, former chair of the Economic Council of Canada and not known for promoting right-of-centre views, recently wrote that business leaders are better than government officials at getting "at the root causes of a social problem that has economic consequences."[31] Senior public servants in Canada, the United Kingdom, the United States, Australia, and New Zealand have been busy relabelling most of what they do into the language of the business world; departmental or strategic plans are now called business plans, and pay-for-performance initiatives have been introduced for senior public servants in these countries, albeit with very little success.[32] The belief here is that somehow one can impose the same discipline on the public sector that one can on the private sector as boundaries between institutions and government departments collapse. However, no one has ever been able to define a discipline for the public sector that compares with either market forces or the competitive requirements of the marketplace.

Undeniably, private-sector actors are more powerful than they were forty years ago. Canada's former industry minister, Jim Prentice, put it succinctly when he said, "Commerce, not politics, must drive investment."[33] His target was state-owned enterprises, not private-sector investments. Regulations, he reported, would be introduced to control the takeover of Canadian firms by enterprises owned by foreign states; he made it clear that private capital looking for investment opportunities was quite another matter. Here he happily extended the welcome mat, and the Government of Canada has, over the past twenty years or so, done away with rules and red tape governing private investment from abroad. The business community and financial markets carefully monitor nation-states and their policies. When national governments do not pursue market-inspired economic policies and an open economy, markets punish them severely, playing havoc with their country's currencies and stock markets. There is no guarantee, however, that market-inspired policies will provide immunity to nation-states against economic problems, as the 2008–09 financial crisis so clearly demonstrated.

Political leaders throughout the Western world continue to send out subtle and less than subtle messages that the private sector remains king. For example, Stephen Harper's Conservative government decided in late 2007 to invite business executives to join Canada's official delegation to the climate-change conference in Bali. The Bali conference, it will be recalled, brought together 190 countries to hammer out a new agreement to replace the Kyoto Accord to deal with the global-warming crisis. Significantly, the Harper government did not invite environmental groups, Aboriginal groups, or opposition MPs to the conference.[34] Nor did it include anyone from Canada's Department of Foreign Affairs, apart from a junior official, who took notes and reported back to the department on what had transpired at the conference.[35] The message could not have been clearer: the government was willing to listen to the private sector but not to the bureaucrats or environmental groups. Those with answers that the government wants to hear tend to have power or at least influence.

The belief that the private sector has the answers has permeated virtually every government in the Western democracies. Public-private partnership agreements have been signed in all Anglo-American democracies to build schools, roads, bridges, and also to deliver public services that in the past were the sole responsibility of government. The Harper government unveiled measures in the 2009 budget to promote public-private partnership agreements more aggressively.[36] These agreements matter when locating power and responsibility.

This is not to suggest that citizens or even shareholders are always willing to bow to business executives. Shareholders, particularly in the United States, not so long ago rose up to bring loose-spending executives to heel. Deference to senior executives has not fared much better of late than deference to politicians and bureaucrats has. Though an alliance of sorts has been struck between political and business leaders under successive governments in Anglo-American democracies, voters, citizens, and shareholders have been less willing to trust them than in the past. Recent changes to corporate governance also have shifted the location of power within the private sector.

Looking for Power above the Political Fray

Citizens in Anglo-American democracies increasingly have to look to the courts to locate power. The United States has long lived with unelected men and women who have tenure and exercise enormous power.[37] This is, however, a relatively recent development in countries with Westminster-style parliamentary systems, but they too are adapting fast. Canada's chief justice stated in a public lecture that law and justice now rest on rational principles. She sent a clear message to Canadians that politicians are no longer fully in charge, a message that no chief justice in either Canada or Britain would have voiced not so long ago. She wrote, "Embedded in the concept of the rule of law is the proposition that there are fundamental and overriding principles of justice binding civilized societies that trump state-made rules when the two come into conflict."[38] Though the courts stand above the political fray, they no longer hesitate to shape the country's social agenda, a responsibility that in the past clearly rested with politicians and bureaucrats.[39] While Stephen Harper and many in his party were opposed to same-sex marriage, he told Canadians there was little that he and his government could do to prevent it because the courts would not let them. The Charter of Rights and Freedoms, which became part of Canada's constitution in 1982, has had a profound impact on the role of the courts, as has the Human Rights Act in Britain.

Judges are not alone in wielding power or influence while operating above the political fray. There is a growing number of officers of Parliament in Westminster-inspired parliamentary systems who sit in judgment on what the government does. They enjoy credibility with some citizens because they have the freedom and mandate to speak truth to political power without fear or favour. They do not have the power to decide, hence they are not responsible when things go wrong, but their views can influence public opinion. The fact that they do not possess power and never have to make policy and program decisions can make them credible voices with voters. Indeed, their ability to make judgments about the behaviour of politicians and, increasingly, of bureaucrats may well influence public opinion.

Recent measures to promote transparency in public institutions also have muddied the waters and pushed individuals farther away from assuming responsibility for their actions. To get around the requirements of right or access to information legislation, government officials have resorted to various means: yellow Post-it notes have often replaced the written memorandum in government, and strong discussion papers have given way to Powerpoint presentations. In at least one case, Canadian government officials actually directed consultants not to commit anything to paper: the Department of Indian Affairs and Northern Development told consultants in a $132,000 contract not to leave "a paper trail in government offices" and insisted that they deliver their findings through oral briefings.[40] There is now a multitude of oversight bodies hovering above political and bureaucratic institutions, all vying for influence; politicians and public servants must learn to deal with or avoid them. In addition, these oversight bodies are free to speak independently of one another: oversight never has a collective perspective.

Looking to the Media and Polls

Pollsters have become modern-day witch doctors. When in doubt or when political leaders want to find a way to capture public support, they ask their favourite pollsters to carry out a survey. If, as politicians are wont to say, the people are never wrong in a representative democracy, they can just point to the people or, more specifically, to the findings of a public opinion survey, as the reason for adopting a given policy or taking a particular decision.

Pollsters, like witch doctors, are never wrong. They simply report what citizens and voters think, and politicians are left to do what they wish with the findings. How can one possibly hold someone responsible for simply delivering a message that voters have generated? But pollsters do have considerable influence in shaping the views of political leaders throughout the Western world.

What about the media? Certainly, the media are vastly different from what they were thirty or forty years ago. Richard Wilson, former cabinet secretary in Britain under Tony Blair, mused in a public lecture, "I sometimes wonder whether the media understand their own power or the impact they can have on the inner workings of government." He added that the media in more recent years have not hesitated to put public servants under the spotlight, explaining that "being attacked in the press ... is a daunting experience for people who chose a career in which, if they are older, they expected to avoid the limelight."[41] The media, of course, have undergone a sea change in recent years: we now have 24-hour television news, radio talk shows, TV punditry, the Internet, and political blogs, all of which have contributed to how the media carry out their work.

The media are less deferential than in the past and much more subjective.[42] The end of deference, the capacity for self-projection, and a more aggressive approach have had a profound impact on all facets of politics and, by ricochet, of public administration. A veteran British journalist, John Lloyd, has pointed out that "the end of deference, celebrated so uncritically, was also the shared assumption of supreme parliamentary sovereignty." He adds: "Day to day sovereignty has bit by bit passed to the media ... A half a century ago, the assumption was that political power trumped all others. Now it doesn't: media power comes closer to trumping all others, at least in some things. It is the power of the media which has been one of the largest shifts in society over the past three decades."[43] Only the most naïve or ill-informed member of Parliament either in Canada or Britain still believes in the sovereignty of Parliament.

Looking to Political Institutions

One thing is clear. Those who wield or claim to wield political power and administrative authority no longer enjoy the deference they once did. Political institutions, political parties, politicians, and the public service have all fallen sharply on the public trust scale. We have seen a spate of books documenting the decline of confidence in government. Several years ago, for example, three well-known scholars, one of whom was Joseph Nye, set out to explain why "people no longer trust government."[44] Peter Hennessy in the United Kingdom concluded that the nineteenth-century government machinery is no longer suited to any of the problems likely to be thrown at governments in future, hence the search for what works without altering in any substantial fashion political institutions, other than chipping away at them.[45] Don Kettl, a leading student of public administration in the United States, wrote that "the federal government is structured for a world that no longer exists."[46] Through all of this, the citizenry has not only become less deferential but is asking for more transparency and accountability from those in power, whoever they may be, whether politicians, public servants, or business executives.

Key observers of politics virtually everywhere in Anglo-American democracies are asking if political parties have been turned into "empty vessels."[47] It is no exaggeration to write that political parties now reflect their leaders, their personalities, and their beliefs rather than the leaders reflecting their parties, their beliefs, and traditions. The result is that political parties have become little more than an election-day machine even though, in the constituencies, parties "still attract members who. are interested in studying policy but are denied any effective capacity to do so."[48] The power to shape public policies now lies elsewhere.

Looking to Bureaucracy

The public administration literature has long held that bureaucracy exerts substantial influence, if not power, in shaping both government policies and government decisions. However, recent developments reveal that all is not well with the state of our government bureaucracies and that they no longer enjoy their former influence. Plagued by morale problems, public servants do not have much public support. Public bureaucracies are being accused of many things – they are bloated, cumbersome, uncreative, lethargic, and insensitive.[49] Derek Bok, former Harvard president, had this to say: "Two-thirds of the public believe that the federal government employs too many people and that they do not work as hard as those who hold private sector jobs. These attitudes are not held only by the uninformed; opinion polls consistently show that respect for government steadily dwindles as one moves up the scale of education and income. Indeed, among the more affluent and better educated, one of the few things that unites the left and the right is their common disdain for bureaucrats."[50]

Public servants themselves are also lamenting their lost of influence, if not power, in shaping public policies. Since Margaret Thatcher set the trend, politicians have all looked for a bureaucracy more responsive to their agenda. The literature suggests that they have been successful.[51] Senior public servants have become more responsive not only to the policy but even to the political wishes of the political executive. Lawrence Martin writes that in Ottawa, bureaucrats now either "fall in line or fall out of favour." He quotes a deputy minister: "When you live in a world where options aren't necessary, I suppose you don't need much of a bureaucracy"; and makes the point that the "government does not want high level bureaucrats to exercise the challenge function."[52] Jim Travers writes that the view among senior bureaucrats in Ottawa is that "instead of sous-chefs helping the government prepare the national menu, bureaucrats complain that they are being used as short-order cooks."[53] Former Canadian prime minister Paul Martin reported bluntly after leaving office, "We have totally destroyed the policy-making capacity of the public service."[54]

Looking to New Voices for Answers

All public institutions in Anglo-American democracies have been told in recent years to reach out to client groups, interested parties, research institutes, and NGOs when shaping public policies. Government managers have also been told to listen to and respond to their clients in delivering public services. I am hardly the first to write that responsibility shared is responsibility shirked.[55]

It seems that politicians and citizens no longer trust government departments to count fish properly (Canada's Department of Fisheries and Oceans has since 1993 had a Fisheries Resource Conservation Council made up of outside members who have a broad mandate to review the work of the department). In June 2005 the minister of finance commissioned a study – the O'Neil report – to review the department's ability to forecast revenue and spending. Tim O'Neil himself argued that the government should seriously consider turning over responsibility for forecasting revenues to the private sector, given that government "forecasts have been consistently off for decades."[56] The Harper government, shortly after coming to power, declared its intention to appoint an independent "parliamentary budget officer" to "ensure truth in budgeting."[57]

Government departments, it seems, can no longer generate truth. Not only are new voices being created or supported, but there is the belief that voices operating outside the government are more credible than even the most senior of government departments, such as Canada's Department of Finance. Harper did make the new parliamentary budget officer part of his accountability legislative reform package, though he stopped short of giving him full parliamentary officer status. Through all of the above changes, our national political and, to a lesser extent, administrative institutions have remained largely unchanged. They cling to established processes and routines and traditional accountability mechanisms.

The reader may well be tempted to conclude that it has become increasingly difficult to locate power and influence in modern society. This book makes this case. But it also argues that the location of power has shifted in recent years, and this shift has enabled those who wield power to sidestep responsibility. Citizens intuitively sense a problem. They see their communities facing political and economic challenges and at the same time see their political and economic leaders and their governments becoming very adroit at shifting blame. They are able to do this because the levers of power are no longer clear, thus allowing organizations to dump problems on one another.

Charles E. Lindblom, a highly respected scholar, maintains that organizations are the ultimate source of power and that they require internal discipline to have external power.[58] The military has been a powerful organization throughout its history partly because it has a single, clear purpose and does not tolerate dissent in its ranks. It settles disputes internally, and its members submit to the organization's common purpose, or leave. From this internal exercise of power "comes the ability of the organization to impose its will externally."[59] The same can be said about the trade union movement. Members understand that their union has a single, clear purpose – to stand up to the employer and secure better wages and benefits for the workers. As John Kenneth Galbraith explained, "If union solidarity, the synonym for effective internal discipline or submission is high, then the chance of winning union demands or of successful strike action is good."[60]

Contrast the above with the Roman Catholic Church. The church has lost a good deal of its power in recent decades. Church attendance has dropped significantly, and fewer and fewer young men and women are joining religious orders. The organization has lost some of its ability to impose internal discipline on its members. The Pope no longer speaks with the kind of authority that popes in past generations did, especially on secular issues.

In this book, I argue that our public organizations are suffering the same fate as the Roman Catholic Church. They can no longer wield the kind of power they once could. This is the result of power becoming more fluid as attempts are made to ensure a wider participation in the exercise of power, through the borrowing of management practices from the private sector and numerous measures to promote greater transparency. The forces of globalization and the apparent inability of institutions, organizations, and formal policy-making processes to respond to current economic circumstances and political expectations have also had a profound effect on the location of power and have made it more difficult to locate.

In large publicly traded companies, power is no longer with the boss, the CEO, to the extent that it once was. However, nowhere is the loss of power more evident than in the public sector. Even the power of presidents and prime ministers is less and less the result of their original will and more the result of accommodating a variety of sources, many of which lie in jurisdictions over which they have little influence. This explains, at least in part, their attempts to centralize power in their own hands and immediate offices.

Public bureaucracy, never a popular institution at the best of times, has also lost power and influence in Anglo-American democracies, a fact that can be attributed in part to having lost credibility in Western society. Bureaucracy once depended on what Galbraith labelled the "conditioned" instrument of power – winning through persuasion, education, and social commitments.[61] This no longer seems to be very effective, at least when it comes from public bureaucracies. Today, power takes new forms and employs new instruments. Compared with even thirty years ago, power is more tangled, more fluid, and more attached to personalities than to institutions and organizations.

All of the above challenges Lindblom's argument that organizations are the ultimate source of power. Where, then, does power now reside? This is the crucial question.

We have witnessed, in recent years, measure after measure to promote public consultations in virtually every sector. We have seen the introduction of access to information legislation and sustained efforts by governments to produce document after document on government programs and their performances. Government departments and agencies have also turned to the Internet to report on their mandates, policies, and operations. Today, there are precious few new initiatives launched without having first been put through focus groups to test public support. Notwithstanding this and many other efforts, there is evidence of growing political apathy, with citizens increasingly believing that nation-states are less democratic than they once were, that government bureaucracies do not work well, and that political leaders are less and less in touch with citizens.

This book's central thesis is that one can explain the above by the growing inability of people outside government and, to some extent, even those inside government, to locate where power actually resides. It argues that our inability to locate power also explains the failure of traditional accountability mechanisms. We have arrived at the point where institutions, organizations, hierarchy, command and control, and the subordinate and obedient model no longer expose who has power, and we are at a loss to locate it. This is all the more remarkable because it appears to hold true in both the public and private sectors, although much less so in the latter.

The book seeks to answer a number of related questions:

- Where is power located and who holds it?
- Has the shift to more transparency served to move the location of power up the ladder?
- If borders and boundaries are collapsing, how can one now define the boundaries of power?
- Did the rigidity of our institutions make more sense in a less transparent world?
- Do we now need to look to personal identity to establish power and responsibility? If so, what are the implications for representative democracy?
- Is it easier for the more powerful political and economic interests to take advantage of opportunities to promote their own interests in a world of ruptured borders, boundaries, and hierarchies?
- When it comes to power, is it the individual or the setting that matters?

1 GLOBALIZATION: I AM NOT TO BLAME, THE DEVIL MADE ME DO IT

I grew up in a small Acadian village in southeast New Brunswick, Canada, some fifty kilometres from Moncton. I attended a one-room school where religion was an important part of the curriculum. We were often invited to contribute five cents to help the Roman Catholic Church save souls in China, India, and Africa. I recall well the faces of poverty-stricken Chinese infants, whom the church called *les païens*, that were posted on *les images* and given to all those making a contribution. I was left to imagine what Third World countries were like, and one could hardly think that some day anyone from my region, other than a missionary, would even visit such a faraway land.

Until recently, rarely a week went by when there was not a local entrepreneur on a flight out of Moncton on his or her way to China. Moncton, with a population of about 100,000 inhabitants, can hardly be described as a major metropolitan centre. Still, a good number of joint and new business ventures have been launched in recent years between local entrepreneurs and Chinese businesses. In 2003, one Moncton entrepreneur established a new plant to produce kitchen cabinets in China. When I asked him why, his response was: "The reason is very simple – I can ship a tree from Canada to China, produce a finished product from my plant there, and ship the product back anywhere in Canada much more cheaply than if I were to take the same tree and process it at my plant in Moncton."[1]

In 2004, OAO Technology Solutions, a large US firm, decided to transfer 140 jobs from Moncton to India, despite only a few years earlier having received provincial government assistance to establish operations in Moncton. The decision, OAO explained, was strictly a business one: it could save money for its shareholders if it ran its operations from India. In January 2008, another large American firm, AOL, announced that it was eliminating 100 jobs from its Moncton operations. Moncton is far from being alone in confronting both the challenges and opportunities flowing from the global economy. Yet the city can hardly be described as one of the most global-oriented communities in the Western world.

It takes only a moment's reflection to appreciate what the rise of the global economy has meant for relations between nation-states and for the location of economic activities, the management of political power, and businesses both large and small. Consider this: Thirty years ago, China held that foreign trade amounted to nothing more than treason, while today it is open for business to virtually anyone with investment dollars. It is becoming an economic powerhouse, made possible in no small measure by foreign investment. Thirty years ago, Canada had an agency with a mandate to control the flow of investment dollars coming into the country. Today, it has an agency with a mandate to do the exact opposite – attract foreign investment. Thirty years ago, Canada sent foreign aid to India. Today, many Canadian businesses hire firms or workers in India to build their websites and service their customers.[2] Thirty years ago, US automakers dominated the North American market. Today, American manufactures are struggling, while some Japanese and European firms are doing well. In December 2007 Toyota surpassed Ford in sales of cars and light trucks in the United States, and in 2008 it sold more cars worldwide than General Motors.[3] By late 2008, the big three US automakers went to Washington and Ottawa, cap in hand, "pleading" for public funds in order to survive, making the point that although we live in a global economy, it is still national governments that are asked to pick up the pieces when things go wrong.[4] Thirty years ago, the Soviet Union dominated Eastern Europe, where private property was not permitted. Today, some of the world's wealthiest individuals are Russian, and capital flows easily in and out of Eastern Europe.

In light of these and other developments, some students of globalization have of late pronounced that globalization will eventually spell the end of the nation-state model, that federations are particularly vulnerable, given that some are in a continuing struggle to maintain national unity, and that national economies are being transformed into regional economies, integrating into the global economy differently and with varying degrees of success.[5]

The nation-state, however, is not about to disappear, and there is little evidence that economic integration at the global or regional levels is promoting new transnational identities.[6] It was, after all, national governments that prevented the collapse of the American and the European banking systems in late 2008 and early 2009. In addition, the US government now spends $4 trillion annually, the Canadian government over $200 billion, and the British government £600 billion, suggesting that they are not about to disappear. The spending power of national governments still matters, constituting an important instrument of political power. The OECD reports that both total government outlays as a percentage of GDP and the size of the central government debt of its member countries have increased substantially between 1980 and today.[7] National governments are free to adopt policies and take decisions that do not square easily with the economic requirements of the global economy, and many still do. The point is that national political leaders and their governments will not easily part with their power.

The financial crisis that first surfaced in September-October 2008 gave rise to a global recession. It led many – even leading private-sector executives – to turn to their national government for help. This response to the crisis showed that although we live in a global economy, we do not live in a global polity. We pay taxes to local, provincial and national governments, not to an international or a global government. In the end, it was taxpayers in nation-states who saved the banking system in the United States and some European states from collapse. Canadians may accept that their government should bail out Canadian financial institutions, but they would not accept its sending funds to bail out an American or a Spanish bank. Many European countries, meanwhile, sought to reconcile the fact that while they had a single currency, they had multiple fiscal policies.

BMW, one of the world's largest luxury car makers, went to the heart of the matter when it argued that if the United States or Canadian government was making funds available to American domestic manufacturers, the same level of funding should be made available to other auto manufacturers located in either country. Failing that, BMW officials insisted, national governments were distorting competition and running the risk of economic warfare between nation-states. Suddenly, globalization had a very different look.[8]

There is evidence to suggest that national governments are re-evaluating and adjusting important aspects of their systems of governance, policies, laws, and regulations because of the rise of the global economy.[9] The question we need to explore is: What does it mean for the location of power and responsibility? Power can look to the voice of the people, to experts, to an independent authority, or to the market for advice and legitimacy.

How the global economy has been defined is largely tied to the voice of the market, the focus of this chapter. Liberal trading and investment norms, new information technologies, deregulation in national economies, privatization and commercialization have all fuelled both growth in the global economy and academic interest in its development. No one, from nation-states to individuals, is immune from globalization. Indeed, even authoritarian political regimes, such as China, Russia, and Libya, have had to cede some control on certain issues in order to compete effectively in the global economy. Proponents of globalization argue that we should trust the market to come up with the right decisions and that we should disturb market forces as little as possible. Recent developments in international financial markets have muddied the waters further. They have led a number of observers to question globalization, its impact, and its capacity to oversee or regulate certain business activities.

The purpose of this chapter is to consider the effect of changes in the global economy on national, political, and administrative institutions. The literature suggests that globalization has led to profound changes in how businesses and national governments go about their work.[10] We know that market and business principles are strongly influencing how globalization is taking shape and changing the world of politics and government. We need to explore how.

This chapter makes the point that although nation-states are not about to disappear, globalization has had a profound impact on the location of power and, in particular, of responsibility, in both the private and public sector. The central argument is that globalization has made it much more difficult to do this and that those who wield power can now take cover under the umbrella of globalization to sidestep responsibility or to justify their actions. Recent events in financial markets have obscured still further the location of power.

No One Understands It

Guy Hands, a highly successful British financier, sent copies of John Kenneth Galbraith's *The Great Crash of 1929* to bankers and investors at the end of 2007. He did so in order to caution investors on the economic turbulence ahead, and hindsight suggests that he was right, given the wild swings in global financial markets that followed. Hands also wanted to make the point that "complex financial instruments have been invented which no one really understands."[11] It seems that only the most advanced specialists now have any idea of what is really happening in financial markets, particularly in the hedge fund industry. Hedge fund managers generally work for privately owned investment funds and thus are not regulated like mutual funds. The managers employ whatever sophisticated financial instruments are available, such as future contracts, options, puts, and leverage to generate high returns to outperform the market. The number of hedge funds has exploded in recent years, making it even more difficult for regulators and investors to understand how they operate. In 1990 there were about 600 hedge funds; by 2000 there were 3,873, and the latest figures put the total at 7,601.[12]

National governments continue to have difficulty regulating the hedge fund industry, not only because it is a hard industry to understand but also because, for the most part, hedge funds are not managed by public corporations and are thus able to operate away from public view. In brief, they are largely unregulated. In any event, hedge fund managers will simply move resources to other jurisdictions if national governments try to control them, given that, for the most part, the funds only trade securities. The driving force behind hedge funds is the search for yield, and hedge fund managers argue that the role of governments should be simple – to stay out of the way. Government intervention will only make things worse, and, in any event, the market itself is quite capable of sorting out winners and punishing losers, even if at times it has to punish the losers severely.

Part of the difficulty in understanding the hedge fund industry is that the industry does not own or run businesses. As the United Nations recently pointed out, "there are very few regulatory restrictions on the types of instruments in which they deal, and they make extensive use of short selling, leverage and derivatives."[13] While in more recent years some hedge funds have expanded their investments to stocklisted companies, their time horizon remains very short. Money easily flows in and out of companies, and many hedge fund managers operate more as speculators than investors. There has been no need to register hedge funds with federal regulations in the United States, and registration remains voluntary, though this may change in light of the 2008 financial crisis. Registration requires regular reviews and more government oversight of risk controls.[14]

Hedge funds are not the only financial instruments operating below the radar. The credit crunch that first surfaced in the United States in the summer of 2008 took only weeks to reverberate throughout the Western world and beyond. By the fall, it had become a worldwide liquidity crisis, and central banks in the European Union, the United States, Canada, and Switzerland decided to intervene by injecting funds into capital markets. Stock markets tumbled around the world, and large commercial banks in the United States saw their market capitalization drop substantially, with some coming close to bankruptcy.[15] In one case, Lehman Brothers, founded in 1850, was forced to file for bankruptcy, and the US Federal Reserve had to come to the rescue to prevent bankruptcy of yet another large investment bank, Bear Stearns. More was to come as bank after bank went to governments in the United States and Europe for help.

Governments everywhere were forced to inject capital into financial institutions and to design interventionist initiatives to stimulate the economy. The financial crisis was global in scope, but it was left to national governments to pick up the pieces. Governments discovered that the market could be trusted, but only up to a point. They also discovered that they had little to offer in terms of solutions, other than throwing money at the problem, and that no one was willing to come forward to accept responsibility for the crisis. The Treasury's intervention to save Bear Stearns suggested to many that profits are always privatized but losses can become the responsibility of the state. For several months at least, there were precious few voices arguing that the role of government was to stay out of the way and let the market select winners and losers. Losers did not hesitate to line up for government hand-outs.

Regional banks in Britain and Germany and local governments as far away as Australia also faced significant financial losses tied to subprime mortgages in the United States.[16] Essentially, the liquidity crisis occurred because one of the securities that was traded in world markets, the Collateralized Debt Obligations (CDOs), ran into problems. In brief, investment banks sold interests in a pool of mortgages, but default and foreclosure rates became considerably higher than had been predicted. Well-known economist Paul Krugman observed, "When you believe in things that you don't understand, bad things happen."[17] Not only did many investors not understand the financial instruments they were buying, they also did not know who had the power to make decisions about their investments.

Central bankers intervened to avert a collapse in financial markets and to avoid future damage to the global economy. They may have sought to identify lessons to be learned from the liquidity crisis, but they were not willing to accept any responsibility. Ben Bernanke, chairman of the US

Federal Reserve, which oversees the US banking system, in the middle of the crisis accused some mortgage lenders of "unfair and deceptive acts and practices that hurt not just borrowers and their families but entire communities, and indeed, the economy as a whole. They have no place in our mortgage industry."[18] Bernanke's predecessor, Alan Greenspan, wrote a lengthy op-ed piece in the *Wall Street Journal* essentially saying, "Don't look at me, blame China or India."[19] Later, appearing before a congressional committee, Greenspan again insisted that the credit crisis was not his "fault," but he admitted that the meltdown in world financial markets had revealed a flaw in his economic thinking. He had always believed that banks, operating in their own self-interest, would look after the interests of their shareholders and the institutions supporting them. His point was that the banks, not he or the Federal Reserve, were at fault.[20] Others blamed the United States government for the crisis by encouraging mortgage loans to unqualified buyers.[21] Still others argued the obvious – that some large financial institutions had proved inept at managing risk.[22] The *New York Times* asked, "Who's to blame?" and came up with this conclusion: "The answer, it seems, is someone else."[23] This was small comfort for those looking to locate power in order to assign responsibility and blame.

While Bernanke blamed mortgage lenders for the crisis, a good number of observers singled out the US Federal Reserve itself for failing to act as a forceful regulator, particularly during the 2001–05 housing boom in the United States.[24] Some also blamed mortgage brokers, others credit rating agencies, and still others investment bankers in the derivative trading market.[25] The *Wall Street Journal* concluded that it was an "example of closing the barn door after all the horses had left."[26]

Alan Blinder, a leading monetary economist at Princeton University, claimed that "the fed and other regulatory agencies were slow on the draw." He added, "They could have made this debacle substantially smaller, not by better monetary policy, but by better regulatory and supervisory policy."[27] International financier George Soros argued that "globalization allowed the US to suck up the savings of the rest of the world and the super-boom got out of hand when new products became so complicated that the authorities could no longer calculate the risks and started relying on the risk management methods of the banks themselves. Similarly, the rating agency relied on the information provided by the originators of the synthetic products." He added, "It was a shocking abdication of responsibility."[28] It may well be that no one had any power to do anything else than close the barn door after all the horses had left, because few actually understood what was going on inside the barn until it was too late.

Identifying those responsible for the liquidity crisis remains to this day no easy task. In the past, banks that arranged mortgages had a strong incentive to work with homeowners to prevent them from defaulting because the mortgage stayed on the bank's books until it was paid. Mortgage lenders, at least in the United States, could hedge their credit-risk exposure by packaging it with other loans and then selling it in financial markets. The market for trading credit-risk expanded substantially during the US housing boom, and $2.5 trillion (US) worth of subprime loans were made between 2000 and 2007, while subprime mortgages grew from $160 billion in 2001 (or 7.2 percent of new mortgages) to $600 billion in 2006 (or 20.6 percent of new mortgages).[29]

Those arranging mortgages took a percentage of each loan once the papers were signed, and they got paid only if they approved the applications. The incentive was to process applications quickly, sign off on the loans, and shuffle the risk to someone else. Investment bankers came up with ways of repackaging mortgages into securities that could be traded in financial markets to attenuate their risks. Thus, those who originally arranged the mortgages had little financial stake in whether or not the loans were eventually paid. Rating services such as Moody's and Standard & Poor's were also paid upfront for their assessments, so could hardly be held responsible when things went bad. In brief, the credit market today is not only global but also the product of many hands.

At best, responsibility for the debacle was shared among several actors, and, at worst, it was lost somewhere between those who originally approved the loans, investment bankers, rating agencies, those who sold asset-backed securities, and those who bought them. The *Wall Street Journal* argued that the financial landscape today is far more complex than at any time in the past and summed up the problem this way: "Traders increasingly sell their credit-risk commitment to other investors in multiple layers, making it more difficult to know where the risk ultimately resides."[30]

To this day, there is little evidence to suggest that international organizations or key political leaders anywhere sought to identify who was responsible for the crisis and to hold them to account. In the end, it was left to the market, with government assistance, to sort things out and for central bankers and national governments to rush to the rescue with public money. Those wielding political or bureaucratic power stayed silent on the sidelines for several weeks. They had no solution to offer even after the crisis was full blown, and they simply handed the steering wheel to the central bankers and said, "Here, now, somehow, you drive." Several months after it first surfaced, they began to look at ways to prevent such a crisis in future. They did eventually come to the rescue with a package to assist primarily the business community and low-income wage earners, to encourage them to start spending more in order to stimulate the economy. The Bush administration even decided, in the immediate aftermath of the crisis, to loosen still further its "regulatory grip" on mortgage lenders and to require only semi-annual rather than quarterly reports on planned debt issues.[31]

The above is a reflection of our time. Henry Mintzberg put it well when he wrote, "Capitalism has triumphed. That was the pat conclusion reached in the West as, one by one, the communist regimes of Eastern Europe began to fall. It has become such an article of faith that we have become blind to its effects. Those effects are highly negative – indeed, dangerous – because the conclusion itself is wrong. In my view, we have confounded the whole relationship between business and government, and we had best clear it up before we end up no better off than the Eastern Europeans once were."[32] The business community, he argued, had never been more influential than it was in the 1980s up to the 2008 global financial crisis, and private-sector values still permeate all of society.[33] The sense of balance was lost, and we lived in a world where it was believed that the private sector could do little wrong while the public sector could do little right. Government intervention was pushed back, and regulatory agencies became hesitant to intervene because of the prevailing view that the business community and market forces would get it right in the end, and that government and its regulatory bodies would inevitably make things worse if they were to intervene too often in the marketplace.[34]

International financial transactions are now carried out on a real-time basis, and transactions are increasingly undertaken by entities other than banks. The foreign exchange market alone witnessed explosive growth in recent years, also with limited oversight. Andrew Sheng, one-time deputy chief executive of the Hong Kong monetary authority, explains that "the supervision and regulation of the global wholesale foreign exchange market is rather special because it is essentially self-regulative." He adds, "Historically the global foreign exchange market evolved offshore largely because of restrictive domestic regulations and tax reasons."[35] Daily trading volume in foreign exchange markets was less than US$1 billion in 1974. Today it is over US$3 trillion and growing.[36] The volatility in currency markets is unlike anything we have witnessed in history. This prompted the British Broadcasting Corporation to report that "the IMF has found it increasingly difficult to influence the world's capital market, whose huge financial flows dwarf its resources, or to correct the huge global imbalances that arise from trade."[37]

It is also no longer possible for national governments to control international capital movements as they were able to do it in the era of fixed exchange rates from 1945 to 1970. Large amounts of highly mobile short-term capital and extremely sophisticated means of communication have made it very difficult for national governments to formulate, let alone implement, policies that regulate or control these assets. Richard Lipsey sums it up in this fashion: "The globalization of capital markets had a lot to do with the breakdown of Breton Woods systems of fixed exchange rate."[38] It also has a lot to do with there being no one, no institution, and little in the way of a process responsible to see that things do not go wrong. What we have instead is a largely self-regulatory world where the key actors are left side-stepping responsibility, blaming one another, and where international organizations such as the IMF no longer have the necessary clout or the instruments to have much of an impact in capital markets.

Individuals are still free to move financial instruments back and forth with a minimum of oversight at the international level. The 2008 financial crisis brought home the point that the economic world has been globalized, while assuming that the global market would somehow self-regulate. When serious cracks surfaced, all turned to their national governments because there was nowhere else to turn. We discovered that the economic and political systems were not harmonized, and people were left scratching their heads, asking where political and economic power were located and who actually held it in this new economic environment.

The Private Sector Still Knows Best

National governments, particularly in Anglo-American democracies, have for the most part accepted that the business community and market forces are much better at picking winners and dealing with losers than the public sector is. Many observers also now subscribe to the view that governments made a mess of things in the 1970s. It will be recalled that at that time it became apparent that governments were unable to deal simultaneously with the issues of unemployment, inflation, balance of payments, and debt. The decade gave birth to the dreaded word "stag-flation" to describe a slowdown in economic growth and rising inflation. It was widely believed that governments were largely responsible for this state of affairs and that consequently they were hardly in a position to show direction to the private sector. Governments, Ronald Reagan proclaimed, had become part of the problem, not the solution, a charge that resonates to this day.[39]

Even people who had supported the ideas of Franklin Roosevelt, Clement Attlee, and T.C. Douglas, who favoured a strong role for government in society, were having second thoughts. John Kenneth Galbraith argued in 1986, "It's more than the Liberal task to defend the system. It is far more important now to improve the operation than enlarge and increase its scope."[40] In Britain, Tony Blair reoriented his Labour Party to give a much larger role to the private sector, even in the delivery of public services. He never sought to turn back the clock on Margaret Thatcher's reforms.[41] Privatization came into fashion in Britain and Canada in the 1980s, and no political leader from whatever political persuasion in either country has since sought to nationalize industries or substantially enlarge the role of government in the economy, other than offering bailout assistance to banks and some multinational firms to deal with the 2008 financial crisis. In some instances, national governments invested in some financial institutions, but they made it clear that it was a temporary measure.

Asked if the private sector has more power today than it had thirty-five years ago when he first joined the Canadian public service, a recently retired deputy minister said, "I saw economic nationalism actually die in Canada while serving in the public service. With economic nationalism came instruments that the federal government had in its policy and regulatory arsenal which gave it an ability to exert control over the business world, particularly foreign businesses. In that sense, the government had more power over the private sector back then than it now has."[42] Economic nationalism may or may not be dead in Canada or elsewhere, but it has taken a different form. The ability to attract foreign investment is now highly valued and constitutes a sure sign of a country's economic health. National governments still go to great efforts to tailor policies that appeal to the private sector in order to locate new economic activities.

It will be recalled that Pierre Trudeau's Liberal government created the Foreign Investment Review Agency (FIRA) in the mid-1970s. Its mandate was to monitor and approve foreign takeovers. A decade later, however, a newly elected Progressive Conservative government replaced FIRA with a new agency – Investment Canada – with a mandate to encourage foreign investment rather than control it. To be sure, the change in policy had an impact. When Investment Canada was established, foreign-controlled firms accounted for only 21 percent of total non-financial assets in Canada, but by 2002 they amounted to about 30 percent of assets.[43] Canada is hardly alone in changing policy and in aggressively pursuing foreign investment; the United Nations observed recently that "many developed countries have used capital controls in the past, but have largely abandoned them."[44]

Today, the ability of a nation-state to attract foreign direct investment remains the litmus test to determine a country's ability to promote economic development. Some countries have been successful. Global foreign direct investments (FDIs) amounted to $916 billion in 2005 with 64 percent of the total going to developed countries. In turn, the five largest host economies – the United Kingdom, the United States, France, the Netherlands, and Canada, in that order – accounted for 75 percent of total FDI inflows to developed countries.[45] Direct investment flows to and from OECD countries are also substantial and remain on an upward trend. In 1990 direct investment flowing out of OECD countries amounted to about US$200 billion, while investment coming in amounted to $180 billion. By 2006 the numbers had grown to $1,120 billion in outflows and $910 billion in inflows.[46] In its review of recent foreign direct investment patterns, the OECD reports some concern among its members about the consequences of globalization – the takeover of prized national firms. However, it insists that the economic advantages far outweigh the disadvantages and labelled its review "Freedom of Investment in a Changing World."[47]

In Canada, the Conference Board carried out a review of the "hollowing out of corporate Canada." "Hollowing out" suggests that when foreign firms buy Canadian firms, the Canadian management and boards of directors are very often replaced by head office people from the parent firms. The Conference Board concluded that "hollowing out" is a myth, and its president declared that "mergers and acquisitions are a positive part of the process of competition for capital and corporate control." Canada's finance minister, Jim Flaherty, responded by declaring that Canada should not be "slamming the door" on foreign investment.[48]

Many nation-states have walked away from policy instruments that would allow them to screen foreign investments. The result is that a business can now invest in countries that suit its business plans but also draw inputs from virtually anywhere in the world through what some have labelled "global sourcing."[49] The Harper government announced measures in 2009 to facilitate still further foreign investment in Canada.[50]

Officials in the economic development field have, in one generation, made the transition from thinking of neighbouring provinces, states, or regions as the competition to thinking of countries halfway around the world. There was a time when the Canadian Department of Regional Economic Expansion (DREE) sought, through financial incentives and other means, to shift jobs from one region of Canada to another to promote balance in the national economy. It was also important for DREE officials to assist the country's political leadership to manage a political space, given tensions that could and did indeed surface between provinces over a shift in employment between regions. DREE is now defunct. Today, the head of Nova Scotia's economic development agency explains that he "competes with India, China, the Philippines, Eastern European bloc countries and now South America."[51]

The economic development field now exists far more in an economic space than in a political one, and that is the way it should be. Indeed, the head of Nova Scotia's investment promotion agency takes great pride in making it clear that, unlike his predecessors, he has a mandate to operate at arm's length from politicians.[52] Though he is an employee of the state, he operates under different rules and likes to portray his work as somehow not government work but more akin to working in the private sector. He and many colleagues in other jurisdictions go to great lengths to make the point that they are not "government bureaucrats" and that they can operate free of politics and politicians and government red tape.

It is no exaggeration to write that, for economic development officials operating in the field, success requires politicians to stay out of the way. It is one thing to object to DREE's attempt to move jobs from, say, Ontario to Nova Scotia, but it is hardly possible to make political hay by blaming market forces or Vietnam's cost competitiveness to explain jobs lost in Ontario or Nova Scotia. Market forces, after all, are economic, not political. One can assign power and responsibility for political decisions, but it is quite another matter when decisions flow out of the hidden hand of the market.

The Atlantic provinces in Canada could, in the past, prove that they had lost manufacturing jobs to Ontario and Quebec because of national policy and the federal government's deliberate economic development efforts in central Canada. It is, however, much more difficult for them to point the finger, for example, at China and its low wage economy and abundant workers to explain their own economic difficulties. The first is a result of political decisions and the impact of public policies in the national context; the second is the result of China's comparative advantages, market forces, and a low wage economy.

The world's one hundred largest private firms now have, on average, affiliates or activities in forty foreign countries.[53] They are not alone, given that many small firms also are increasingly locating some of their activities abroad. There are several reasons for this; they include higher costs of production at home, the limited size of the local market, and the search for lower taxes. More efficient means of transportation and communication are also important factors in the rise of the global economy. It is easy to appreciate that today's integrated global financial markets and global production and supply chains would not exist without the information revolution and an efficient transportation sector.

A firm, however, will still look to a number of key factors when selecting a location for its activities. The availability and quality of human resources is one.[54] China, for example, has no difficulty in finding a workforce for a variety of economic sectors, notably for its manufacturing sector, where workers receive modest wages and limited social benefits. But there are other factors. International organizations report that countries now employ a number of instruments to attract foreign investment: match-making services, feasibility studies, some legal support, human resources development and training, information provision, and, in some instances, financial incentives.[55] In short, the power to locate economic activities is shared between market forces and the ability of governments to construct a framework that appeals to private-sector investment. The framework, however, is considerably less interventionist than it was thirty years ago.

At the risk of stating the obvious, countries that offer a business-friendly agenda and provide cost advantages stand a much better chance of attracting new private-sector investment than those that do not. In brief, public policy advisers and specialists are still telling national governments that laissez-faire economics works in the global economy. Lester Thurow maintains that "anti-globalization is an anti-capitalist argument" and that it is "a futile argument, since capitalism is the only proven system."[56] He is not the only economist or public policy specialist to hold this view.

A business-friendly agenda calls for deregulation, the reduction of red tape, low corporate taxes, privatization, tariff reductions, and free trade. Many Western countries have followed this route. Anglo-American democracies, particularly since the Thatcher and Reagan days, have promoted the privatization of state corporations, lower corporate taxes, and freer trade. The OECD reports that its member countries have also launched ambitious measures to reduce red tape and promote deregulation of their economies.[57]

It will be recalled that for many observers, Margaret Thatcher showed the way to self-sustaining economic development and success in the global economy through a policy of privatization, some reduction in public spending, and a strong reliance on the private sector or free market economics. It will also be recalled that before Thatcher came to power, Britain depended on heavy borrowing and at one point had to turn to politically sensitive borrowing from the IMF, which imposed some constraints on the country. The Thatcher reforms and their successes in revitalizing the British economy inspired other political leaders and other jurisdictions, large and small, to privatize state corporations, cut red tape and regulatory policies, and attempt to cut government spending.

In one generation, Anglo-American democracies also went from a belief in a strong positive role for the state in managing the economy to embracing free market economics and downplaying the role of government. Those who argued against tampering with the machinery of government and the status quo became the new reactionaries. What mattered was the entrepreneur, the individual. Margaret Thatcher had a message for those who wanted to prosper in Britain and in the global economy. She said, "There is no such thing as society. There are individuals, men and women, and there are families. And no government can do anything except through people, and people must look after themselves first."[58] For Thatcher, the individual, the entrepreneur, the business community, property rights, a certain hostility to government intervention in the economy, the reduction or removal of state controls, and lower taxes were key to economic growth. Individuals and private firms compete, not national governments, and competition holds the key to higher productivity and economic growth. The solution, then, is to throw economic power up in the air and let the most capable individuals and private firms grab it as best they can.

Advocates of a business agenda insist that it is the best way forward for national economies in the global economy, and they happily point to success stories other than Britain's to support their claim, including Ireland's economic miracle. As is well known, for several years Ireland was transformed into the Celtic Tiger, able to reduce its external debt while at the same time keeping inflation in check and lowering unemployment. Agriculture lost its standing as the country's most important economic sector, and at one point exports accounted for about 75 percent of national output, which was higher than anywhere else in Europe, and well over a thousand overseas companies decided to locate their activities in Ireland.

There are three main reasons for Ireland's temporary success: it developed a highly competitive cost base for business; profits derived from manufacturing and qualifying services are subject to a 10 percent tax rate; and companies engaged in research and development activities and developing patents in Ireland can do so tax free. Ireland's economy prompted *Fortune* magazine to observe, "Other countries look enviously at an Ireland that has transformed itself in one generation from a threadbare country on Europe's periphery to the second-richest (on a GDP-per-capita basis) in the European Union. Scarcely a week goes by without a national delegation visiting Dublin to learn how the Celtic Tiger was conceived and, more important, whether it can be cloned."[59]

The Celtic Tiger got badly mauled, however, by the financial crisis of 2008 as the media began to report on the "Celtic catastrophe." Economists started to take stock of Ireland's success from a different perspective and concluded that "greed, easy credit, immigration, massive foreign investment inflows and government spending fuelled the boom."[60] In brief, Ireland's success was built on debt, and many observers began to question the wisdom of turning "power" over to market forces. Economists argued that one way out of the economic difficulties for Ireland was to lower interest rates and devalue its currency. But Ireland no longer holds power over these economic levers – the European Central Bank now sets monetary policy. It seems that, much as governments made a mess of things in the 1970s, globalization made a mess of things in 2008. This makes it still more difficult for those setting out to locate power.

Advocates of a pro-business agenda, however, are not about to admit defeat. They can still point to some US states to make their case. Arthur Laffer and Stephen Moore argue in their *Rich States, Poor States* that high taxes, not incomes, redistribute people. Americans, they write, are uprooting themselves to relocate to low tax, business-friendly, high-growth areas.[61] In Canada, some observers have established a link between restricted trade policies and a regulatory climate inhibiting foreign investment and a period of economic stagnation (circa 1970–85) and the period of sustained economic growth (circa 1985 to today) that followed, which introduced a more liberal regulatory climate in both trade (NAFTA) and foreign investment.[62]

What about the business community itself? Why would a relatively small entrepreneur from Moncton, New Brunswick, wish to locate a kitchen cabinet plant in China? The answer is straightforward – because it makes business sense to do so. It is for the same reason that large American conglomerates such as Bausch & Lomb set up a plant in Ireland. Private firms will naturally pursue opportunities to lower their costs, become more efficient, increase profit margins, try to secure a larger share of their market, and pay less tax. National governments, meanwhile, will happily accommodate legitimate businesses that are searching the world to pursue new opportunities by responding as best they can to the needs of private firms and their investment plans. Again, their role is to provide the policy and infrastructure framework to encourage private-sector investment.

I put another question to the Moncton entrepreneur who set up a plant in China: "Which government would you rather deal with – the Government of Canada, your government at home, or the Chinese government? His response: "The government in China because government officials are there to make things happen; they can be remarkably flexible when you are bringing investment and machinery into China. They can tailor things to what you need. Canadian government officials have set policies and programs to deliver. Senior government officials in Canada may be flexible for large businesses that have political clout in Ottawa, but when it comes to my level they are set in their ways and are much less flexible."[63] Bureaucrats in Anglo-American democracies no longer seem to have the ability to make deals. A good number of public servants themselves accept this criticism and acknowledge that Ottawa has become so bureaucratic and fixated on rules, processes, and transparency that it is almost impossible to get anything done with business representatives any more. They also point to the problem of the growing number of oversight bodies constantly looking over their shoulders.[64] The power that bureaucrats once had has dissipated to the point where only when a file they are working on grabs the attention of the national media and the country's political leadership can they move things forward at a reasonable speed.

In any event, for entrepreneurs dealing with two governments, things are very often better for them than when they are dealing with just one. For one thing, it enables the entrepreneurs to compare the advantages provided by one against the other. It also enables them to apply pressure on their home government to grant concessions or special tax breaks to avoid losing jobs to another country. I asked a senior federal official why a Moncton-based entrepreneur would find it easier to deal with the Chinese government than with the Canadian. His response: "I am not surprised. Authoritarian states like China and Singapore have a much greater capacity to say, 'This is where we are going,' and make it stick than we do. They have fewer oversight bodies to deal with than we do, and the media are far less intrusive. Government officials have the delegated authority to strike deals, make decisions. They can certainly give the appearance that they are all moving in the same direction. We no longer have that authority, and we do now have dozens of oversight bodies always looking to strike if we make a bad decision. That, in a nutshell, is why."[65]

That said, governments in Anglo-American democracies have also reoriented their bureaucracies to promote their country's economic interests. Nowhere is this more evident than in the departments and agencies responsible for foreign affairs. Governments have been overhauling their diplomatic functions to extend the commercial and trade activities of their diplomats. Donna Lee and David Hudson write that business interests are increasingly being "formally integrated in diplomatic systems," and traditional diplomacy has been recast into the pursuit of national economic agendas.[66]

A senior official with Canada's Department of Foreign Affairs says that the organizational model under which Foreign Affairs officials operate around the Western world is "past its best before due date." She explains that things are vastly different today from what they were even twenty years ago:

> The ability to communicate in microseconds has changed things substantially. Prime ministers and presidents are no longer captive of their foreign affairs departments like they once were. They can pick up the telephone and speak with anyone. CEOs of large and well-known multinationals now have almost instant access to heads of government. They are free to speak their minds and to pursue their own economic interests. We are there to defend the position of our department, and the same can be said about other Foreign Affairs officials elsewhere. This model simply doesn't work anymore. We can no longer compete for the attention of our heads of government. This is as true in London, Paris, and Washington as it is in Ottawa.[67]

She adds, "Bill Gates is better informed, more influential, and has far better access to heads of government around the world than any Foreign Affairs minister."[68]

Asked if the department had been retooled to focus on promoting trade and economic opportunities, another Canadian Foreign Affairs official explained, "Trade has always been a part of foreign affairs and the work of our offices abroad, but it now dominates our work, certainly a lot more than in the past." He added, "trade was the very first interest to be globalized."[69] I also asked two other senior officials in the department whether international organizations should be overhauled. Their answer was short and to the point: "Yes."[70] One added, "Departments of Foreign Affairs do not bring tanks or trade. They bring policy and a capacity to manage issues. The question is: Is there still a market for this? I am not sure."[71]

Foreign Affairs officials are faced with yet another difficulty – the desire of subnational regions to integrate more fully in the global economy. Both Michigan and Ontario, for example, have less and less reason to be concerned with the economies of, say, Vermont or Nova Scotia. The traditional east-west trade between Canada and the United States is giving way to a north-south pattern. It is becoming more and more difficult for national governments to define a national economic interest that speaks to all its subregions. Ontario premier Dalton McGuinty recently spoke to this development when he said that his government will consider introducing a surcharge on Hyundai and Kia vehicles unless Korea opens access to its domestic markets. McGuinty explained that he has "a responsibility to find new and creative ways to protect our workers and our jobs."[72] Canada's auto-manufacturing sector is concentrated in Ontario, and the premier, unlike the Canadian prime minister, does not need to balance the interests of that sector with those of the non-renewable energy sector, for example, which is largely concentrated in Western and Atlantic Canada. Thirty years ago, subnational regions were better integrated into national economies, and the Ontario premier had no good reason to muse about launching a trade war with a foreign country. This, if nothing else, makes it more difficult for citizens to sort out which order of government has power over international trade issues.

We need to underline two points here. First, most countries in the Western world and elsewhere have liberalized their investment environment to attract foreign investment and to promote a more competitive economy. The business community has responded. Second, the international architecture in place to establish the rules of the game – the

International Monetary Fund (IMF), the World Bank, the United Nations and its agencies, the General Agreement on Tariffs and Trade (GATT), now the World Trade Organization (WTO), and the Organization for Economic Co-operation and Development (OECD) – has, in the opinion of Kevin Lynch (Canada's top public servant between 2006 and 2009 and a director at the IMF between 2004 and 2006), remained "largely unchanged," notwithstanding the "dramatic events of the last sixty years."[73]

It is beyond the scope of this work to review the strengths and weaknesses of international organizations. In any event, it is a well-travelled territory in the international relations literature.[74] International organizations are bureaucratic organizations. They are path-dependent, they often favour the status quo and can be slow to react to new developments and changing circumstances. They survive year after year, with little or no cuts to their operations, and it is not always clear who has the power to change their orientation. They may well be costly to run and overstaffed, but who is to know, how is one to know, and, better yet, who should or even could be doing something about it?[75] Gordon Brown, Britain's prime minister, echoed the views of Kevin Lynch by pointing out that international institutions date back to the immediate post-World War II days, but he went further by calling for "an overhaul of global institutions to deal with new priorities."[76]

Change at the international level is negotiated between member states, with some having far more influence than others. Political leaders in national governments do not always have the time or, for that matter, the interest to focus on the work of international organizations. In addition, in many instances, international organizations no longer have the policy instruments to intervene, and it is doubtful that member states would wish to give them too much political or economic clout to intervene in capital markets or to get in the way in the flow of foreign investment. Flexibility holds distinct advantages for political leaders, and for this if for no other reason it often suits nation-states to avoid clarity of purpose in international organizations. Notwithstanding the above, we do know that some international organizations – notably the IMF and the World Bank – have been responsive to the policy fashion of the time, both of them aggressively promoting privatization and pushing client nations to pursue a pro-business agenda.[77] Particularly in recent years, they have urged countries to embrace the global economy by requiring their governments to open up their borders to international trade, foreign investment, and privatization.

Lastly, it is important to stress that nation-states have given up power to regional trade agreements such as NAFTA and the WTO and to financial markets. As a result, national governments have lost some of their power to international forces, particularly on broad economic issues such as fiscal stabilization policies, monetary policy, and exchange rates and tariffs.[78] The Canadian government, for example, launched one of the most ambitious program review exercises in its history in 1995, but the motive had more to do with international financial markets than domestic politics. It will be recalled that in December 1994 Mexico was plunged into a currency crisis and the Mexican economic miracle came to an abrupt end. Within weeks, the Canadian dollar also came under attack. Given its high accumulated government debt, Canada became the focus of scrutiny by international financial markets. In early January 1995, the *Wall Street Journal* described the Canadian dollar as a "basket case." The *Journal* ran an editorial on 12 January titled "Bankrupt Canada?" and declared, "Mexico isn't the only U.S. neighbour flirting with the financial abyss." It went on to argue, "If dramatic action isn't taken in the next month's federal budget, it's not inconceivable that Canada could hit the debt wall and have to call in the International Monetary Fund to stabilize its falling currency."[79]

The editorial had a major impact on those in the Cabinet who were hesitant to cut government spending; indeed, the deputy minister of finance, David Dodge, later described it as a "seminal event" in the politics of the 1995 budget.[80] The result is that $29 billion in spending cuts was made and nearly 50,000 public service jobs were eliminated or transferred to other jurisdictions.[81] Given the Dodge comments, one can assume that without the *Wall Street Journal* article and international financial markets, the government would not have been nearly as successful in its 1995–97 program review exercise. The Chrétien government could, and did, invoke the international financial markets to justify its deep spending cuts. It made the case that this was not something it wanted to do, but international financial markets had forced its hand.[82] Some of the power to craft a country's fiscal framework had to some extent slipped out of the grasp of national governments and shifted to the international business community.

Staying Put but Not Standing Still

Globalization has also had a profound impact even on businesses that have decided to stay home. The competitiveness of the global economy reaches down to small firms in small communities as well as to large firms in large urban areas. Firms may decide to stay home, but the competitive nature of the global economy will know where to find them. The Moncton entrepreneur who set up a plant to manufacture kitchen cabinets did so to ensure that his business would be competitive at home, not in China.

In the fall of 2007 I met with a senior forestry executive from Quebec who spoke about recent developments in his sector. He outlined far-reaching changes in virtually every aspect of his industry. He reported, for example, that logging is no longer anything like it was thirty years ago. Today, he explained, a logger is an entrepreneur who must buy a highly sophisticated and expensive machine to remain in business. "We now," he said, "have automated and computer-guided machines that are costly and have to operate some twenty hours a day to be economically viable. The entrepreneur runs his machine for ten hours and hires someone else to operate it for the other ten hours. At the end of the day, we run a computer printout that tells how many minutes were taken for lunch, for a health break, or for any other reason. This is the way it works. This is not because we are hard-driving business executives who take pleasure in seeing people work ten hours a day. It is quite simple: either we do it or we do not survive. If we do not do this, the competition from Brazil will drive all of us out of business. That is what competition is now all about."[83] Put another way, he was saying, "Don't blame me, blame globalization."

For small businesses as well as large, globalization means that foreign influences are felt in their operations and communities. To be sure, businesses, large and small, will pressure governments wherever they are located to adjust their policies so that they can compete better, given the requirements of the global economy. Chrysler, for example, told the Canadian government in early 2008 that it needed to come up with an automotive policy that "helps the industry or the country risks losing future investment."[84] The president of Chrysler LLC explained that it was "all about us being more competitive" and called on the government to "do things that are so unique that industries want to come here." He pointed out that "building a new plant in Canada that would assemble 200,000 vehicles a year would cost $800-million (U.S.), compared with $250-million in China and perhaps $450-million in Mexico." Further, he said, "We can get approvals in other states here much faster than in Canada. If you're competing with an investment in different locations and others are faster, you lose out." He insisted, however, that he "was not asking any government to bail Chrysler out."[85] He later had a change of mind, of course, as did other US-based automotive manufacturers.

Globalization was forcing Chrysler to act, and in turn Chrysler executives argued that it should be forcing the Canadian government to respond. If not, Canada would lose important new investment. The global marketplace now holds the power to decide where jobs should be located, and it is left to both Chrysler and the Canadian government to accommodate its requirements.

The Internet Makes It Possible

The Internet opens up much of the world to small businesses. It enables entrepreneurs and aspiring entrepreneurs to establish contact with potential clients all over the world and ship their products everywhere without having to establish costly regional or representative offices.

In March 2000 two entrepreneurs, with modest funding from a handful of venture capitalists, established VistaPrint, a website to provide online printing services, primarily to small businesses. They designed an automated and integrated graphic design and print process that connects large printing presses directly to the customers and their computers. VistaPrint's printing process is fully automated so that it requires a minimum number of staff to run its operations.

In seven years, VistaPrint has grown from a concept developed by two young aspiring entrepreneurs to a publicly traded company with well over a billion-dollar (US) value in market capitalization, which generates over $500 million in annual revenues. The Internet-based order-processing systems receive and store tens of thousands of individual print jobs daily and, using complex algorithms, efficiently aggregate these jobs for printing as a single press-run. VistaPrint's systems search pending individual print jobs, select those with similar printing parameters for combination into a single larger aggregate job, and calculate the optimal allocation of print orders that result in the lowest production costs and on-time delivery. This enables VistaPrint to significantly reduce the costs and inefficiencies associated with traditional short-run printing and to provide customized finished products in as little as three days from design to delivery.

VistaPrint correctly maintains that it has come up with what is called a disruptive business model. Its impact is being felt by small printing businesses in communities throughout the Western world and beyond. In April 2000, VistaPrint had 500 customers. By early 2009 it had over

17,000,000 in more than 120 countries. The firm was established in the Boston area, but by 2009 nearly 40 percent of its revenues came from non-US markets. It achieved this by setting up nineteen localized websites so that customers could order in their own language and currency high-quality business cards, brochures, envelopes, flyers, calendars, and a variety of other marketing tools at a substantially lower cost than from the local printing shop.

VistaPrint now has over 1,400 employees, and its main operations are still in Boston. However, its head office is in Bermuda (for tax reasons); its call centre to assist customers is in Jamaica (because of low-cost and highly qualified personnel); a printing plant in Windsor, Ontario, services the North American market (because of its geographic location and, at the time it was established, to take advantage of the lower Canadian currency); another printing plant is in Venlo, Netherlands, to service Europe (because of its strategic transportation links); and its European marketing operations are in Barcelona, Spain (because of access to highly qualified personnel). VistaPrint has over 70 employees in its Barcelona marketing office, which includes "50 multi-national employees."[86] Its 19 regional operations, meanwhile, are all located in cyberspace, with little overhead cost.[87]

VistaPrint located its operations in various countries for reasons of efficiency, but also to take advantage of tax benefits. VistaPrint Limited is a Bermuda-based company because Bermuda does not currently impose any tax computed on profits or income, which results in a zero tax liability for profits recorded in Bermuda. The Jamaican operation is located in a tax-free zone, so VistaPrint pays no tax on profits generated there.[88]

VistaPrint is, of course, not the only firm to use the Internet to develop a disruptive business model. The Internet is enabling small firms, not just large transnationals such as Coca-Cola and General Electric, to drive global integration. This, combined with the integration of financial markets, is also shifting power in several ways; the days of hierarchy with clearly defined boundaries and a fairly clear nationality have given way to the Web or to a façade with no physical offices or presence. The new business organization is in many ways a stateless or multistate "global web," consisting of production and marketing activities linked together by computers, e-mails, and satellites.[89] Its loyalty is to its shareholders, to clients, to market forces, and to the Internet that made its success possible. Nation-states, for the new business organization, are relegated to second-tier concerns, to be managed and accommodated or avoided, depending on the business requirements.

Locating Power in Cyberspace

The market has been unleashed on a world scale, and countries that are unwilling to throw their markets wide open are left out in the cold. At the risk of sounding repetitive, countries that go further in reducing corporate taxes, cutting red tape, and privatizing state corporations tend to see their economies prosper more than those that do not. To be sure, globalization has created wealth as well as the occasional financial crisis. Countries and regions, starting with Britain, that once lagged behind have moved up the ladder by embracing Thatcher's laissez-faire economics model.

The Internet, the lowering of trade barriers, and international financial markets that operate in real time, however, are making it increasingly difficult for national governments to control their own economies and to identify who actually wields power, either political or economic. Whatever else may be said about the Internet, it has promoted more open political systems and encouraged a free flow of information. Given that national governments can no longer manage or even control the flow of information to its residents to the extent that they could only thirty years ago, some observers believe that new communication technologies are transcending physical space.[90] In brief, the Internet has become a powerful autonomous force for economic and social change across physical boundaries.

Manuel Castells argues that the new information age disempowers individual workers, since they have become "lean individuals, farmed out in a flexible network whose whereabouts are unknown to the network itself." He adds, however, that the new networks "do more than organize activity or share information. They are the actual producers and distributors," so power in network societies is no longer concentrated in institutions such as the state but is "diffused in global networks of wealth, power, information and images and transmuted in a system of variable geometry and dematerialized geometry."[91] The Internet promotes what is labelled "many to many" rather than "one to many," the classic television approach to communication.[92] The result is that "the ubiquitous nature of the Internet has rendered the implementation of purely nation-state based regulations rather difficult, making international action in more policy fields even more urgent."[93] Power, it will be recalled, requires two parts to work: somebody to give a command and someone with an obligation to obey. The new information age is making it more difficult to pinpoint who is giving a command and who obeys.

Bill Gates once envisaged "friction-free capitalism"; that is, the information age would enable customers to know the best price and the best quality of goods at all times, while businesses would know exactly what customers wanted and would produce it quickly. His point is that the Internet serves to extend the marketplace around the globe in real time and that economic power would in future rest in the hands of the consumer.[94] Put differently, economic power should be easy to locate, since one only needs to look to the consumer.

Gates was not forthcoming on the role of national governments in friction-free capitalism, but one can conclude that he saw a limited role for them. Friction-free capitalism is yet to arrive (companies downsize, workers continue to lose their jobs, and small print shop owners go out of business in communities around the world because of firms like Vista-Print), and not all customers are happy with the new marketplace. Still, Gates joined the chorus that sings the praise of free market economies. He writes: "Capitalism, demonstrably the greatest of the constructed economic systems, has in the past decade clearly proved its advantages over the alternative systems. As the Internet evolves into a broadband, global, interactive network, those advantages will be magnified. Product and active providers will see what buyers want a lot more efficiently. I think Adam Smith would be pleased."[95]

Bill Gates is a charter member of the "superclass," a class that has an international perspective and wields considerable influence if not direct power. The opinions of its members matter, and they have access not just to one another but also to key political leaders. Samuel Huntington writes that members of the superclass "have little need for national loyalty, view national boundaries as obstacles that thankfully are vanishing, and see national governments as residues from the past."[96]

David Rothkopf has established that the superclass comprises 6,000 individuals. He explains that these elites have varied resumés, not just wealth. They are powerful because of who they are, where they meet (for example, at the annual Davos conference), and because their opinions often receive wide media coverage. Rothkopf identified the 6,000 individuals on the basis of their "ability to regularly influence the lives of millions of people in multiple countries worldwide."[97]

The problem is that the great majority of these individuals exercise power and influence transnationally, while laws and regulations are the product of nation-states and are confined within the borders of nation-states. It is possible to determine who the members of the superclass are, but only for a relatively brief period because of their transient nature.

Rothkopf insists that publishing the list would be an exercise in futility because it would be obsolete the day after it was published.[98] It is also very difficult to document their power and where and how they exercise it, because the superclass prefers to exercise its influence away from the public eye. A discreet telephone call to a prime minister, to a newspaper editor, or the head of a large multinational can move an idea or a project along without any public fanfare.

Everyone Benefits from Laissez-Faire

Tom Courchene, one of Canada's leading economists, contrasts the old economic paradigm with the new. He writes that in the industrial age, "the principal economic dynamic was government-driven, nation-centred capitalism. Now in the information age, the principal dynamic is commerce-driven, globe-centred capitalism." Nation-states may well have been in the past better able to control nation-centred capitalism, and voters may have been better able to hold government policy makers to account. Things are not so simple for globe-centred mechanisms because, leaving aside market forces, we do not know which institutions to turn to when holding someone, anyone, to account.

Canada, Courchene argues, is less and less a single east-west or national economy. He believes that the Canadian government should permit private-sector initiatives in the new economy unless the government can demonstrate that they are contrary to the public interest. This would reverse the burden of proof now placed on companies and would, for example, "enable Canadian banks to merge without waiting for decades for the right Finance Minister and the right political moment to come along to give their blessings."[99]

Globalization, the information age, a widespread belief in a free market economy, coupled with the view that government bureaucracies have become inept and that government intervention in the economy is more often than not unwise and unproductive have all served to limit the role of nation-states. Put differently, for several reasons, national governments can no longer do what they did in the past. Until the recent financial crisis erupted, first in the United States and then around the world, national governments believed that it was not their responsibility to deal with economic bubbles of one kind or another, but they did not answer the question: Whose responsibility is it to do so? The question has become even more perplexing since the economic downturn of late 2008. If governments made a mess of things in the 1970s and then financial institutions made a mess of things in 2008, where should power and responsibility now lie?

National governments soon realized that they did not have the tools, let alone the capacity, to deal with the situation. They began to throw money at the problem, uncertain if it was the right medicine. The policy capacity of their public services, as we will see in later chapters, had been run down and was thus not equipped to provide the solution, particularly to those problems originating outside their borders. It also remains to be seen whether national public services still have the capacity to deliver new programs to stimulate the economy efficiently.

We know that national and international issues no longer respect boundaries and that nation-states can no longer act as self-determining entities; the locus of power has shifted, and it is now shared among many different agents.[100] Samuel Huntington's widely quoted definition of the term "Davos Man" still resonates. As noted above, he wrote that individuals now see "little need for national loyalty"; they believe that "national boundaries are thankfully vanishing, and see national governments as residues from the past whose only useful function is to facilitate the elite's global operations."[101]

How, then, does one locate power and responsibility in a borderless world run by individuals and organizations without boundaries and with limited hierarchies? It seems that we should no longer focus on institutions but should look to corporations and especially to individuals. How can one do this in the case of truly stateless corporations born on the Internet? In addition, for the most part (leaving aside the power of military intervention), power in the global economy today involves asymmetrical negotiations, making it even more difficult. Shared responsibility, the operations of the global economy and international financial markets, and the reach of the Internet in both the political and economic spheres have also enabled those who wield political and economic power to sidestep responsibility in exercising their power.

Given that the private sector is a dominant actor in the global economy, we need to explore who has power in the modern firm. Decisions are now taken in a number of places in large firms and in complex multinational business organizations – by directors, senior executives, managers, front-line workers, and shareholders.[102] We shall explore these issues in the next chapter.

2 THE PRIVATE SECTOR: SOMEONE NOW HAS POWER, BUT WHO?

In the spring of 1997 Raymond Garneau, the long-serving chair of the board and president-CEO of Industrial-Alliance, Canada's fifth largest insurance company, invited me to sit on the company's board of directors. Before I agreed to serve, I asked, "What do you expect from me, what would be my role, given that I know precious little about the life insurance business?" His response: "I wish some of the other members of the board would ask me the same question. There may come a point when you and other members of the board will have to decide to fire me. Essentially, your role boils down to this. You and the other board members will have to decide whether I stay or go."

Things are far more complicated today. There was a time when senior management reported to the president-CEO, who in turn had near absolute authority to run things as he saw fit. The board would play a broad oversight role and concentrate its efforts on assessing the performance of the president-CEO, albeit with varying degrees of effort and success. James Gillies, quoting the chair of the United States Steel Corporation, compared the value of directors of companies until the 1990s to "parsley on fish – decorative but useless."[1] He added that retiring chief executive officers, when reflecting on their careers prior to the 1990s, would always refer to "their" management teams and "their" companies. The boss, senior management, and hierarchy were important, and if one wanted to locate power, one did not need to search very far. Business schools, meanwhile, offered no courses on corporate governance until the 1990s.

Things began to change in the mid-1990s. The misuse of assets, highly publicized fraud cases, conflicts of interest, and spectacular failures were all thought to be linked to weakness in corporate governance. This led both governments and the private sector to introduce measures to strengthen corporate governance, which has now become a field of specialization in its own right, with books, seminars, workshops, and consultants always at the ready to explain new requirements and to report on the role and responsibilities of boards of directors.

Recent advances in communications have also served to redefine the relationships, not only between shareholders, senior management, and boards of directors but also within the firm itself. New communication technologies have enabled senior management to shift power and responsibility almost at will, depending on the circumstances and requirements. In addition, governments everywhere in Anglo-American democracies are more and more often striking partnership agreements with the private sector to deliver public services.

All of the above is not without implications for the location of power and responsibility. This chapter explores the issue by looking at changes in corporate governance and other recent developments in private-sector management practices. The central argument is that power in the private sector, much as in the public sector, will wish to avoid scrutiny. Those who wield power – again, much as in the public sector – will attempt to avoid taking responsibility when things go wrong, although they will want to be highly visible when there is success to be claimed. Powerful personalities capable of driving change are now highly valued, highly visible, and highly paid. The focus is on them and less on their management teams.

Somebody Needs to Be Responsible

Bertrand Russell observed that it has been "customary to accept economic power without analysis."[2] The thinking is that economic power, more than other forms of power or influence, is born of competition in the marketplace. There has for some time been a widely held consensus in Anglo-American democracies that arbitrary power and monopolies are unhealthy and that competition is one of the surest and simplest ways to avoid both.

The market is, or at least ought to be, open to everyone willing to compete, and ultimately it is the market that should decide who has economic power. The best will flourish, and those who cannot compete will disappear, and in the opinion of many, that is precisely the way it should be. That said, there are many forms of economic power; that of the local entrepreneur in his or her community is very different from that of a large multinational or transnational firm. The individual shareholder has a degree of ownership in a large firm but has no power and virtually no voice in the management of the enterprise. The same is obviously not the case for small owner-operated businesses.

As is well known, there have been efforts in recent years to strengthen the hand of shareholders in their dealings with management. Corporate scandals came to dominate the news all too often in the 1990s and early part of the following decade. Bre-X, Cinar Corporation, Livent Inc., and YBM Magnex International in Canada, and Enron, WorldCom, Adelphia, and Global Crossing in the United States come to mind. Outright fraud, cases of flagrant conflict of interest at senior levels, abuse of perks by senior management, and gross mismanagement led first to a crisis of confidence, particularly among investors, and then to public- and private-sector leaders demanding more stringent corporate governance requirements. The goal was to make clear, or at least clearer, who was responsible for what in the corporate world. But in the process, the measures may have muddied the location of responsibility further.

There was a time when the president-CEO of a publicly traded firm could say, "I'm in charge and therefore responsible." Even if nothing happened, one could point the finger at someone. Today, influence, if not responsibility, is in many instances shared between the president-CEO, the board of directors, and a host of organizations and groups promoting community interests or goals, notably the environment. This is not to suggest for a moment that better checks and balances on senior management are inherently bad. Rather, the point is that they have made it more difficult to establish who has power, influence, and responsibility. Today, only when a CEO becomes a superstar in the eyes of the media or shareholders can he or she say, "I'm in charge and therefore responsible."

The corporate governance reforms introduced in recent years in North America and Western Europe have a number of things in common. For the most part, they focus on the role of the board of directors, senior management, financial reporting, and transparency. The various reforms in Canada, the United States, and Europe have had a profound impact, at least on publicly traded companies. The impact has been felt at every level, from the board of directors and CEOs down to middle managers and financial officers. It has also relocated power and, in the process, made assigning responsibility considerably more difficult.

The reforms have created a new and highly profitable industry of consultants. From a virtual standstill as recently as the mid-1980s, there is now a veritable army of consultants roaming North America and Europe, ready to provide advice for a fee on how companies can and should approach corporate governance. But that is not all. There are today many magazines and journals on the topic, and centres of excellence on corporate governance have been established on many university campuses throughout North America and Europe. Moreover, we have codes and principles of good governance to guide senior management and members of boards of directors.[3]

The Reports

It will be recalled that in December 1994 the Toronto Stock Exchange Committee on Corporate Governance tabled a seminal report, *Where Were the Directors?* The report, commonly known as the Dey Report, broke new ground. It stated, "Investors and other parties interested in the welfare of corporations which failed or which have been significantly restructured have frequently been dissatisfied with the performance of their boards and management,"[4] and it concluded that there had been "several instances of corporate breakdown attributable in part to ineffective governance."[5] It outlined the key responsibilities of boards of directors: those relating to the stewardship of the corporation; the strategic planning process; the identification and monitoring of the principal risks of the business; the appointment, development, and succession of senior management; the implementation of an effective communications policy; and the adoption of relevant and reliable internal systems to enable the board to fulfill these responsibilities.

The report presented a series of recommendations designed to strengthen the effectiveness of boards of directors. It proposed that a majority of directors be "unrelated" – that is, free of relationships and other interests that could or could be perceived to interfere with the exercise of judgment in the best interests of the corporation. It prescribed a number of governance-related functions to be carried out by the board, normally through board committees. These include: (i) the process of constituting the board, which would entail recruiting new directors and assessing the effectiveness of the existing board and the contribution of its individual members; (ii) assessing management, which would entail meeting with management to establish objectives and to monitor progress in relation to these objectives; and (iii) establishing and administering the corporation's system of governance.[6]

In the United States, Kenneth Lay, former Enron chairman and chief executive officer, essentially argued, following the firm's high-profile debacle, "I take the blame, but I am not to blame." He pointed the finger at Enron chief's financial officer, Andrew Fastow, as the one who should be held responsible.[7] The Enron catastrophe, among others, gave rise to numerous urgent calls to repair corporate governance in America. It led the United States Congress, the Senate, and President Bush to sign into law the Sarbanes-Oxley Act in 2002. The Sarbanes-Oxley reforms were designed to enhance financial disclosure, strengthen the hand of external auditors, punish white-collar crimes, establish limits on the behaviour of corporate officers, and strongly encourage, if not require, boards of directors to assume a stewardship responsibility.[8]

Canada, meanwhile, followed the findings of the Dey Report with still more initiatives, including the Saucier Report, which sought to strengthen corporate governance practices in Canada. The Toronto Stock Exchange specifically called on the board of directors of "every corporation" to assume "responsibility for the stewardship of the corporation."[9]

The United Kingdom introduced similar measures. A number of its firms have signed on to a combined code of good governance. The code has a preamble that outlines what is expected of "listed companies in the United Kingdom." It then spells out in considerable detail how "listed companies" should deal with shareholders, how new internal controls should work, and what the role of the board of directors and its chair should be, and it outlines processes to be followed to establish performance-related remuneration.[10] The United Kingdom, however, did not go as far as the Americans did under the Sarbanes-Oxley Act. Indeed, a number of firms decided to list their stocks in London rather than in the United States to avoid dealing with Sarbanes-Oxley.[11]

Europe also introduced measures to strengthen corporate governance, largely because of the increasing cross-border activity of institutional investors, the growing importance of stock markets in Europe, and the need to promote transparency.[12] There are different approaches among European countries, but there is less and less "disparity between them" on corporate governance measures, and the issue is now "at the top of the Board agenda" of many publicly traded firms.[13] Thus, globalization is being felt in corporate governance, as it is in many economic sectors. Boards of directors and senior management everywhere became convinced that they needed to fall into step or risk losing investments and credibility on the world stage.

Consultants in corporate governance are no different from those found in other fields. They have clients and they are in the business of generating new work and turning a profit. Though they are not solely responsible for it, corporate governance continues to expand as new requirements and activities are added in several areas, including financial reporting and auditing. The boards of directors are now expected to have a much broader and more rigorous agenda than simply making sure that the corporation has the right chief executive officer.

Today, things are different on many fronts for boards of directors when compared with even twenty years ago. They are now called upon to take part in succession planning, including "appointing, training and monitoring senior management."[14] They are expected to establish a strong working relationship with "members of the senior management team" and to set "the tone at the top" as well as the "ethical tone for the corporation."[15] They are also expected to play a key role in producing a corporate strategy and in evaluating the performance of their colleagues on the board. Individual board members are asked to evaluate, on a continuing basis, whether "the information they receive from management is sufficient to discharge their responsibilities effectively."[16] And this is not all. They are expected to "stay on top of the issues," enrol in training and educational programs, and gain a full understanding of the statutory liabilities to which individual board members are now subject.

Publicly traded companies now have charters or guidelines to respect. A typical charter lays down in specific terms the "responsibilities" and "obligations" as well as "qualification standards" for members of the board of directors. The guidelines are quite detailed and run the full gamut, from evaluating the work of the chief executive officer to assessing the firm's resources and to understanding risks and the factors determining the firm's success. Board members no longer simply go along for the ride; they are now "partners" with senior management in establishing the firm's broad strategic direction, exercising "business judgment," and establishing management, operational, and financial objectives.[17]

Directors are now expected to accept responsibility, or at least part of it, when things go badly in a publicly listed company. Being held responsible for something is one thing, but determining precisely what role the board and individual board members should play is another. McKinsey recently joined forces with the Anderson Governance Group and the Institute of Corporate Directors to sponsor a series of surveys to provide the answer. The surveys reveal that as recently as the late 1990s, half of the members of boards of directors reported that they had little or no understanding of what was going on in the firms they were being asked to govern. However, by the early 2000s the surveys reported that there had been a significant shift and the "utility of board decisions" had "increased dramatically." Board members now believe that they need to be more involved in strategic development and to become more hands-on in assessing the quality of management plans and even how the corporate strategy should be implemented.[18]

Thus, the role of boards of directors has expanded considerably in recent years, and they now hold some power and responsibility for establishing both strategic direction and good management of publicly listed companies. More to the point, power and responsibility are shared between boards of directors and management far more than they were thirty or even fifteen years ago.

I consulted with individual board members to gain an appreciation of how they see the recent changes. One long-serving member (first appointed in the mid-1990s) of the board of the Canadian National Railway reports that the changes in corporate governance are like "night and day," completely different from the way things were in the mid-1990s. He explains: "The liability issue or the possibility that someone will take legal action against you for your decisions or lack thereof has significantly changed how directors go about their responsibilities." In addition, he claims that much more is expected of directors today and the contribution of individual directors is now reviewed on an annual basis: "If you have not influenced anything in a year or two, you will not stay on the board. We now do our homework; if not, we go off the board. In addition, we now say 'no' to management on things, which we hardly, if ever, did fifteen years ago."[19]

Several board members of other publicly listed companies whom I interviewed in Toronto in January 2008 *all* reported that boards play a much more activist role than they did fifteen years ago. One remarked, "No more rubber stamping of things management wants. It does not, however, mean never-ending confrontations between the board and management, but it does mean that senior management knows that it can no longer dominate everything."[20] No more rubber stamping means that boards of directors have to carve out a distinct role, a role that empowers board members to orient the firm's strategic direction and also to take important decisions. If anything, the role of board members may expand still more in the years ahead. The 2008 crisis in financial markets has led many observers to urge boards of directors to play an even greater role in relation to management.[21] As their responsibilities expand, it means that many CEOs and their management teams have lost some of their power.

It Is a Different World

Corporate governance reforms have come at a cost. The role of the chief executive officer has been altered, and CEOs, together with senior management, can no longer bestride the corporation like a colossus, as was often the case until the 1990s. Those who do, those who are able to muscle their way through corporate governance charters, guidelines, and transparency requirements, are the superstars of the business world. These superstars are those who, through the force of their personalities, can "deliver for shareholders." There is now an annual ranking of the world's best presidents/chief executive officers.[22] The superstars have power on the basis of their reputations, and boards of directors are careful in their dealings with them for fear that they will go elsewhere.

The political leaders who crafted the Sarbanes-Oxley Act were not content to let legal prosecutors deal with those who had committed fraud or misrepresented financial reports. Their primary focus was to prevent future wrongdoing by enlarging the role of boards of directors and by introducing a number of disclosure requirements. In doing so, they forced most CEOs to share not only the limelight but also the responsibility for the corporation, its stewardship, and its strategic direction, even down to succession planning in its senior ranks. Gone are the days when the board was limited to firing the CEO and hiring a new one if the need arose. The need did not surface very often, if only because the CEO and senior management had a firm hand on all the levers of power and controlled the flow of information to the board of directors. CEOs now have to deal with a variety of measures that force them to respond to the wishes of their boards and also to seek their advice and approval on a number of issues and to deal with a growing number of reporting requirements. These requirements tend to place more emphasis on compliance than on judgment.

Power and responsibility are more apparent when one exercises judgment than when one relies on compliance. Responsibility is also more apparent when the onus is on someone to perform and to be held responsible for the performance. This is not to suggest for a moment that today's CEOs are without power. The superstars, from Bill Gates and Steve Jobs to Warren Buffett, still wield considerable power. All in all, CEOs still have access to the levers of power – if less so than in years past. They still control the information that flows to their boards, still meet with financial analysts, and still decide in large measure who gets promoted and who does not. They shape the company's strategic plan and represent the company to the outside world. The one important difference is that most must now share some of their power with their boards and deal with many more demanding transparency requirements.

Executive compensation, for example, is today much more in the open than in past years. Stock options and bonus practices are treated as compensation expenses, and bonuses are declared and regularly made public. Financial statements are prepared in accordance with more demanding accounting practices, and all corporations are required to report certain basic financial information to their shareholders. "Frameworks" are required to monitor the management of business opportunities and risks, and processes have to be put in place to guide and monitor relationships between corporations and investment dealers.

All of the above, however, comes at a financial cost. Not long after the Sarbanes-Oxley Act came into force, a number of studies were produced showing that the cost of complying with the act amounted to about $3 million annually in 2006 for companies with revenues of $6–7 billion a year. Other studies suggest that the total cost of the legislation could, over time, be as high as $1.4 trillion when measuring changes in market value around "key legislative events." Still other studies suggest that the compliance costs have come down in more recent years as auditors became more familiar with the Sarbanes-Oxley requirements.[23] It is not at all clear, however, how one could possibly isolate the impact of the legislation on the market value of individual firms. Some studies, meanwhile, suggest that the legislation may have had the opposite effect because it has lowered the cost of borrowing for firms that have improved internal control measures.[24]

Whatever the various studies may report, a number of senior corporate executives insist that the financial cost of implementing corporate governance measures has been high, and few of them will acknowledge that the measures entail many benefits, including lower borrowing costs. Senior managers argue that the reforms have inhibited their ability to manage and have bureaucratized management processes, thus slowing down decision making. In short, they have been built on the premise that senior management cannot be fully trusted. An emphasis on greater transparency, whether in the public or private sector, sends a signal that, left on their own, some managers make bad or self-serving decisions, hence the need for greater control and more oversight bodies and requirements. Transparency, it appears, has also had an impact on members of boards of directors. One board member of a major Canadian corporation recently told me that he refuses to fly on the corporation's private jet because there is now a requirement to make public the names of all those who use it.[25]

Shareholders, on the other hand, and those who sit on boards of directors approve of the reforms because they enlarge their own role, influence, and profile. Many individual shareholders also welcome attempts to strengthen corporate governance because, if they make the effort, they can gain much more information on the business, its operations, and the remuneration of its senior executives than at any time in the past. However, many large institutional investors and senior management hold a different view.

Independent observers have reviewed the impact, both positive and negative, in terms of the cost of compliance with the Sarbanes-Oxley Act and similar requirements elsewhere. They report that many firms reconsidered their organizational form in the immediate aftermath of the Sarbanes-Oxley reforms. Some maintain that, for a number of firms, going private could well be an "attractive response" to the act. Indeed, three students of business reported on the greater frequency of publicly listed companies doing just that; they noted that the tendency to go from public to private was greater among smaller firms and companies that already had high inside ownership.[26] Others came to the same conclusion. In a paper prepared for the RAND Corporation, three observers of American economics maintained that the act does not encourage smaller firms to access the public capital market.[27] Not only is compliance expensive for smaller firms, but entrepreneurs have little patience for elaborate reporting requirements, preferring to focus their efforts on enlarging their businesses.

There are, of course, a number of factors that influence a firm's decision to go private, and the corporate governance requirements on publicly traded companies are an important one. *Business Week* explains:

"The flexibility is alluring. In private equity, there's less annoyance from the Sarbanes-Oxley Act, the controversial regulations passed in 2002 to police publicly held companies."[28] Some leading institutional investors insist that "governance is superior at private firms, as decisions can be made much quicker."[29] Mark Woodward, CEO at the high-tech Serena firm, explained the rationale for moving from a public to a private organizational model: "Being public means that Serena was spending $2 million a year on achieving and maintaining Sarbanes-Oxley compliance." He added that public companies "are now so worried about regulations that they only provide bland information," so they went "from lots of information given to some people, to very little information given to lots of people."[30] But this seems to defeat the purpose of Sarbanes-Oxley to promote greater transparency. It is also important to note that low interest rates for the past fifteen years or so have allowed private equity firms to access capital in financial markets to buy out shareholders and take companies private. A number of students of business have expressed concern over the recent trend to privatize public companies. Michael Useem at the Wharton School, for example, suggests that the recent exodus of publicly traded firms is a "sign that the ascent of widely held companies over the past century might be cresting. With capital in fewer hands, there are fewer checks and balances coming from other stakeholders."[31]

Niagara Corporation announced in 2004, two years after Sarbanes-Oxley came into law, that it "was going dark" and would be "delisting its common stock." In 2003, just twelve months after Sarbanes-Oxley, more than 200 firms in the United States went dark, up from 67 in the previous year.[32] "Going dark" means that firms cease to report to the Securities Exchange Commission by deregistering their common stock, though they continue to trade in the over-the-counter market. It appears that the decision to go dark is not solely in order to cut costs to meet compliance requirements. The findings of a comprehensive review reveal that "insiders may be using the veil of deregistration in order to decrease their legal risk ... thus having the perverse effect of decreasing transparency."[33]

Going private or dark offers a number of advantages. There is considerably less need for transparency or, in the case of going private, to share power with others and to respond to the financial analysts. Going dark also means that firms and their senior management can sidestep the elaborate institutional infrastructure and legal requirements that have been put in place to promote good governance.

In brief, stronger corporate governance requirements have shifted power and responsibility in publicly listed companies, while going private or going dark have brought down a veil of secrecy on formerly listed public companies. In the first instance, the location of power and responsibility has been muddied, and in the second it has become hidden or much less evident to those on the outside. Going dark also means that it is more difficult to identify who has power.

Power and Responsibility within the Firm

A long-serving employee of the National Bank of Canada compares the responsibility of a bank manager today versus twenty years ago when she was first appointed branch manager. Twenty years ago, she had delegated authority to approve mortgages or loans up to $300,000. Today, the local bank manager has virtually no authority to make any loans. All loan requests are sent to the risk assessment centre at head office for review and decision. The local branch manager is, of course, free to make a recommendation, but it is the centre that takes the decision. The centre, in turn, relies almost exclusively on Equifax's formula to establish a credit score to arrive at its decisions.[34]

"What," I asked, "do branch managers now do to keep busy?" Her answer: "They manage staff, pay close attention to clients, and do a great deal of public relations activities." She laments the passing of the old way of doing things, saying that it made for much better decisions and management: "You knew the client, and the client knew that it was you who made the decision. You met clients at social gatherings, at the grocery store, and you felt that they did not want to let you or anyone down. Today, things are different."[35] In other words, the client felt responsible to the local bank manager who approved the loan. It is much easier to let down a process, a formula, or a risk assessment centre located far from one's community than it is to let down your local bank manager.

A senior official with another Canadian bank has a similar take: "All decisions are now-hard wired into computers. We now have one manager managing three or four branches, making sure part-time workers are on time, the windows clean, and things like that. They are not much different than managers of fast-food outlets like McDonald's. Communities no longer recognize them or value their presence because today they simply have no power."[36] He claims that things really began to change when investment bankers took over the banks. He suggests that this new generation of bank executives decided to centralize decision making at head office or in their own offices and saw no reason why local branch managers should have any "power other than perhaps approving some car loans."[37]

He maintains that relying on sophisticated but incomplete risk assessment techniques and on impersonal "hard-wiring" investment decisions, rather than on the track record and economic potential of businesses and individuals, tends to make borrowers less responsible. He longs for the day when banking executives base their decisions on judgment of character and are held directly responsible for the decisions. He is not alone.

The increasing emphasis on risk management and reliance on established formulae to assess risk motivated Jamie Dimon, CEO of JP Morgan Chase, to urge his senior managers and peers to turn back the clock and "have people who you know and whom you trust, people who are transparent and have character, to look at the risk." He stressed the importance of common sense and having people in place "with good judgment."[38] It is better to hold individuals responsible than simply to rely on a formula put together by head office and outside consultants into which a multitude of individuals feed information. It is also easier to locate power in a local branch manager than in a risk assessment centre.

IT Has Changed Things

Developments in communications and information technology also have had a considerable impact on the location of power and responsibility within firms. They have strengthened the hand of senior executives in controlling their organizations, if only because people and processes are now monitored in a way that was not even conceivable thirty years ago. In traditional hierarchical organizations, senior executives established the business plan, middle managers told subordinates what to do, and front-line workers performed assigned tasks. In turn, middle managers informed their superiors of the outcomes. It was a classic case of employing carrots and sticks to get things done, to get managers and their employees to do what senior management expected.

Extensive use of communications technologies now makes it far easier for senior executives to monitor, evaluate, and control all parts of their organizations if they decide to do so. This development alone has shifted power within organizations away from middle management and front-line workers. People can now communicate in real time through e-mail, fax, and video conference. It is no more difficult for a senior executive in New York to contact a subordinate in Vancouver than it is to contact a subordinate on the next floor or down the hall. In addition, IT makes it possible for top management to establish elaborate reporting and evaluation requirements to which employees down the line or in offices thousand of kilometres away must respond.

The impact of IT on the organization and decision making of firms has been hotly debated in business schools. Some insist that IT has been a force for centralization, while others argue the opposite. To be sure, IT has considerably increased the information available to top management and boards of directors, and provided the instruments to centralize decision making.

However, IT can also promote a form of decentralization. It can easily and quickly disseminate information to all corners of the globe. Hand in hand with developments in IT, new organizational models have taken form in recent years. The flat organizational structure, which tends to centralize decision making, and a matrix model, which generates a great deal of information and data, have been joined by a network model, which promotes decentralization and informal communication networks that connect all parts of a firm. All have advantages and drawbacks, and it is up to senior executives and their boards to adopt the right model to fit the circumstances and the firm. The point is that developments in IT have enabled senior executives and their boards to centralize decision making if they so decide or to empower front-line managers and their employees if it makes business sense to do so. Locating power in this environment is far more difficult than it is under the traditional organization model.

No matter the model, developments in IT have given senior executives the upper hand because of the level of detailed information that computer-driven systems can generate. IT makes it easy to collect, analyze, move, and share information. It also makes it easier for senior executives to monitor performance, evaluate approaches and opportunities, provide rapid feedback, and control activities.[39]

It is easier today for managers to set the ground rules, intervene whenever they wish, and control the organization and staff. Indeed, IT has enabled organizations to decentralize their operations, motivate their knowledge workers, and promote creativity in their operations because it allows senior executives to control quality assurance and monitor risk management. In short, senior executives now have ready access to many sources of knowledge, and they no longer have to rely exclusively on managers down the hierarchy.[40] Indeed, it is no exaggeration to write that fairly independent decentralized decision makers have been replaced by centralized decision makers, able to control operations by being connected to front-line managers and workers.[41]

In brief, IT has enabled the private sector to decentralize operations to respond better to their clients' competitive pressure for timeliness and quality while centralizing power. In addition, regional offices can no longer operate as free agents to the extent they could thirty years ago because executives up the ladder now have access to superior information, enabling them to monitor, evaluate, and control their activities.[42]

The power to make decisions is also much less static than it was thirty years ago. It can move up or down to accommodate changing circumstances, of the month or even the day. While this makes business sense, the client is no longer certain who has the power to make decisions, at least when dealing with local or regional offices. The same to some extent also applies to business organizations. It explains the rise in the private sector of superstars or successful leaders who show the way to success.

Shifting Power between Business and Government

Numerous authors have commented of late on the growing power of the business community in general and of large transnational corporations in particular. This increase in power comes from various sources and is employed at various levels. To complicate matters, the power and influence of businesses can now be exercised without leaving a trace.

The business world today has access to several levers of power in its dealings with government.[43] Size, together with its reputation for administrative efficiency when compared to the public sector, leaving aside large Wall Street firms, has given the business community a level of credibility that it did not enjoy thirty years ago. The political power of the private sector in the global economy is often tied to the size of some of the large transnational companies compared with a number of small national economies.[44] When Microsoft speaks, national governments listen very carefully in the hope that it may locate some of its activities in their nation or region.

To be sure, the 2008 financial and credit crisis revealed weaknesses in the private sector, particularly in the financial sector. However, when political leaders throughout the Western world decided to establish committees to advise them on dealing with the crisis, they turned to the business community in virtually all cases. In Canada, for example, finance minister Jim Flaherty assembled an eleven-member Economic Advisory Council to provide advice to the government. Nine of the eleven are leading members of Canada's business community, and another member, Jack Mintz, is an economist with very close ties to the private sector. Flaherty explained, "In this time of unprecedented economic turmoil, I am bringing some of Canada's best minds together to find solutions and help launch a timely recovery."[45] Similar committees with a strong private-sector bias were set up in other countries, including the United States and Britain. Thus, governments now turn to the business community for advice and guidance in both good and bad times.

In any event, many in the business community no longer wait for governments to call. They have in recent years turned to the lobby industry to make their views heard by governments. Leaving aside the United States, which has a long-established lobby industry in Washington, the growth in the number of lobbyists – for example, in Canada and the United Kingdom – has been truly remarkable. More will be said about the lobby industry in a subsequent chapter.

Public-Private Partnerships

Back in 1983, John Kenneth Galbraith wrote that "government and business are widely regarded as mutual enemies."[46] Times have changed. Governments in Anglo-American democracies, beginning with that of Margaret Thatcher but continuing to this day, have come to accept that the private sector is far more efficient than government at getting things done. Whether the reputation was earned or whether politicians were responsible for promoting it, bureaucracy has had a "bad press" for a number of years. In time, public servants themselves came to doubt their own institutions.

Bureaucracies in all Western democracies began to emulate the ways of the private sector. One former senior Canadian public servant maintains that things have gone too far. He writes:

Without blushing or even without a second thought, we now talk about our "customers" or "clients" in a way that would not have occurred to public servants three or four decades ago. And this is just the tip of the iceberg ... Sometimes the results of this attempt to reinvent the public sector into the private sector are quite bizarre. I recently visited a well-meaning colleague who proudly presented to me the organizational renewal efforts of a high-priced foreign consultant that consisted in, among other things, the translation of all terms of public administration and parliamentary democracy into private sector equivalents, including the reinvention of members of Parliament as the shareholders of the corporation and Cabinet as the Board of Directors.

He also reported that by the early 1990s, with the new public-management approach in vogue, a Canadian deputy minister waxed "expansively about what he believed to be the renewal and transformation of his own department. This is really serious stuff," he said. "It's just like the private sector."[47]

Governments have emulated the private sector in many ways. For example, to introduce private-sector efficiency into the public sector, they have set up public-private partnerships to undertake capital projects and deliver public services. These partnerships have been employed to build bridges, schools, prisons, and hospitals and to deliver health care, waste management services, and even social services. In the United States a public-private partnership agreement was struck to restore the Statue of Liberty. In Britain, Tony Blair's chief of staff described public-private partnerships as a "Conservative idea that works."[48] In Canada, the Harper government pledged to "make more frequent use of public-private partnerships."[49]

Marcel Massé, once Canada's top public servant and later a senior minister in the Chrétien Cabinet, explained in the mid-1990s that "governments everywhere have felt the need to streamline bureaucracies and turn more and more of their traditional programs over to the private sector."[50] What Massé had in mind for Canada were the public-private partnerships that became popular in the 1980s and 1990s in other Anglo-American democracies. The enthusiasm for such arrangements has not waned in recent years, despite the 2008 financial crisis. Public-private partnerships gave life to the call widely heard in the 1980s that governments should "steer" and the private sector should "row." They can take various forms, but the one of interest to us is the "true" or "substantive" partnership, where there is "joint responsibility for decision-making" and "risks and goals are shared."[51] Having joint responsibility and sharing risks and goals, however, does not clarify who has power and who holds responsibility when things go wrong. Indeed, it does the opposite.

The widely held belief that management in the private sector is far superior to that in the public sector has led politicians to turn over activities traditionally run by government bureaucracies to the business community to manage and deliver. Recent measures include load shedding, by which the public sector withdraws from providing certain services in the expectation that they can be provided by others; make-or-buy policies, by which government bureaucracies are required to compete with the private sector to see who should deliver selected services; contracting out certain activities; and forming partnerships with private-sector firms that assume certain responsibilities or deliver public services.

Politicians, including many on the left, continue to see significant benefits in public-private partnerships: they reduce the size of the public sector and promote more efficiency in delivering public services, which are ever-expanding. In brief, they concluded that these partnerships were a sure way to bring private-sector expertise and capital to the public sector.

Certainly, the private sector can bring benefits to the table. Large private firms have highly specialized in-house expertise; some can access sophisticated financial instruments, they know how to calculate risk, and many have a well-honed capacity to cut costs when necessary. They can also assume up-front costs on projects to enable governments to provide new services on infrastructure projects without having to show these costs in their budgets. There are numerous projects in every Anglo-American democracy that would not have been built without public-private partnerships, just as there are many partnership arrangements by which private firms deliver public services, operate prisons, and manage public schools. Partnership networks have also sprung up in many jurisdictions to provide a forum for interested government departments and others to share lessons learned.[52] There is now a substantial body of literature that explores the strengths and weaknesses of public-private partnerships. A good number of authors argue that the partnerships "are an effective means of pursuing collaboration, cooperation and coordination in the many areas where business and government have common or compatible objectives."[53]

These partnership arrangements, however, are having an impact on the location of power and responsibility inside and outside government. Officials in a government department, reporting on how they were able to make a public-private partnership work, put it well when they wrote, "Individuals, organizations and governments must relinquish their control mentality when trying to manage resources and they must form partnerships that recognize the importance and necessity of each Partner's role in the successful implementation of common goals."[54] Relinquishing control also means relinquishing power and responsibility.

The problem is that the public and private sectors often have conflicting goals.[55] Partnership arrangements can provide opportunities for one partner to blame the other when things go wrong. In addition, governments require new staff to negotiate and monitor partnership arrangements, which in turn makes government thicker and less accessible and individuals less responsible. It also makes it difficult for people outside the partnership arrangements, particularly those outside government, to keep track of how power and responsibility flow back and forth between the two partners.

Students of government have produced numerous case studies to assess the contribution of public-private partnerships. The verdict: partnerships have been successful in delivering major projects and public services on schedule and within budget. Advocates of the concept insist that the partnerships are beneficial for both sectors. The argument is that governments and taxpayers gain from the private sector's resources and its knowledge of ways to improve the quality of public service, while private firms gain new markets.[56]

There have, however, also been a number of concerns. Some insist that it has become increasingly difficult to determine who is responsible for what. The argument is that historically the private sector was never accountable to the public at large, and partnership arrangements are now changing that. Also, it has proved to be very difficult to put in practice David Osborne and Ted Gaebler's notion that "steering" belongs in the hands of politicians and "rowing" should be in the hands of managers and the private sector. Osborne and Gaebler never answered how one could separate those who "steer" from those who "row" and then hold both responsible for their decisions, either collectively or individually.[57] In addition, in some cases, those responsible for steering did not stay around long enough to "oversee and accept responsibility for the direction taken by the rowers."[58]

In a detailed study of a public-private partnership involving the Government of Canada and a private firm, Jennifer Berardi concluded that "the direct lines of accountability and responsibility that are typically enjoyed in traditional public sector organizations are not always applicable in a partnership arrangement."[59] Again, under partnership agreements, it is extremely difficult to pinpoint who is ultimately responsible for what.

It is hardly possible for a public-private agreement, however well thought out, to provide for all developments and make provisions for all constraints in the construction of a major capital project or the delivery of a public service. Commercial confidentiality requirements can seriously inhibit the flow of information to those outside government and the relevant firm, making public-private partnerships less transparent than regular government programs.[60] One thing is clear: public-private partnerships have blurred the dividing line between the two sectors.

Blurring that line is not without implications. It not only makes it more difficult to determine who has power and who holds responsibility, but it also mixes two sectors that have or should have distinct values. Jane Jacobs identified a set of values that exists in each of the two sectors but are incompatible. The private sector, she said, values initiative and enterprise, invests for productive purposes, and is thrifty, optimistic, and open to inventiveness; the public sector values obedience and discipline, adheres to tradition, respects hierarchy, and is exclusive.[61] The point she was making is that having government operate like a business or have businesses run government and deliver public services suggests that profit and competition should now be introduced inside government, even though traditionally they have had no role in the public sector.[62] It also makes it very difficult to establish power and responsibility employing the subordinate and obedient model. Increasingly, we need to look to a model that relies less on hierarchy to see who has power and to assign responsibility.

Other factors also have shifted power around in the private sector. The role of boards of directors, developments in communication technology, going dark to avoid transparency requirements, and the importance of networking with governments and with other businesses have made hierarchy less important than in years past. These developments have made businesses thicker, given the need to add staff and processes to deal with the above requirements. Thicker business organizations in turn encourage the promotion of strong leaders with strong personalities who are able to plough through elaborate processes and get things done.

3 POWER OPERATING ABOVE THE FRAY

Roméo LeBlanc, a senior minister in the Trudeau government and later governor general of Canada, once told me, "Lawyers are the only people in the world who can regain their virginity; all you have to do is appoint them judges." He explained that overnight, some of them go from being fiercely partisan to having a disdain for politicians and all things political. "You meet them at airports, and they are eager to profess their complete loyalty to you and your party and their willingness to get involved and give a helping hand. You promote their nomination to the bench. Later, when you see them at airports, they will avoid you; some do not want even to make eye contact with you. Overnight, they change. Politics is suddenly unhealthy and to be avoided. I always find it quite amazing and amusing."[1] They change, of course, because we expect them to operate above the fray, to be non-political, to call a spade a spade without fear or favour from political leaders, and to arrive only at objective decisions rather than the kind that politicians and public servants make. Judges are hardly alone in operating above the political fray. Agents of Parliament, a growing breed in recent years, also are non-political, although they are accountable and responsible – or, at least, ought to be – to Parliament, the most political institution in the land. But that is not all. There is a growing inclination in all Anglo-American democracies to move responsibilities and activities out of the political orbit.

Citizens have lost confidence in political and bureaucratic institutions and systems. The World Values Survey has been tracking the level of confidence in various institutions since 1982 and reports a general decline in both political and bureaucratic institutions. Canadians, for example, have more confidence in major private companies than they have in either Parliament or the public service.[2] An ideological climate has set in that celebrates market liberalization, managerialism, regulations, and processes that are able to operate in isolation from politics. It seems that routine events and crises are no longer interpreted through the lenses of political institutions, notably Parliament.[3]

What does this mean for the location of power and responsibility? The courts certainly have power, and, if nothing else, agents of Parliament have influence. The latter occupy a new zone, one that has never been properly defined. Even if they do not hold power, their work, particularly in recent years, has had a profound effect on both the location and the management of political power. In this chapter, we seek to define this zone, its powers and influence.

The Courts

Ronald Dworkin wrote in his widely read *Law's Empire* that "people often stand to gain or lose more by one judge's decision than they could by any general act of Congress or Parliament."[4] He added that the question is no longer what power the Supreme Court has but how its vast power should be exercised. The question matters because increasingly judges in their efforts to "enforce the whole Constitution" are also exercising "pure political judgement."[5] This in turn explains why many observers are trying to sort justices into two camps: conservatives and liberals; at the risk of oversimplification, one could say that conservative justices tend to obey the Constitution, and liberal ones try to reform it according to their personal convictions.

The debate is no longer limited to the United States, and in recent years we have seen a spate of books from other countries on the growth of judicial power.[6] Countries such as Canada and Britain, whose courts have historically played a limited role, now have judiciaries that are far more interventionist when dealing with the policies or potential policies and decisions of elected governments.

In the United States the legislature, the executive, and the judiciary were created separate and equal as the country was born in the aftermath of the American Revolution. The US courts have long been described as the "guardians of the Constitution," and judicial independence is held to be a fundamental value of American political life. James Madison, one of the founding fathers of the United States and widely recognized as the father of the US Constitution, believed strongly in "checks and balances" to limit the power of individuals and branches of government. He wrote in the *Federalist Papers*: "The accumulation of all powers, legislative, executive and judiciary, in the same hands, whether of one, a few, or many, and whether hereditary, self-appointed, or elective, may justly be pronounced the very definition of tyranny."[7] The courts in the United States have for some time represented a source of power distinct from politicians and other government officials.

Things were different in the Westminster parliamentary model. Here, power rested with the Crown and gradually shifted, first to Parliament, then to the executive, and more recently to the courts. As Adam Tomkins points out, power in England started with the Crown as "great monarchs ruled England well into the Tudor period."[8] The struggle for power in Britain until the nineteenth century was between the Crown and Parliament. In addition, the debate over the separation of powers essentially centred over the ability of Parliament to hold the Crown to account for its decisions. Put differently, in Britain the judiciary and the public service were derived from the powers of the Crown and did not enjoy a separate or distinct status in law. The courts belonged to the monarch, and they operated under his guidance.

Britain has no constitution, only precedents. This is not to suggest that there were no disagreements between those who held or sought power; there were frequent and at times violent disagreements between monarchs and their barons. However, the barons never turned to the courts to seek redress because both the law and the judiciary belonged to the king. Ultimate power and authority were firmly in the monarch's hands, and the judiciary had no personality distinct from the king. Well into the eighteenth century, it was easy in Britain to locate most of the political, administrative, and even judicial powers: one had only to look to the monarch.[9]

The Magna Carta, the Bill of Rights, and the Act of Settlement served to limit the power of the Crown or at least to hold it to account. As is well known, the barons revolted against tax increases and took London by force in 1215. They made King John agree to a document limiting his power, and in return they renewed their oaths of allegiance to him. King John was later to renege on the document, but his successor King Henry III reissued a shorter version of the Magna Carta. The document contained a number of provisions, including freedom for the church, new feudal rights, judicial rights, and the establishment of a council consisting of the most powerful men in the country, working for the benefit of the state and not simply for the king. This council, though subservient to the monarch, would in time form the basis of Parliament. Thus began the long struggle that established Parliament or, rather, the king in Parliament to become a completely sovereign authority, at least in theory. As a result, the Magna Carta set in motion a number of reforms to strip away some of the power that had been concentrated in one individual. For this and related reasons, it has been described as "perhaps the most important legal document in the history of democracy."[10]

It will be recalled that Parliament issued a Declaration of Rights, which was read to William and Mary during the ceremony when they were offered the crown in 1689. The "rights" are those enjoyed by Parliament, not by individuals, and its central provisions remain in force to this day. The legislation essentially laid the foundations for affirming the ultimate sovereignty of Parliament.[11] It restricted many royal prerogatives, placed some power under the direct control of Parliament, and declared that raising money for the use of the Crown "by pretence of prerogative, without grant of Parliament" to be illegal. It also gave Parliament the ability to control the identity of the monarch by altering the line of succession (so much for the divine right to rule!) and made Parliament master of its own affairs. One student of British politics summed up these developments very well when he wrote, "Power started with the Crown, but it continues to be vested in the Crown only because, and for only as long as Parliament continues to wish it."[12] In brief, the Declaration of Rights, confirmed by the Bill of Rights in December 1689, saw to it that sovereignty was vested in the king or queen in Parliament and not in the king or queen alone, a seminal moment in the development of the Westminster model.

By the end of the nineteenth century, Parliament had forced from the Crown virtually all the power it wanted. It would have been hard to find anyone by then claiming that Parliament did not in practice possess unlimited legislative authority. Walter Bagehot, the most celebrated student of government in Victorian Britain, maintained that Parliament and, more specifically, the House of Commons, by then firmly held the upper hand. He wrote, "No matter whether it concerns high matters of the essential constitution or small matters of daily detail, the House of Commons can despotically and finally resolve it ... It is absolute, it can rule as it likes and decide as it likes."[13] With respect to the role of Parliament and its relations with the monarch, Bagehot wrote that the "Queen must sign her own death warrant if the two Houses unanimously sent it up to her."[14] After the period when the monarch ruled with an iron hand, one could look to Parliament, for a while at least, to locate political power.

The courts, like all other institutions, took a back seat to Parliament. C.D. Yonge observed in 1868 that the first principle of the constitution was "the omnipotence of Parliament." Justice Willes asserted in 1871, "Acts of Parliament ... are the law of the land; and we do not sit here as a court of appeal from parliament ... We sit here as servants of the Queen and the legislature ... The proceedings here are judicial, not autocratic, which they would be if we could make laws instead of administering them."[15] In 1872 Chief Justice Cockburn and Justice Blackburn wrote, "There is no judicial body in the country by which the validity of an act of parliament can be questioned. An act of the legislature is superior in authority to any court of law ... and no court could pronounce a judgment as to the validity of an act of parliament."[16] A few years later, Sheldon Amos claimed that "in one sense Parliament can do anything, because it can pass a law which by the existing Constitution must be recognized in every Court of Justice in the land."[17] One would be hard pressed to find many judges, if any at all, in Canada making that same observation today. Even in nineteenth-century Britain, members of the judiciary knew their place in the pecking order, and Parliament was on top. The courts, until the era of the Charter of Rights and Freedoms, could check government only if it acted ultra vires of statutory authority.

Today the courts in Canada, and increasingly even in Britain, show considerably less restraint in defining their role and substituting their own policy judgments for those of elected MPs.[18] One would have to search far and wide to find anyone, particularly in Canada, still willing to make the case that Parliament remains supreme under the Westminster model. At one point the monarch was all-powerful. Later, power shifted to Parliament or the king or queen in Parliament, and it has continued to shift to the courts and other bodies.

The incorporation of the European Convention of Human Rights, for example, into Britain's domestic law has had considerable impact on the location of power in Britain; the courts are playing an increasingly important role in reviewing the constitutionality of parliamentary statutes. Section 6 of the 1998 Human Rights Act provides that it is "unlawful for a public authority to act in a way which is incompatible with a convention right" and defines "public authority" as "any person certain of whose functions are functions of a public nature."[19]

In Canada, the Charter of Rights and Freedoms continues to have a considerable effect on Canadian politics. Those who put forward claims under the Charter are in no mood for compromise. They seek straight answers to their grievances, the kind of answers that are not always forthcoming in the less than clear-cut political bureaucratic world. There is every indication that Canadians are turning to the courts as a source of power in search of straight answers. Canada's federal government published a performance report on the Supreme Court in early 2009 which revealed that the court received 602 leave applications in 2007, up from 445 in 1991. The Supreme Court attributes this change to an assertive population that is "more willing to challenge the perceived wisdom of its leaders – often in court."[20] Canadians, it seems, are growing disillusioned with the workings of representative democracy and are losing patience with government by debate and discussion.[21] It may well be that they prefer the courts and their clear-cut answers.

Canada's chief justice explains that the Charter has introduced a new set of constitutional limitations on the legislative and executive branches of government. Canadians, she points out, can "now go to court to challenge laws and government acts not only on the grounds that they exceeded the grants of power, but also on the grounds that they violate fundamental rights." She insists that the Charter has changed the constitutional role of the courts, not only quantitatively but qualitatively: before the Charter, the courts' role in defining the boundaries of power of the legislature and the executive meant that they were mediating between different levels of government and sometimes between the citizen and government; today, the courts are "required to mediate conflicts between individuals and minorities on the one hand and the majority-elected government on the other."[22] This in turn has shifted power away from the executive and legislature to the courts.

Judges appear to relish their newfound power. They now decide on virtually all matters of public policy. It will be recalled that the Supreme Court was asked to consider whether Quebec had a constitutional right to secede unilaterally from Canada. The court ruled that Quebec did not possess such a right and based its decision on four fundamental rights: federalism, democracy, constitutionalism, and the rule of law. Canada's written constitution dates back to 1867, and one would be hard pressed to see these principles in it, certainly in pre-Charter days. The Canadian Senate, it will be recalled, was established as a check on democracy and federalism, both of which were only reluctantly embraced. As Adam Tomkins writes, it may be more accurate to say that Canada in 1867 was based on principles of "elitism, racism, sexism and imperialism than on the four good things that the Supreme Court identified."[23]

Still, some Canadians appear increasingly willing to turn to the courts rather than to Parliament to counterbalance the power of the executive. We know, for example, that parliamentary scrutiny "has generally occurred during the legislative responses to judicial invalidation of acts by the Supreme Court."[24] Some observers also believe that judicial activism promotes greater democracy by giving more power to citizens.[25] In some instances, the courts have looked beyond the Charter to stop the government from changing policy direction. When the New Brunswick government decided to eliminate its early French immersion program in March 2008, some parents challenged the decision in court. The judge ruled that the government's decision did not violate the Charter of Rights and Freedoms, but he said that the government had not allowed sufficient time for debate on the issue. He added that the minister's decision "was unfair and unreasonable" and on this basis "quashed" it.[26] The government decided not to appeal but to go back to the drawing board. It initiated a new round of public consultations and subsequently revised its plan by introducing early immersion in grade 3. The important point is that the court essentially ignored the substance of the issue but decided that a democratically elected government had adopted a wrong process in taking a policy decision. It forced the government to initiate a new one.

The New Brunswick government was in for another surprise when it decided to overhaul the delivery of health-care services in the province. Ostensibly, to cut costs and eliminate duplication, it planned to reduce regional health authorities from eight to two. Mike Murphy, the minister of health, declared that the changes would save nearly $20 million over five years.[27] He explained that the legislation contained a provision (section 17) that denied the right to challenge the proposed reform before the courts. A recently retired Supreme Court judge, known for being a strong advocate of minority language rights while on the bench, agreed to be part of the citizens' group taking the provincial government to court. He dismissed out of hand the minister's claim, insisting that no legislative body in Canada any longer has such power.[28]

The Canadian government reacted strongly when the Supreme Court struck down a law forcing young offenders guilty of serious crimes to be sentenced as adults unless it could be proved that it would be unfair to do so. The justice minister, Rob Nicholson, argued that the court was supporting "soft treatment for young offenders" and showing insufficient deference to "parliamentary decision making."[29] It is important to note that the courts have expanded their power over time so that the shift has not been as discernible to citizens as it would have been if it had occurred more quickly.

It is now well established in Canada that the legal system, judges, and the courts require independence from the government of the day. The courts, for example, are free to find guilty and punish even a government minister who has acted unlawfully, and the government must do as the court wishes.[30] More to the point, the courts now have a personality that is distinct from the government of the day, and they hold considerable power. Allan Hutchinson argues that "the Supreme Court of Canada is as political in its decisions as those of its American counterpart." He adds, "Let there be no mistake, the Supreme Court is a powerful body and, as importantly, an ideological one at that."[31]

In his study of the impact of the 1982 Charter of Rights and Freedoms on Canada's judiciary, Christopher Manfredi maintains that the Supreme Court has shown "little restraint in building up its own review of judicial review or in asserting its own pre-eminent authority over the development of Charter-related constitutional principles."[32] He reports that interest groups, preferring to pursue their political agenda through the courts rather than through politicians, have contributed to the expansion of judicial power. In the process, Canadian politics is being transformed, in that difficult or divisive issues are increasingly being submitted to the courts for resolution rather than through the political process.[33]

In his comprehensive review of the work of Canada's Supreme Court, Donald Songer concluded that "while it is still fashionable in many circles to think of the work of courts as divorced from the often disdained world of politics, both the empirical analysis of the Court's decisions and the views of the justices expressed in interviews provide strong support for the thesis that one must understand the Court as a court of law *and* a political court."[34] Put another way, the courts have become political actors but without having to deal with the constraints politicians have to contend with, including transparency requirements and seeking re-election.

Manfredi and Songer are not alone in claiming that judges are increasingly willing to assert their "pre-eminent authority." Ian Greene makes similar observations but argues that "most Canadians are satisfied with the quality of judicial decision making, and Canadian courts have made important contributions to thinking about the nature of judicial independence and impartiality."[35]

Raymond Bazowski writes about the "judicialization of politics," suggesting that the courts have intruded into the policy-making arena and that conflicts that are political in nature are being transformed into legal issues to be resolved "in an impenetrable institutional setting."[36] Some observers insist that self-serving special interest groups (feminists, gays and lesbians, and minority language groups) have turned to the courts to secure rights that they would not have been able to obtain through the political process.[37] Others, however, argue that public opinion surveys reveal that Canadians prefer the courts to political institutions and that they are more likely to agree than to disagree with controversial Supreme Court rulings.[38]

This is not to suggest that elected politicians are completely at the mercy of the courts. Canada's Charter of Rights and Freedoms includes the notwithstanding clause (section 33), which allows the federal or provincial governments to enact legislation to override some sections of the Charter. Some provincial governments, including the Quebec government, have turned to the notwithstanding clause to override minority language rights. However, the notwithstanding clause has not been employed by any Canadian government in recent years. Canadian politicians understand that any political decision to override the Charter of Rights and Freedoms would not be welcomed by Canadian voters. Bazowski maintains that the notwithstanding clause has less and less been a "credible option for governments because its public legitimacy had declined in recent years."[39] Thus, if one is looking to locate political power in Canada, one increasingly has to look to the courts and not just to elected politicians.

The debate is no longer whether the courts have power – this is now widely acknowledged. Rather, the debate centres on how judges should be appointed. The thinking is that citizens and their elected representatives have more democratic legitimacy than judges, and they should be consulted on how and who should be appointed to the courts. Others, however, argue that judicial appointments are too important to be left in the hands of politicians, a less-than-subtle message that politicians should have less power than they currently have.

In 2006 Britain established the Judicial Appointments Commission, which was designed to "maintain and strengthen judicial independence from the Executive and the Legislature." The secretary of state for constitutional affairs explained, "In a modern democratic society, it is no longer acceptable for judicial appointments to be entirely in the hands of a Government Minister. For example, the judiciary is often involved in adjudicating on the lawfulness of actions of the Executive. And so the appointments system must be, and must be seen to be, independent of Government."[40] The commission squares nicely with the current climate of cynicism and mistrust about political power and bureaucratic influence. There is an inherent belief that judicial appointments will be better because they will be made above the political fray. Baroness Prashar of the Judicial Appointments Commission explains that the commission is "required to select solely on merit and to only select people of good character."[41] That is a requirement that the political power is apparently not able to meet. In short, political power cannot be trusted to make the right decision when it comes to appointing judges.

Canada has followed Britain's lead in making judicial appointments more transparent. It has not, however, been as successful as Britain. Lawyers wishing to be considered for an appointment to the bench are asked to apply to the Commission for Federal Judicial Affairs. Judicial advisory committees, made up of law enforcement associations, members of the bar, and the general public, are established to review candidates. Appointments are still made by the governor general on the advice of Cabinet from a list of names recommended by the advisory committee.

The prime minister has recently established a process to consult MPs before making a decision on appointing Supreme Court justices, which thus far has met with little success.[42] The prime minister still makes the final decision on Supreme Court justices and provincial chief justices, and if he has his eye on a candidate he will get his way.[43] In these cases, merit is in the eye of the prime minister, and a past association with him or her, or with the political party in power, matters. In a recent study of the Supreme Court of Canada, Donald Songer observed a "moderately strong relationship" between the federal party that appointed a judge and his or her policy preferences. He writes that "notwithstanding disclaimers that judicial ideology is not actively considered in judicial selection," three of the Supreme Court justices whom he interviewed confirmed their belief that this is so.[44]

Officers of Parliament

The location of political power, influence, and responsibility has also been made less clear by the work of officers of Parliament. They have had a presence in politics for some time: the first independent auditor general of Canada was appointed in 1878. The role of the auditor general down through the ages and until the early 1980s was straightforward: to ensure financial probity and compliance with appropriation authority. The Office of the Auditor General was mostly staffed by accountants, and it had a narrow and well-defined mandate. But things have taken a dramatic turn in more recent years, not only with the role of the auditor general but with other officers of government, making the management of political power considerably more difficult.

Agents of Parliament such as the auditor general have sought to break out of the traditional boundaries to establish new turf for themselves, but not necessarily at the urging of Parliament. Indeed, they now appear to function as free agents accountable to no one but themselves. To be sure, they cannot be subordinate or accountable to the government of the day because that in itself would compromise their *raison d'être*. But, once established, agents of Parliament, like other bureaucratic organizations, will wish to expand their sphere of influence. Parliament has not been effective in its dealings with them. Predictably, opposition parties and the media support an expanded role, while those on the government side of the House do not. Political parties that supported agents of Parliament while in opposition can very quickly turn sour on them once in power.[45]

The Office of the Auditor General once had clear boundaries defining its role and responsibility. Its purpose was to assist the Public Accounts Committee of the House and to report to the committee the results of its investigations of financial probity and compliance with appropriation authority.[46] Today, nearly 60 percent of its budget goes to "qualitative" or "soft reviews" that "bear little apparent relationship to efficiency or economy in use of funds, human resources or material."[47] A good number of reports published by the office have little to do with financial probity. They are essentially political documents, in that they stake out policy positions or explore issues that have nothing to do with financial audits. Yet the office continues to insist on its non-political nature even though it regularly engages in policy debates. Neither it nor the media bothers to explain that qualitative or soft reviews can never be as certain or conclusive as financial audits. The office has also become particularly adroit at attracting media attention, and it now reports its findings to the media as much if not more than to Parliament.

The Canadian auditor general, it will be recalled, became a media star during the sponsorship scandal. There was talk on a number of open-line shows of "Sheila Fraser for prime minister," and she was described as a "folk hero with the electorate."[48] The office has successfully created its own distinct voice, and it views Parliament as just another consumer of its reports. Its activities are no longer based on the exact work of accountants but increasingly on "soft" policy work. The voice may not be partisan, but it is political. It is sufficiently influential that the prime minister, ministers, and senior public servants must invest time and effort to deal with it. The office continually seeks to expand its sphere of influence and has become an important policy actor in its own right, a far cry from its original mandate.

In recent years, the Office of the Auditor General has produced a wide range of reports that are far removed from financial audits. In 2008 it published a report examining whether the Canadian government suc- cessfully manages risks associated with invasive alien plants, seeds, and pest and plant diseases that might enter the country. In 2007 it published a report that examined Canada's ability to keep its borders "open and secure." The report prompted Sheila Fraser to underline "the need for effective targeting methods so that low-risk people can enter while appropriate action is taken for those who are high-risk." In the same annual report, the office published still another report that was highly critical of the ability of the Department of Foreign Affairs and International Trade to manage human resources. In 2005 it published a report highly critical of the government's ability to manage horizontal issues, claiming that central agencies "do not provide enough leadership or guidance to various federal organizations."[49]

The above-noted chapters in the annual reports are mixed in with financial audits. The chapters are given the same legitimacy as the financial audits, yet they read much like consulting reports, containing many points that could be challenged or are open to interpretation. The auditor general, at least in the eyes of the media and of Canadians in general, speaks with an authority and influence that consultants do not enjoy. The basis for this credibility, however, is based on straightforward financial audits.

The Canadian privacy commissioner held a press conference in June 2002 to announce a Charter challenge to the RCMP's video surveillance activities in Kelowna, British Columbia. He was doing so, he explained, after being unable to persuade the solicitor general to "exercise his responsibility and instruct the RCMP to take down the camera."[50] His press release made no reference to consulting Parliament in initiating this action. He did report, however, that he had consulted a former justice of the Supreme Court, who "prior to his retirement, wrote many of the Supreme Court's most important decisions on privacy rights."[51] Cabinet ministers, MPs, and public servants no longer, it seems, command the respect of Canadians seeking advice.

There are now ten or eleven officers of Parliament, depending on how one counts, including the newly created parliamentary budget officer to "ensure truth in budgeting." Although initially Harper's proposal was to give the office full officer-of-Parliament status, he had a change of mind once he was in power. The officer, for the time being at least, reports to Parliament through the Library of Parliament.[52] Regardless of the status, the mandate of the parliamentary budget officer is still not clear. Allan Darling, the consultant hired by the Library of Parliament to define the mandate, explained that the office's area of responsibility "could mean almost anything, but essentially, the role is best summarized as an officer to assist Parliamentarians to understand what is being put forward in the documents provided by the government, either as budget documents or expenditure estimates and to provide appropriate analysis that would help the members understand those documents."[53]

The government's insistence that the office was created to "ensure truth in budgeting" could not have been lost on the minister of finance and his officials, who apparently could not be as credible as a parliamentary budget officer. It was not long before the parliamentary budget officer was embroiled in a political controversy. He began to challenge the government's spending estimates, its economic forecasts, and its projected revenues. He questioned whether the government's 2009 economic stimulus package would actually create the 189,000 jobs it projected,[54] and he said it would "push the country to the brink of a persistent deficit."[55] He was able to arrive at this and other conclusions with a handful of employees, while the 800-strong Department of Finance could not.

The media has given the budget officer wide coverage, and overnight he made the transition from an obscure bureaucrat to someone in high demand by journalists. Indeed, in some ways he is playing the role that the leader of the opposition once played; also, he enables the media to challenge the government without having to do the leg work. Veteran MP Carolyn Bennett went to the heart of the matter when she observed that the parliamentary budget officer should "work for parliamentarians, not the public." She took exception to his "habit of releasing reports to the public the same time as he gives them to the MPs requesting the information, or tables them in the Commons and Senate."[56]

The fact that officers of Parliament have been created without clarifying how they fit into the constitutional framework does not seem to bother Canadians or the media. The officers all speak from a narrow viewpoint or from their mandate or interest, and no one is charged with bringing a broad overarching perspective. The result is that those in government have several independent officers constantly looking over their shoulders from different and at times conflicting (privacy versus access to information) perspectives. Opposition parties view officers of Parliament as their natural allies and do not want to challenge them, let alone hold them to account; best to let them wander wherever they want in the hope that they will uncover a situation embarrassing to the government.

Again, Canada is hardly alone in turning to officers of Parliament or to those operating above the political fray to shed light on how political leaders exercise power. Although Britain, for example, does not have as many officers of Parliament as Canada, there, too, the number has increased in recent years. The tendency to enlarge one's mandate is also evident. The UK National Audit Office saw its mandate expand in the early 1980s to include, like its Canadian counterpart, value-for-money audits. The 1983 National Audit Act formally made it an officer of the House of Commons and gave it the power to report to Parliament at its "own discretion on the economy, efficiency and effectiveness with which government bodies have used public funds."[57] The mandate of the National Audit Office is no longer restricted to investigating financial probity and compliance with appropriation authority. Its focus has shifted away from the details of expenditure to broader and more subjective investigations related to value for money, much as in Canada (though its Canadian counterpart also includes performance reviews). However, the relationship between Britain's Committee of Public Accounts and the National Audit Office appears to be much stronger than that between the Public Accounts Committee and the Office of the Auditor General in Canada.

In short, officers of Parliament serve various purposes. They perform audits, look after judicial appointments and access to information legislation, and perform various oversight roles. New officers of Parliament have been created in recent years without any effort to define a constitutional niche or to clarify how they fit into the existing constitutional framework.[58] It is not at all clear how they are to be held accountable or by whom. They all have one thing in common – they are independent and are free to voice their views even when they may be serving the interest of their own organizations. For the most part, they answer to themselves and play to the media. They operate above the political fray, and the media turn to them for material, slip-ups, and political miscues with which to challenge government officials. The media will not want to challenge parliamentary officers or their findings because they can always be counted on to generate material embarrassing to the government.

There are, however, some drawbacks. Creating new officers of Parliament without defining a constitutional niche in which they should operate leaves these officers to expand their mandate almost at will, without anyone holding them to account. They become media personalities, acting as judge and jury on virtually all aspects of government activity. They also become influential individuals, at least in the eyes of the media, and citizens are left to sort out, for example, who has the financial numbers right – the minister of finance or the parliamentary budget officer.

It is interesting to note that officers of Parliament are not an invention of Westminster parliamentary systems. If anything, they constitute yet another example of the Americanization of Canadian politics (see, among others, fixed election dates). In line with the checks and balance nature of the American system, the US Congress has long had independent offices to review in considerable detail the work of the executive. The work of the US Government Accountability Office (GAO) looms large in Washington, as it regularly produces reports that require a very high level of expertise. It is an exceptionally rare occurrence for such reports to say anything positive about government departments and agencies. Indeed, their continued relevance often depends on their finding fault. The GAO reports on such issues as "military readiness," "information security," "disability programs," and the list goes on and on.[59] Again, no effort is made to explain that such reviews can never be as certain or as conclusive as financial audits.

There are other congressional offices also overseeing the work of the executive branch. The Congressional Budget Office, for example, undertakes a number of functions for Congress, though to protect its objectivity it maintains that its "reports contain no policy recommendations."[60] It does, however, carry out a "re-estimate" of the president's budget proposals and prepares economic and budget outlooks. The Congressional Budget Office inspired the Harper government to include in its 2006 accountability package the Parliamentary Budget Office to ensure truth in budgeting. Nothing was said about how this new office squares with the Westminster parliamentary model or how it would affect its traditional power structure.

Protecting Venerable Institutions from Politicians

Jim Travers, a leading Canadian journalist, writes: "A Canada without the RCMP is unimaginable. An RCMP that isn't competent or trusted by Canadians is unacceptable."[61] It will be recalled that the RCMP became embroiled in 2007 in one scandal after another, with finger-pointing, cover-ups, and public embarrassments. It stood accused of corruption, nepotism, mismanagement of its pension fund, and interference by senior officers in political campaigns.[62] Extensive media coverage and the resulting public outcry forced the government to call for an independent review of the force. The review reported that the RCMP had "significant" weaknesses and called for sweeping changes.[63]

The solution? Ensure somehow that the RCMP operates away from politicians and other government officials and bureaucratic requirements. In the interest of giving more independence to the RCMP, the report urged the government to turn responsibility for the force over to a new board of civilians. The traditional government machinery was no longer up to the task, a conclusion which the Harper government accepted.

The new civilian board, in place since December 2009, is responsible for the RCMP's financial affairs, resources, services, property, human resources, and procurement. The purpose is to make the RCMP a standalone and independent entity, separate from the federal government. More to the point, the organization is no longer to be directed by politicians or public servants. The problem with the RCMP, it seems, was tied to the work of politicians and public servants, and a new locus of power is being created.

The RCMP, "after 134 years of operating in insular, hierarchical, paramilitary fashion," is to be transformed, according to the report, "to restore trust in the institution."[64] The report's central message is that politicians, public servants, and the traditional hierarchical structure linking it to politicians and the government were no longer up to the task and that the RCMP needed to operate beyond their reach to regain credibility. The RCMP would, after 2009, be responsible to a management board made up of several prominent Canadians skilled in corporate leadership and management. However, to whom and how this management board would be responsible is not clear. This question, it seems, became less important than the need to take politicians and other government officials out of the picture in running the RCMP.

Other public organizations also have recently been moved away from politicians and government officials. It appears that as things become more important to the national interest, the greater is the desire to move them outside political or bureaucratic power and influence. This phenomenon is evident in many Anglo-American democracies, not just in Canada.

The Bank of England was founded in 1694 and nationalized in 1946. As is well known, the bank acts as the "bankers' bank," establishes monetary policy, and manages the United Kingdom's foreign exchange and gold reserves. One of Tony Blair's first initiatives when he came to power in 1997 was to "give independence to the Bank of England," a decision he called "pivotal."[65] Alan Budd, chief economic adviser to the British government between 1991 and 1992, observed that the government was asking the bank "to succeed where politicians had failed."[66] This sums up the problem well, and to the surprise of no one the key to the bank's future success was to take politicians out of the picture. A new consensus emerged in Britain that it was necessary to turn over the conduct of monetary policy to an independent Bank of England. Politicians, whether from the Labour or Conservative Party, came to believe that this was necessary to ensure market credibility for the country's monetary policy.[67]

Canada and the United States had much earlier moved responsibility for monetary policy away from the hands of politicians. Many policy decisions are today taken by non-elected bodies, decisions that have wide implications for both economic and social policies. A case in point is the US Federal Reserve's rescue of Bear Stearns in 2008 to prevent a bankruptcy filing and to help a $29 billion takeover by JP Morgan Chase. Paul Volcker, a former Federal Reserve chairman, said that the decision went to "the very edge of Fed's lawful and implied powers."[68] The fact that the chair and members of the board of governors of the Federal Reserve are not politicians may well explain why the decision did not dominate the media and why the general public showed only limited interest in it.

In Canada there are many other areas of government activity that have been turned over in some fashion to non-government officials. New centres of power and influence are constantly being created to shape, guide, or even second-guess government decisions. As already noted, it seems that bureaucrats can no longer be trusted even to count fish properly. As also noted earlier, Tim O'Neil, the author of a report on government forecasting, argued that the government should seriously consider turning over responsibility for forecasting revenues to the private sector, given that government "forecasts have been consistently off for decades."[69]

The Canadian government also decided in the mid-1990s to move responsibility for managing airports from one of its departments to not-for-profit corporations without share capital. Airports are now the responsibility of boards of directors with members drawn from local municipalities, the federal and provincial governments, and the region's business and professional communities. The reason for the transfer of responsibility was in part the result of the federal government's desire to cut spending by downloading responsibilities to other orders of government or to community groups. But it was also the result of politicians buying into the thinking that they and public servants have no business running airports; best, they were told, to turn things over to professionals.[70] The same can be said about ports. Indeed, parts of every sector and every government department are now tied in some way to outside groups, to sectoral experts, and to the private sector to guide their work.

When Stephen Harper sought advice on Canada's continued military presence in Afghanistan, he turned to an "independent panel" made up of "eminent" and "knowledgeable" Canadians.[71] He did not turn to the Department of Foreign Affairs or to a parliamentary committee. Harper's decision to appoint an independent panel was widely approved in the media.[72] Indeed, precious few voices were heard in society or even in Parliament critical of Harper's decision.

The above speaks to politics and governing by other means. Political competition over policy and decisions by politicians and public servants no longer enjoy the public standing and credibility that they once did. This may well explain why fewer and fewer citizens want to be involved with political parties and why volunteer political activity is no longer regarded as a civic virtue. In fact, it is the opposite. The media are constantly on the lookout for appointments to boards or commissions to see if there is any link to the party in power. The media applauded, for example, the fact that the last two governors general, Adrienne Clarkson and Michaëlle Jean, had no political affiliation. They argued that Clarkson had "removed the tarnish of political patronage that had marred previous appointments."[73] In other words, citizens should avoid joining political parties and being politically partisan if they wish to avoid tarnishing their image. Citizens understood the message well and are now resorting to other means of influencing public policies.

The above is not without implications for the location of power and responsibility. New centres of influence are being created – whether in the judiciary, with officers of Parliament, or with bodies outside government – carrying responsibilities that were traditionally tied to politicians and public servants. We now have a cacophony of centres of influence all vying to be heard. The new centres have made government bigger, more cautious in certain areas, and certainly more bureaucratic.[74] Officers of Parliament have reporting requirements that have to be met and processes that have to be respected. Government departments need to hire new staff in a wide range of areas: to manage the relationship with officers of Parliament; to keep an eye on non-government bodies that are managing airports, delivering services, and managing public-private partnerships; to participate in various policy networks; and to generate advice for the politicians.

4

THE SHIFTING POWER OF PERSUASION: POLITICAL PARTIES, THE MEDIA, PERMANENT POLITICAL CAMPAIGNS, AND POLLS

We already noted that Richard Wilson, a former British cabinet secretary, mused in a public lecture, "I sometimes wonder whether the media understand their own power or the impact they can have on the inner workings of government." He added that in more recent years the media have not hesitated to put public servants under the spotlight, explaining that "being attacked in the press ... is a daunting experience for people who chose a career in which, if they are older, they expected to avoid the limelight."[1] If public servants today have more power or influence, the media will be much more aggressive in shedding light on it. However, given their propensity for anonymity, public servants in turn may well go to great lengths to camouflage their influence. Politicians, of course, welcome favourable attention, but they want to manage their media relations carefully so as to shift blame or even responsibility to others, notably public servants, when things go wrong.

The media's power is unique. It is tied to their ability to shape a policy agenda and to influence voters, politicians, and public servants to take positions that they would not otherwise take. In brief, theirs is a power of persuasion and agenda setting, a form of soft power. As a result, it is difficult to pinpoint precisely who in the media and which pollsters have influence on any given issue or at any given period. Although their influence is not static and shifts over time from individual to individual and even from issue to issue, it is a form of power. Steven Lukes extended Weber's definition of power when he wrote, "A may exercise power over

B by getting him to do what he does not want to do, but he also exercises power over him by influencing, shaping, or determining his very wants. Indeed, is it not the supreme exercise of power to get another or others to have the desires you want them to have – that is, to secure their compliance by controlling their thoughts and desires?"[2]

The media have of course undergone a sea change in recent years with the advent of twenty-four-hour television news, radio talk shows, TV punditry, the Internet, and political blogs. The new media involve many different sources, and they deliver content differently.[3] But even the old media have changed. Forty years ago, political columnists were rare. Today, according to a leading Canadian columnist, they are "almost a dime a dozen." Forty years ago, we are told, journalists "worked hard on collecting facts, cross-checking them, reading documents and talking to people." But "this kind of work is now considered hopelessly old-fashioned."[4] The media now take a different approach, one that is less deferential and much more subjective.[5] Journalists themselves readily agree that the role of the media has changed substantially in recent years.

Pollsters, too, have become an important part of the political and policy-making processes, advising political leaders, lobbyists, and others who are able to pay for their services. The media and public opinion surveys have in turn fuelled the rise of permanent election campaigns. The goal, even in power, is increasingly to govern with an eye on high public approval – hence the term "permanent campaign." This development also has shifted the location of political power.

In this chapter, we look at the role of the media and their influence. We seek to understand the reasons for the shift of power towards the media and how the media have been transformed in recent years. We also look at how political leaders have turned to pollsters for guidance and at the growing influence of public opinion surveys in shaping public policy and government decisions.

Searching for Answers

There are a number of reasons to explain the power shift towards the media. One is that political parties no longer provide citizens with clear answers, so people turn to the media because there is little alternative. Party allegiance has been waning throughout the Western world for years, and consistent voters have become rare when compared with forty years ago. Recent studies in Anglo-American democracies have telling titles: "Parties without Members," "Empty Vessels?" and "Parties without Partisans."[6] The media, meanwhile, provide relatively easy access for citizens looking for quick answers to political and economic questions.

In the past, political parties had a fairly consistent voice, and the print media were often associated directly with a political party. In fact, many newspapers were openly tied to a particular political party and promoted the party's agenda.[7] The line separating political parties from one another was discernible in several ways, including their direct association with newspapers. Things are vastly different today. Newspapers, for the most part, are no longer willing to identify with a political party, and while some of the electronic media may have an ideological bias, most also shy away from being directly aligned with a party.

However, the media are not without limitations. They are increasingly on the lookout for political gaffes, and they enjoy making the news rather than reporting it. This, as much as anything, explains the rise of "war rooms," not just during election campaigns but in permanent campaigns. War rooms are designed to counter political attacks and to create problems or controversies for the opposition. War rooms essentially have one client: the media.

The media also will not hesitate to create controversies for a particular political party. Consider the following. In the 2008 Canadian general election, Liberal leader Stéphane Dion had to take a question three times from a television journalist, perhaps because of a hearing disability or a poorly phrased question. Dion clearly flubbed his answer twice. However, he had an understanding with the journalist that the tape-to-tape interview allowed for retakes. The television network decided not to respect this understanding and broadcast the parts of the interview showing Dion's initial confusion. The network's head of news explained that the "decision to broadcast an awkward interview with Liberal leader Stéphane Dion" was taken "because its news value outweighed an understanding that the disputed portions should not be aired."[8] Veteran journalists maintain that there was a time, thirty or forty years ago, when such an understanding was invariably respected.[9]

The adversarial nature of government-media relations is now evident in all Anglo-American democracies. Politicians have to be constantly on guard lest present and past events or incidents, however small, are brought up and cast in a negative light. The London *Times*, for example, ran a front-page story under the headline "Cameron and the Sex Clinic Mystery." David Cameron, Conservative Party leader, was asked if he had ever been to a particular clinic to check if he had a sexually transmitted disease. He responded that he had once gone there, along with college friends, during his student days at Oxford at the height of the 1980s AIDS scare. The test result was negative.[10]

One doubts that the *Times* would have run such a non-story on its front page in the pre-Watergate era. It is also a far cry from the days when journalists respected boundaries and considered some things off-limits: Churchill's heavy drinking, Mackenzie King's prostitutes, and Franklin D. Roosevelt's polio. But no more. Former British prime minister John Major laments a "breakdown in trust between the Government and the media."[11] Robin Sears explains that a whole new generation of journalists began to see themselves as "Woodward and Bernstein"; the word was that "politicians are crooks and liars, and it's our job to get them."[12] He adds that "gotcha" journalism is "easy to write and avoids the tedium of having to know anything about the policies or goals of the government you are covering."[13] David Taras, one of Canada's leading students of the media, insists that "the quality of journalism has deteriorated" and adds that "citizens are increasingly deprived of the vital information they need to make decisions about their communities and their lives."[14]

There are other forces at play. Competition for high-profile and highly paid positions in the media, as in professional sports, has reduced compliance with professional codes, ethics, even rules. In an "anything goes" environment, all media became tabloid media.[15] One veteran Canadian journalist insists that working in a highly fragmented media and competitive environment is forcing the hand of print journalists to produce articles quickly. He explains: "Before our newspaper went online, a journalist was expected to produce a solid article a day. Now, journalists are expected to report all new developments online. There is no time for reflection or in-depth reporting."[16]

Michel Cormier, a veteran CBC/Radio-Canada journalist, also points to an increasingly fragmented media. He talks about citizens as journalists with mobile telephones, giving licence to everyone to become a photojournalist. He explains: "This and blogs have put enormous pressure on the mainstream media to run after stories as they develop. This comes with a price – more substantive and reflective work is less and less evident." He adds, "There is also a greater focus on media stars than in years past. The individual journalist with a high profile has come to matter a great deal."[17]

The presence of new media was strongly felt in the 2008 Canadian federal election campaign. It will be recalled that when Prime Minister Harper announced a cut of $45 million in funding for the arts, Michel

Rivard, a leading Quebec artist, produced a video protesting the government's decision. The video was funny, to the point, and devastating, and within seven days it had been viewed by 500,000 people. The impact was subsequently widely reported in the mainstream media, and many believe that Harper lost several constituencies and probably a majority mandate in Quebec because of the video.[18]

Many people welcome the new media. New communications technologies enable governments, businesses, large and small, and individuals to voice their views in an innovative fashion. The Internet has already had a profound impact on election campaigns, and it has also contributed to permanent campaigns. The Rivard video is just one example. The leaders of all political parties in the 2008 Canadian election campaign were forced to jettison candidates whose past misdeeds were uncovered by blogger activists and were reported on the Internet and, later, in the mainstream media.

The Internet, Google searches, and political bloggers have introduced a new dynamic in election campaigns: one's past. The Internet is highly accessible, easily searchable, and a virtual permanent repository of everything the media publish, and this strengthens the impact of journalism. As a *Toronto Star* journalist put it, "A news organization's journalism can now reach more people, in more places around the world, at greater speed than ever before. No longer does today's printed news become tomorrow's recycling bin throwaway."[19] This often makes the individual or the candidate the centre of attention rather than the political party or a policy proposal. One only has to Google a name to access a political candidate's past deeds, good or bad.

Political bloggers are increasingly read by the mainstream media and by political observers. Some have become opinion leaders because of their background in politics or government. Others claim to have insider information because of their close ties to political leaders, and still others prefer the freedom from restrictions or profit motives that mainstream journalists must always bear in mind. Some bloggers happily identify with political parties (in Canada, Jason Cherniak with the Liberals and Ezra Levant with the Conservatives), and they can exert influence on political debates. *Newsweek*, for example, reports that Bill Clinton lost some of his political standing in American politics because he had "no allies in the blogosphere to point out his grievances for him."[20] Given that bloggers never rest, they have become an important part of permanent campaigns. In addition, the media's fragmentation has made it difficult for politicians and others to reach the mass public.

The Internet also has the potential to turn every utterance by every local candidate into a controversial issue that national leaders have to address. This explains why national leaders and their political advisers try to impose a "command and control" approach to their party's candidates.[21] After the Canadian 2008 election campaign, one veteran journalist reported that he could never have imagined the extent to which local candidates could be muzzled. Many of them avoided candidates' debates because they had been told not to participate for fear of going off-message or creating problems for the leader.[22] Thus, the media have, perhaps unwittingly, strengthened the hand of party leaders and their close advisers at the expense of local party candidates.

William Cross, one of Canada's leading political scientists, recently observed that Canada's political parties are no longer effective vehicles for policy study and development. They neither offer voters a meaningful opportunity for involvement in the policy-making process nor do they regularly generate policy alternatives for consideration and examination by those in elected office or in the senior bureaucracy. It is fair to say that Canadian parties now see their primary role as being electoral machines.[23] Tom Axworthy, one-time chief of staff to Pierre Trudeau, writes that in Canada in the 1960s, if one was interested in policy, the place to be was on the floor of a party convention. That, he says, is simply not a recognizable model today.[24]

Television cameras at the 2006 Liberal Party leadership convention revealed near-empty rooms where delegates might be expected to be found discussing the party's policy agenda. The cameras found the delegates at gatherings with leadership candidates and their supporters. The focus was on how well the leadership candidates were doing. The delegates knew full well that the best way to influence the party's future was to concentrate their efforts on who would be the next leader rather than on the party's policy platform. They knew that in the end the platform would be crafted by the newly crowned party leader and his close advisers.

It is hardly possible to overstate the point that the competition in contemporary politics is now between a choice of personalities rather than between political parties and their policies. The one constant in recent years is that political parties have lost their place to the "celebritization" of party leaders.[25] It will be recalled that senior Canadian Liberal Party members, including former ministers, won "sustained applause" at a party convention when they spoke about "party oligarchy" replacing "party democracy" and about Paul Martin's top-down approach to governing after pledging to be different from Jean Chrétien on this front. One former minister said that she and her colleagues are "fed up with platforms that have not even been run by the party membership. We're fed up with the fact that campaign ads can be approved by focus groups on Bay Street instead of by Liberal Party members."[26]

The Canadian Conservative Party held a policy convention shortly after Stephen Harper led the party to victory in the fall of 2008. Delegates were informed that Harper would appear only "briefly" at the convention and that "rarely does a convention do a government much good. They are rarely important, but occasionally can cause real headaches." Perhaps for this reason the total time scheduled for debating party constitution and policy matters was down 30 percent to eight hours from the eleven and a half allotted at the 2005 convention. Moreover, the party scheduled feel-good events that overlapped with many of the policy workshops.[27] It is no exaggeration to write that party policy conventions are there to be managed by party leaders and their key advisers, not to generate new policies.

Political parties in Anglo-American democracies are now primarily concerned with winning power for their leaders and have little interest in analyzing political or policy issues that are not connected to winning the next election. This has always been the case, but it is much more apparent today. In a comparative study, Pippa Norris maintains that the loss of support for political parties is particularly evident in affluent, established democracies. She explains that there are various aspects of modern society that lead to a weakening of the bond between citizens and political parties. For example, some individuals are now much more able to become self-reliant. Well-educated people pick and choose what they want from government and ignore the rest. This suits the political, intellectual, and economic elites just fine. One can also easily appreciate why a small group of political advisers with easy access to the elites would wish to produce election campaign platforms in a vacuum, working with the leader.[28] It is neat, tidy, and easy to control. It also reduces the chance of committing political gaffes, something that has gained importance in an era of 24-hour-news television channels and political blogs.

The problem is that interests not represented by this inner circle of political elites may be frozen out of the political process. The alternative is for individuals with no political or economic power and with genuine policy concerns to join interest groups to promote their point of view. But as Robert Young points out, this serves to degenerate parties "further into domination by leaders and their personal entourages, who play the politics of image and strategic vagueness, who take office with little sense of direction, and who end up as brokers among interest groups."[29] Power brokers also prefer operating away from public view, exerting their influence quietly so as not to stir up new opposition to their policy preferences. More to the point, it is becoming increasingly difficult for non-political groups to sort out who, either in or outside government, have power and influence. The economic elites can always hire lobbyists to sort things out for them and identify who to talk to in government. Not so the average citizen.

The lack of formal policy-making processes tied to a political party permits party leaders and their inner circles to pick and choose which interest groups they will respond to and which issues they will address. With sophisticated public opinion surveys always available, political leaders can tailor their response to the survey results. There is a much better chance that the concerns of average citizens will be heard when broad policy preferences are prepared rather than when this responsibility is concentrated in a few hands. Similarly, the concerns of the average citizen in shaping policies are less likely to be taken into account when political power is so concentrated in the hands of some individuals. In other words, the hollowing out of political parties is not without significant consequences for representative democracy and the location of power. If nothing else, it places even more pressure on other political institutions and makes it more difficult for citizens to establish where political power and influence are located. In brief, if one is trying to locate political power, one should be looking somewhere other than at political parties.

The Media: Do They Have Power?

If you were to ask politicians and senior public servants in any Western democracy whether the media have power, the answer would be an emphatic yes. They would, likely to a person, echo Richard Wilson's view that the media do not appreciate the extent to which they have power or the impact they have on the inner workings of government.

Few politicians today believe that they have any chance of winning an election without a carefully worked-out media strategy. Media, communications, and spin specialists are now key elements, not only of election campaigns but also of the political and policy processes within governments. This involves attempts to shape tomorrow's news headlines rather than simply reacting to them. In brief, one must always be at the ready with effective sound bites, instant rebuttal capacity, public opinion surveys, and competent media spin specialists to promote political success.

It is hardly possible to overstate the importance of the media in shaping voter perception in an era when loyalty to political parties continues to decline. The media will, however, more often than not focus on two things: party leaders and missteps. This and their capacity to cover "crisis situations," real or imagined, have led many to suggest that governments are now in "perpetual election campaign" mode.[30]

Party leaders are at the heart of news management, a circumstance that has strengthened their hand in dealing with their parties and establishing party policies. Indeed, judging by the media focus, party leaders now appear to be the only substantial candidates in an election race. How one does in an election campaign and in the televised leaders' debate can affect the election itself.[31] Increasingly, the objective of all parties at election time is to sell their leaders to the media, rather than their ideas, policies, or party. A study by leading students of election campaigns has observed that "Canadian elections, in common with elections in other Westminster-style systems, as well as with presidential elections in the United States, inevitably turn on the question of who – which individual – shall form the government."[32] If the leader secures a majority, it is generally assumed that the party is in his or her debt, not the other way around.

Party leaders – with the help of spin doctors, pollsters, and partisan advisers – run the national campaign, keep a watchful eye on the media, and try as best they can to control campaign developments. Recent history in many countries, particularly in Canada, has shown that a sure recipe to win power is to hug the political centre. It is, of course, no sin against representative democracy if parties converge on the political centre. But when they do, voters must look to other matters in deciding how to vote. Some may choose to abstain, and there is evidence that this is in fact happening, given the decline in voter turnout in recent years and the weakening of party loyalty. Party leaders and their advisers are well aware that the media greatly influence how electors view their credibility and competence; hence the need to score points on air and to avoid blunders. The challenge for party leaders is less one of defining policy preferences than of avoiding political gaffes: the media are always at the ready to pounce.

The above explains the rise of what Christopher Hood and Martin Lodge describe as "a new politico-bureaucratic class of spin doctors shouldering aside public servants" with more traditional analytic skills.[33] They are a key component of a government's news-management model. They are the hired hands whose job is to manage the media. In the process, they have become influential in their own right, trying to control voices on the outside. Whether or not it is the result of a more aggressive media, governments in Anglo-American democracies are increasingly in the business of spinning stories and winning the headlines every day.

In short, governments have had to learn the business of news management and to develop an instinct for political survival so as to be perceived as winners before the television cameras. Christopher Foster, a former British senior civil servant, goes so far as to say, "If one cannot find a means of detaching ministers – including the Prime Minister – from too much daily absorption in the media preventing them from progressing the real business of government, we cannot have a genuine representative democracy which works."[34]

Permanent Political Campaigns Staffed by Contract Professionals

The gap between political campaigning and governing is much narrower than it was a generation ago. Whether on the campaign trail or sitting in the Prime Minister's Office, Jean Chrétien had this advice for aspiring politicians: "The art of politics is learning to walk with your back to the wall, your elbows high, and a smile on your face. It's a survival game played under the glare of light. If you don't learn that, you're quickly finished. The press wants to get you. The opposition wants to get you. Even some of the bureaucrats want to get you. They all may have an interest in making you look bad."[35] It is interesting to note that Chrétien places the media at the top of his list of those having an interest in making politicians look bad.

There is a premium on never letting one's guard down, on always appearing to be in control, and on honing skills as a communicator, especially before television cameras. Reg Alcock, the former Treasury Board minister in the Paul Martin Cabinet, compared governing to flying a 747: "When you fly a 747 over the Atlantic Ocean, you want the nose of the plane to point straight or slightly up – if it starts to point down, you have a problem. Once the nose points down for any amount of time, it becomes very difficult to pull it back up. The same applies in government. You never want to let up, to have your eye off the ball because when you start losing public support, it is very difficult to get it back."[36]

A good number of politicians now maintain that good government means "perpetual campaigning." Australian Prime Minister John Howard said shortly after his 2004 election victory that he was "a great believer in perpetual campaigning and that the government campaign to win the next election had already begun."[37] The following factors are all contributions to permanent campaigns: the new media; the blogification of the media; political reporting; negative campaigning; the rise of political consultants and professional campaigners and spin specialists; single issue movements; the use of focus groups to review policy issues; the larger and more senior partisan political staff in ministerial offices; the staff and increased resources allocated to members of Parliament; the growing number of swing voters and those unwilling to identify with a political party; increases in spending on government advertising and public opinion surveys; the development of a voter data base; and spending restrictions during elections campaigns but none outside the campaign period.[38]

It will be recalled that shortly after Stéphane Dion was elected Canadian Liberal leader, the Conservative Party unleashed a negative ad campaign to "define" him as a weak leader. The general election was still nearly two years away, but the Conservatives lost no time in putting Dion on the defensive.[39] The costly ad campaign had little to do with policy differences between Canada's two main parties. Rather, it had everything to do with how elections in Canada – and elsewhere, for that matter – are now won or lost; that is, how political leaders are perceived.

Barely a month after the 2008 election campaign and on the eve of a Liberal leadership campaign to replace Stéphane Dion, Tom Flanagan, a leading strategist for the Conservative Party, mapped out a negative campaign plan against one of the leading candidates, Bob Rae. He explained, "I would go heavily negative against Rae early and do whatever damage I could." He added that if Rae wanted to have a chance at winning, he would "have to take the first punch in the mouth, swallow the blood and keep coming."[40] The main target he selected was Rae's management of the Ontario economy when he was provincial premier during the recession of the early 1990s.

Westminster-inspired parliamentary systems – and, here again, Canada is no exception – have been adding resources to the offices of both ministerial and MPs' offices in recent years. In addition, they have given new financial resources to political parties to assist them in holding the government to account and to define policy positions. Things have not worked out as intended. In both Canada and Britain the added resources have been applied to partisan purposes, not to research on policy issues or on strengthening the ability of MPs to hold the government to account. MPs in Canada have earmarked the bulk of the new resources to deal with their constituencies. More and more MPs see their main role as promoting the interests of their constituencies and acting as ombudsman for their constituents. They regard this role as the surest way to be re-elected.[41]

It may be that MPs attach a great deal of importance to constituency issues and to their ombudsman role because they have precious few opportunities to influence anything else. One veteran observer of Canadian politics exemplified the extent to which Parliament has been brought low by noting that MPs are increasingly turning to the Access to Information Act in order to get information from the government. This he describes as "ridiculous and an affront to Parliament."[42] Former prime minister Pierre Trudeau spoke to the declining role of Parliament when he declared that "MPs are nobodies" beyond fifty yards from Parliament Hill. A good number of MPs responded that the opposite was in fact true – that they were important in their communities but were nobodies in the nation's capital.[43]

Parliamentary committees have also been given more resources, but here again expectations tied to these new resources have not been met. MPs do not invest much of their time and energy in the work of parliamentary committees. Their work on a committee in Canada accounts for only about four hours weekly when Parliament sits. This estimate assumes that they attend all committee meetings, which they do not. They also do not have access to much expertise when crafting their participation. More importantly, they see limited political advantage in their work with parliamentary committees. As one Canadian official remarked, "An MP would trade all his or her work on a Parliamentary Committee for the chance of being seen for fifteen seconds on the evening news on television asking a tough question during Question Period." She added, "Visibility matters a great deal to MPs, and much more often than not there are no journalists covering Parliamentary Committees, let alone television cameras."[44]

In Canada, parliamentarians now receive, among other documents, more than ninety reports on plans and priorities, a similar number of departmental performance reports, and various reports from some forty

Crown corporations – but they spend precious little time going over them because they see few benefits in doing so.[45] In consequence, if one is looking to locate influence, let alone power, one needs to look elsewhere than to MPs or parliamentary committees.

Ministerial offices have also expanded in recent years, both in terms of resources and in staffers enjoying higher classification and status, compared with public servants forty years ago. They also enjoy greater influence, especially in their dealings with public servants. This is a result, at least in part, of the growing importance of news management, which has strengthened the hand of politically partisan advisers. News management is often regarded by many public servants as a partisan activity, and some have simply decided to turn the steering wheel over to the politicians and say, "OK, now you drive." But spinning tomorrow's headlines is not without implications for how power and influence are distributed in government or for relations between elected politicians, their advisers, and public servants. Political or even administrative slip-ups have to be managed publicly or generated – depending on where one sits – and public servants are reluctant to be drawn into such activities.

Partisan politics has lost the amateur quality that it once had. In addition, we have witnessed in recent years throughout Anglo-American democracies a shift away from political parties to candidate-centred campaigns that call for a new type of political actor – the professional political consultant. The need for well-thought-out political strategies, the use of new technologies, brushing up a candidate profile, and dealing with a more educated and literate public have given rise to a political consultant industry. Political marketing professionals are in demand, and no political leader goes without having them by his or her side. These professionals bring a variety of expertise to politics: fundraising, media creation, media relations, image making, and polling. Whatever we may think of political consultants and their impact on representative democracy, studies in the United States reveal that political campaigns that hire consultants are more successful than those that do not.[46] We have every reason to believe that the same is true for Canada.

Political scientists generally take a dim view of political consultants, with some suggesting that they bring a rather "cavalier approach" to representative democracy.[47] Political consultants may well bring stronger skills to campaigns than party faithfuls, but they are ambitious, always on the lookout for the next contract. They owe their loyalty to political candidates and future contracts less than to political parties, and they are exclusively focused on electoral success.

The arrival of political consultants has to some extent pushed aside party activists and the permanent party organization. Political parties may well begin to resemble business organizations more than social movements. Political consultants are transient, if only because there is no guarantee that they will be working in the same locale in future, while political parties in the past sought to promote a fixed capacity. Whatever loyalty consultants have is a moving target, shifting from one candidate and one community to another. The voter, meanwhile, is left looking at the battalions of political consultants promoting their clients or candidates by exploiting whatever advantage is at hand, real or manufactured.[48] As a result, the role of political parties has been sidelined.

Pollsters: Modern Day Witch Doctors

Martin Goldfarb, a pioneer in public opinion surveys in Canada, once observed that they are to the politician and the policy maker what the stock market is to the financial analyst.[49] Pollsters are now omnipresent, advising prime ministers, party leaders, political candidates, senior bureaucrats, lobbyists, and the media. In brief, they have become a vital part of governing. They are increasingly visible in the media, reporting on the political fortunes of a party leader or on public support for a proposed policy initiative, and all political leaders have a pollster or two at hand to advise on political strategies and policy.

Public opinion surveys have had a profound impact on the location of power inside government, shifting it to prime ministers, party leaders, and their close advisers. Not only are party leaders the media stars in election campaigns, but they no longer need to rely on local candidates or even cabinet ministers to know where voters stand on any given issue. Public opinion surveys are more reliable, more objective, more to the point, and easier to cope with than ministers or party candidates. They can also be employed to deal with any public policy issue. Surveys can enable prime ministers and their advisers to challenge the views of ministers. After all, how can even the most senior ministers dispute what the polls say?

Pollsters, better than ministers, can assist a prime minister in deciding what is important and what is not, what is politically feasible and what is not. A politically loyal pollster, always at the ready with data, can be particularly helpful in dealing with the problem of political overload, of "spinning" the media, being able to ferret out inside information, and defusing the feeling of being overwhelmed either by events or by the number of matters needing attention. A pollster can also advise the prime minister on "hot button" issues. In the past, regional ministers, respected and valued MPs on the government side, and senior public servants assumed these responsibilities.

Politicians, journalists, and voters regard public opinion surveys as scientific and accurate. Surveys have become an indispensable tool for senior public servants, if only to convince their political masters that they have tested the political waters or are on the right track in promoting a policy prescription. Government departments now spend over $30 million dollars on public opinion surveys every year.[50] Canadian departments sponsored 562 public opinion surveys in 2006–07, led by the Department of Health, which had 101 projects. The Privy Council Office, which serves the prime minister but has no program to deliver, spent close to $1.5 million on surveys to support twelve projects. One PCO project was designed to track "changing attitudes of 4,000 Canadians towards government priorities" and was commissioned on three separate occasions in one year.[51]

The federal government commissioned a review of government polling in 2007. The author of the review expressed concern over the increasing reliance on polling, saying that he was "astounded" by the high number of projects, pointing out that they amounted "to over two polls per business day." He added that though he did not see it as a serious problem, he did uncover some "breaches of the rule that prohibits the government from conducting polling about politicial preference or voting intentions."[52] Polling has thus become an important tool for prime ministers in managing their permanent election campaigns. If not active in actually shaping policy, polling now plays a key role in selling the prescriptions and in developing the government communications strategy. Christopher Page maintains that governments make use of polls to decide how to sell what they have decided to do rather than to assist them in deciding what to do.[53]

As already noted, prime ministers and party leaders have their preferred pollsters, and in Canada over half of the country's major polling firms are tied to either a political party or a media outlet.[54] When a leader's favourite pollster meets with the party's caucus or participates in its policy convention, his or her findings are well reported in the media. The party is told of its chances in the next general election and about what needs fixing, a message that party leaders ignored at their peril.

The role of pollsters has been debated by political scientists since they first appeared on the scene in Canada in the 1960s. Some have made the case that public opinion survey results are transient and do not speak to the values of a political party, that they fuel leader fixation by focusing on how well party leaders are doing. They also inhibit the ability of leaders to lead, take risks, create and lead an informed public opinion, and stand for something more than what the popular sentiment of the moment dictates. Polls have shifted power away from career public servants, from local party candidates, from political parties and their volunteers, and from regional ministers who in the past had been able to claim, with some legitimacy, to represent the views and preferences of their regions. They have contributed substantially to the rise of permanent election campaigns and a new breed of political adviser. The resulting changes once again favour political and economic elites, well-organized groups that can afford to pay for public opinion surveys, and the political and economic interests of privileged individuals.

Revisiting Classical Liberal Theory

Classical liberal theory suggests that the media should perform four key functions in a representative democracy: informing the public; scrutinizing government; staging a public debate; and expressing public opinion.[55] Some would sum up the role of the media even more pointedly by claiming that their role is to supervise government on behalf of the people.[56] One would assume that their role would have increased in importance in recent years, with political parties losing their way and their traditional bond with citizens.

To be sure, the media still inform the voter. Indeed, they are probably better suited at informing voters today than at any time in the past. Twenty-four-hour news channels, the Internet, and access or right to information legislation in all Anglo-American democracies have turned governments into fish bowls. The media now have a great variety of instruments to shape what people know and what they think about politics, public policy, and government.

It is important to recognize that, like politicians, the media operate in a volatile world. The media can no longer count on regular readers or viewers. They must compete, as never before, not only within their own sector but also with cable television, twenty-four-hour news channels, and political bloggers, some of whom have easy access to politicians – all competing for attention and clients. The pressure has led to a change of leadership in the media. Experienced journalists are being replaced by "accountants, bankers and financial managers."[57]

Journalists increasingly report that they are constantly pressured to produce quickly and to cope as best as they can with a never-ending flow of information emerging from an incoherent world of government departments, agencies, research institutes, and communication specialists.[58] Competition to break the news, to be the first to identify and interpret new developments, is leading to the media's "tabloidization or infotainment." The emphasis on scandals, on the search for "dirt," may sell newspapers but could well erode trust in public institutions. Some observers believe that trust in politics and trust in the news media go hand in hand.[59]

Bill Fox, who experienced the media both as a long-serving journalist and as director of communications for Prime Minister Brian Mulroney, writes that Ottawa now governs by risk avoidance and that "the strategy recognizes the media's preoccupation with gossip instead of governance." He quotes a colleague, Elly Alboim, a highly respected "media sage" in Ottawa, who writes that even if an issue is "important," it does not get covered if it isn't "interesting." The consequence, he says, is that the policy makers can routinely operate publicly, though in private they are interacting only with elites and the powerful, because what they are engaged in attracts no attention and fits none of the new models or criteria for political coverage. Put differently, presidents or prime ministers skilled at managing the media, which are geared towards lifestyle and personal habit issues, can now preside over policy development away from the distracting glare of the media.[60] More to the point, the media have tremendous influence on a government's policy agenda but not on policy substance.

The above may well challenge the liberal theory of the independence of journalists, which is linked to their "ability to follow the uninhibited dictates of their conscience."[61] But there are other forces at play. Whatever the cause, journalists are now on the receiving end of managed news, spin specialists, and sophisticated communication strategies. The adversarial relationship between media and government is not a one-way street. We know, for example, that some government officials saw 9/11 and the terrorists' attack on the World Trade Center as a "very good day to get out anything we want to bury."[62] Journalists now expect to be managed or conned by government spin specialists.

Once spun, however, the media have come to distrust government even more, and this has increased the distrust on both sides. For journalists, spin is simply another word for not coming clean and telling the truth.

Governments have reacted with attempts to conceal even more and to manage news precisely at a time when access to information legislation was making its mark on government administration.

The pressure to generate eye-catching news bites, along with the post-Watergate environment in which journalists and government officials now operate, has often pushed aside serious coverage of important public policy issues and placed a premium on "gotcha journalism." It has also led governments in all Anglo-American democracies to staff ministerial offices and government departments with communications specialists, a development that has in many instances fuelled the adversarial relationship between media and governments.

In Canada, CBC news anchor Peter Mansbridge had a "gotcha" moment in an interview with Stephen Harper during the 2008 general election campaign. Mansbridge pushed the prime minister throughout the interview for his handling of the Canadian economy, given the looming recession. In reference to the sharp drop in the stock market, Harper said, "I suspect some good buying opportunities are opening up with some of the panic we have seen in the stock market in the last few days." Sensing immediately Harper's faux pas, Mansbridge pounced: "Do you really want to say that?" The clip, suggesting that Harper had little concern for the average Canadian, was replayed on the evening news for several days. Mansbridge had his gotcha moment.[63]

Testimony from current and former politicians and public servants reveals that the media have a profound impact inside government and that the change has altered the location of power. Three things have changed: the role of the centre is different and in some ways considerably more powerful than in years past; the role of the media and the business of news management is now much more persuasive or "stronger"; and elected politicians and their partisan advisers are much more present in the day-to-day activities of public servants.[64] British Prime Minister Gordon Brown recently overhauled 10 Downing Street in response to the requirements of the new media and permanent election campaign. He turned the Prime Minister's Office into an "open-plan war room staffed by advisers, enforcers and media spinners." The room has "plasma television screens that beam in twenty-four-hour news channels and speaks to the growing importance of the media in the art of governing."[65] President Obama spoke about the changing role of the media at Walter Cronkite's memorial service. He said that in Cronkite's days, the media focused on "what happened today," while now they focus on "who won today."[66] The emphasis now is thus on the individual and how well he or she performs and less on institutions, organizations, and substantive policy issues.

Senior public servants maintain that the presence of the media is constantly felt inside government and that the media are mostly interested in the drama of individuals; like Obama, they are convinced that the media are in a constant search for winners and losers to make good headlines. Richard Wilson spoke about the power of the media and their ability to report something that might be "inaccurate, but with the media the story has a way of becoming the reality."[67] As Robert Armstrong, a former British cabinet secretary, noted, "There has never, in my experience, been a time when considerations of political spin did not enter into the business of news management, but it seems to be that the balance has now swung too far in that direction."[68] On the pervasive presence of partisan political advisers, Armstrong told the *Spectator* that the lines separating partisan political advisers and public servants "have been blurred."[69]

I consulted journalists at the national and local levels to get their take on the power of the media. They are not convinced that the media have as much power as political and bureaucratic leaders believe. One spoke about "press release journalism" and "telephone journalism" because news organizations, including the print media, no longer invest the necessary resources for in-depth reporting. Another argued that journalists now have to be instant experts in all facets of public policy and all sectors because news rooms are shrinking. Yet another did not deny that the media have a great deal of influence. But he argued, "It is much less concentrated than it was thirty years ago. There was a time when you could point to several news organizations and say, 'There is where the power lies.' Today, power and influence are spread out to print, electronic, and political blogs. The individual journalist or blogger can have a great deal of influence so that the power of the media is spread out all over the place to individuals rather than to news organizations."[70]

Governments have grown in recent years and put out a great deal of information. For the most part, however, it is written in such impenetrable bureaucratese that even the most competent journalists have a difficult time interpreting it. Government officials are in the business of protecting their units, their departments, their ministers, and the government. They are assisted by spin specialists and a new breed of adviser in the prime minister's and ministerial offices. Political missteps and glaring bureaucratic errors or waste is what the media want to report.

The focus now is on the individual politician or public servant who has screwed up, much less so on organizations.

This is true despite countless measures to promote transparency in government. These measures have also contributed to permanent campaigns and to the adversarial relationship between the media and politicians. The call for greater transparency holds many benefits: it has the potential to eliminate corruption, promote citizens' participation, and enhance accountability. Greater transparency would also serve to expose those who have access to the levers of power. In the next chapter, we shall explore the extent to which transparency has shed light on where power is located.

5   WHEN TRANSPARENCY MEETS POWER

I had breakfast in Ottawa a few years ago with a senior public servant. We were discussing access to information legislation. He illustrated a point by placing two blackberries on the table in front of him. He explained that one was accessible under access to information legislation but the other was not. I said, "It seems to me that it defeats the purpose of the legislation," to which he replied, "Well, that's the point."[1] I also recall the expressions on the faces of the chief executive officers of the big three US automakers when they were asked by members of Congress whether they had come to Washington in private jets to ask for government assistance in November 2008. They were visibly uncomfortable, and one could sense that they felt it was no one's business other than their own how they travelled from Detroit to Washington.

The call for greater transparency has been in vogue in recent years throughout the Anglo-American world. Few want to be seen, publicly at least, to be opposed to greater transparency. Politicians (particularly when in opposition), the media, the academic community, citizens, and interest groups have all welcomed greater transparency in both the public and private sectors. However, though they often shy away from saying so, those with direct access to the levers of power are a good deal less enthusiastic about it.

Former British prime minister Clement Attlee summed up his opposition to transparency even before transparency came into fashion when he observed, "No government can be successful which cannot keep its secrets."[2] The reader should not assume that Attlee's views belong to a different era or to the period immediately after the Second World War. Jean Chrétien delivered the very same message when he chaired his first cabinet meeting in 1993, some ten years after Canada passed the Access to Information Act.[3]

The call for "the right to know" now resonates widely in society and in the public and private sectors. Christopher Hood writes that "transparency is a term that has attained quasi-religious significance in debate over governance and institutional design."[4] The end of deference, the rise of interest groups – with many calling for open government so that they can exert greater influence – and the media have made transparency an important feature of the government's policy- and decision-making processes. Transparency means truth, and who can be against truth? It takes a brave soul to challenge publicly the merits of transparency. To be sure, opposition parties, the media, and shareholder groups have every interest in wanting greater transparency because, when it comes to power, they have nothing to lose and everything to gain. They are on the outside looking in, and greater transparency provides more and better opportunities for them to see how decisions are made and to uncover embarrassing gaffes. They also see transparency requirements as a way of identifying vulnerable points in the activities of those who hold power in the public sector.

There is today an insatiable appetite for information about all facets of public life. Leading politicians are high-profile public figures, and we want to know all we can about their private lives. By focusing on this, the media have altered the nature of what information should be made public. Nothing, it seems, is off-limits any more; the public has the right to know everything. Public servants, meanwhile, have lost their anonymity. To some extent, so have citizens, since we want to know who gave how much money to which political party. In addition to access to information legislation, we also have disclosure laws that cover many areas, notably, party financing and lobbying activities.

This is all well and good for those on the outside looking in, and they can count on the support of virtually everyone outside government or the business community to press for still more transparency. Being against transparency is akin to being against democracy or in favour of backroom deals and even corruption. But those on the inside, particularly those with power, hold a different view. Otto von Bismarck, the Iron Chancellor who had power and knew how to use it, once observed that "to retain respect for sausages and laws, one must not watch them in the making." Mel Cappe, who was clerk of the privy council under Jean Chrétien, warns that transparency is not always a good thing. He writes that it "squeezes the creativity out of the bureaucracy, to the extent it was ever there. Every problem is blamed on someone. Every decision is second-guessed with the benefit of hindsight. No one says, 'Nice try – too bad it didn't work.'"[5] Oscar Wilde, a keen observer of those who held power in society, wrote that "truth is rarely pure, and never simple."[6]

In this chapter, we look at transparency in both the public and the private sector. The Watergate scandal, among many other developments, led many to believe that there were all kinds of machinations going on inside government and that there was an urgent need to shed light on how those with power make decisions. Similarly, the collapse of Enron, Lehman Brothers, and World.com, among others, suggested that transparency was no less important in the private sector, if only to protect shareholder interests. It is perhaps as a result of high-profile scandals in both sectors that it is no longer possible to think about transparency in the public sector in isolation from the private sector, since the "peak of modern transparency talk in both spheres seems to have been reached at the same time in the 1990s."[7]

Transparency in the Private Sector

One can point to several reasons for the current state of the relationship in society between the powerful and less powerful; as already noted, these include the end of deference, better educated citizens, and the new media. The relationship is certainly vastly different today from fifty years ago. Indeed, a politician of yesteryear would not recognize government today, with its emphasis on transparency.

We are informed, for example, that C.D. Howe, Canada's minister of industry after the Second World War, would review his extensive stock portfolio on the basis of the government's decisions and the information he had learned inside government during the week. No one thought anything of the fact that Howe was an active investor and a minister at the same time: "There was no chorus of claims that he was corrupt or that his decisions were tainted by his own personal interests. It was felt that he would never take a decision as minister that was not in the public interest. Howe saw no contradiction between doing good for his country and doing well for himself. There was a high level of trust in public officials."[8] Transparency, to the extent that it mattered in the 1950s and

1960s, was mostly limited to government. The private sector was by definition "private," and it was only in the late twentieth century that the word transparency "entered the lexicon of corporate governance."[9]

Transparency in Howe's day was limited to Question Period, whatever the media could get from their government sources, and annual reports from the auditor general. But those days are long gone. Consider what former president Bill Clinton was recently required to do when President Obama appointed Clinton's wife as secretary of state. Clinton agreed to disclose the names of every contributor to his foundation, Clinton Global Initiative (CGI), since its inception in 1997, to refuse donations from foreign governments, and to cease holding CGI meetings overseas.[10] It seems that Michael Moore's observation, "You should start from the position that anyone important is lying. Force them to tell the truth,"[11] now resonates more and more in the Western world in both the public and the private sector. It appears that we have lost trust in anyone with power and that the cure is to open the books wide so that we can see not only the decisions that were made but also how they were made. More to the point, we now want to know how both sausages and laws are made.

There are now a number of groups whose only purpose is to promote transparency in all things. For example, Democracy Watch has a mission to "clean up and make governments and corporations more accountable to you."[12] Transparency International, meanwhile, stresses "fundamental values of integrity, transparency and accountability" in the private sector.[13] Among other things, the organization is on the lookout to promote anti-bribery measures and to promote greater transparency in private business dealings and between the public and the private sector. Transparency, the argument goes, holds the promise of eradicating corruption and promoting politics-free solutions.

These and many other groups are constantly on the lookout for those who wish to avoid transparency requirements. They believe that transparency enables voters to assess better the work of public institutions and shareholders to evaluate businesses. They argue that transparency makes both public and private sectors more efficient, reduces or even eliminates corruption, encourages citizen or shareholder participation, and enhances accountability. Powerful individuals, they insist, are beset with the temptation to abuse power, to take advantage of situations, and to promote their own interests. Accordingly, the powerful require transparency so that they can "release their grip on themselves to change, which is otherwise psychologically hard to do."[14] In any event, transparency is the most important instrument that those without power and influence can use to keep an eye on those who have.

Government officials believe that their private-sector counterparts do not have the same demanding requirements that they do. This is true, but things are changing. Michael McCain, chief executive officer of Maple Leaf Foods, came face to face with demanding transparency requirements when it was discovered that products from his firm were killing people. It will be recalled that in the summer of 2008 meat products from Maple Leaf contained listeriosis, and DNA tests revealed that the death of several Canadians was attributable to it.[15]

McCain and Maple Leaf Foods were plunged into a crisis, with the media demanding immediate answers to the most pressing question: "How soon did Maple Leaf Foods know that there was a listeria problem and how quickly did it act?"[16] It was not enough for the firm to argue that it responded "with lightning speed." Within days, the media also demanded that the firm open up its decision-making process and make public internal exchanges, including e-mails, to establish that it had informed the public as quickly as it could.[17]

The other important question, of course, was how this could ever happen. Who, the question was soon asked, was responsible for regulating the food industry – the government or the firm through self-regulation? It appears that the responsibility was shared between the Canadian Food Inspection Agency (CFIA) and Maple Leaf Foods. Michael McCain took responsibility for the problem but insisted that there were "hundreds of provincial meat plants across the country operating under significantly lower standards than those applied to his company."[18]

The CFIA reported that, in carrying out its mandate, it does not work alone; its officials collaborate continually with public-health authorities and with "stakeholder partners," including "producers and processors."[19] Firms now assume part of the responsibility for food inspection; consequently, as in so many other sectors, it is no longer possible for anyone to single out a culprit to be held responsible when things go wrong. It was later learned that the CFIA had not informed the relevant health officials in Ontario, where the plant was located, until it was too late, and Maple Leaf Foods concluded that the CFIA was primarily concerned with getting the paperwork right rather than dealing with the crisis at hand.[20]

The federal government appointed an independent investigator, Sheila Weatherill, to probe the bacteria outbreak at Maple Leaf Foods. For reasons that were never made clear, Weatherill's terms of reference prevented her from assigning blame. Still, she pointed to a long list of communications failures, to intergovernmental protocols that were poorly understood, to vague policies, and to the fact that the CFIA carried out only three of the required twelve quarterly audits between 2005 and 2007.[21] In the end, it was not possible for Canadians to hold Maple Leaf Foods, the federal government, or the provincial government directly responsible for the death of twenty-two Canadians who ate contaminated meat. For those with power, transparency not only has limits; it also needs to be managed.

Publicly traded firms must today manage more and more demands to open their books, to deal with securities commissions, and to demonstrate social responsibility, particularly but not exclusively relating to the environment. Indeed, every incident seems to generate new transparency requirements, or "sunshine" laws, directed at the private sector: nutritional labelling of one kind or another, new reporting requirements on toxic pollution after an environmental mishap, and new financial standards after high-profile accounting scandals. In brief, the notion of a democratic deficit is no longer restricted to the public sector. Adrian Henriques maintains that "transparency is required whenever power is exercised," and private and publicly traded "companies suffer from a democratic deficit."[22] The democratic deficit the private sector is now expected to deal with includes trust and the pursuit of the public interest, however defined. One sure way of tackling the democratic deficit is through greater transparency.

The private sector has seen the definition of "public interest" expand considerably in recent years. Still, the concept remains poorly defined and seems to mean anything and everything, including what a news editor decides it means.[23] As a result, the notion of public interest drifts between what "the public might like to know" and what "the public ought to know because it affects them."[24] All firms above a certain size now have on staff someone to look after public interest issues, community relations, and the media.

It is now in the public interest to know who owns companies, both private and publicly traded ones, how a firm deals with its shareholders and stakeholders, how its senior managers are compensated (including stock options), and how a firm relates to relevant communities, interest groups, and the environment. Firms are now expected to retain the trust not only of shareholders but also of relevant community leaders and indeed of the general public. Unethical behaviour by some senior private-sector executives, which invariably gets media attention, is one factor that tipped the balance towards much greater transparency in the name of promoting the public interest. Other factors include the rise of public interest groups and, again, a decline across the Western world in deference to those who wield political and economic power.

Trust and transparency, the argument goes, go hand in hand. Firms should only harbour secrets that go to the very heart of their survival and competitiveness or those they are required to keep confidential under privacy laws. Where, then, does public interest come in? This is the grey area, where firms very often wish to expand the confidential space, while others – notably, public interest groups and the media – wish to narrow it. They insist that the greater the transparency, the greater the trust.

Public interest groups push for transparency in all things. Many will not accept, at face value, a firm's argument that it needs to protect information tied to its commercial interests. Many groups also insist that their actions benefit people beyond their membership. In order to defend the interests of customers, clients, and citizens, interest groups maintain that they need full access to all relevant information. Only by having such unencumbered access can they protect individuals from purchasing unsafe or subpar products or from making bad investments. Public interest groups also make the case that we live in more diffuse, if not disjointed, political and economic environments, and transparency is the best way to ensure accountability. These groups invariably can count on the media's support in the call for greater transparency.

There are some 20,000 recognized "public groups" today in Canada. They range from the Canadian Manufacturers' Association, which exists essentially to promote the interests of its members, to the Canadian Coalition on Acid Rain, which, it claims, exists to benefit all Canadians. A number of such groups need government funding to remain viable. The argument is that Canadians should be able to have their voices heard and that public funding is required to ensure a somewhat level playing field. The argument also goes that consumers need protection against big business, and if they cannot afford to look after their own interests, the government should step in by funding groups and associations that will do it for them.

The appetite of public interest groups for free and easy access to data from the private sector is not easily met. As they push private firms for more and more information to be made public, the firms just as certainly push back on the grounds of safeguarding their commercial interests. Increasingly, public interest groups are turning, with some success, to the courts and to government agencies and regulations to pry out more information and also to ensure that the refusal to divulge information is not made unilaterally by corporate management. There are now government bodies in most jurisdictions to which public interest groups can appeal to overturn a firm's decision to withhold information.

Transparency in the Public Sector

There is a widely held view that because politicians represent the public and because public servants are employees of the state, they should be held to a higher standard of integrity than their private-sector counterparts. This explains why politicians and public servants enjoy particularly rich pension plans so that they will not have to look after their own economic interests during and after their careers. If they cannot be held to a high standard of ethics, society will pay the heavy price of a breakdown in trust between citizens and their governments. Governments agree. In its 2006 Speech from the Throne, for example, the Harper government insisted that "no aspect of responsible government is more fundamental than having the trust of citizens."[25] Trust is not given automatically. There are core values that underpin trust in a representative democracy: fairness and democratic equality, a belief in political and administrative institutions based on the integrity of individuals who serve in them, and formal decision-making processes to ensure that public funds are spent in an honest and transparent fashion.

There have been no lack of attempts in recent years to strengthen the bond between government and citizens. Indeed, we have seen throughout the Western world a plethora of new measures designed to promote integrity, transparency, and trust in the public sector. The measures in place today would have been unrecognizable, and likely unacceptable, to those serving in government forty years ago. C.D. Howe, for one, would certainly not recognize the current environment, and one can easily speculate that he would not wish to serve under its requirements.

What changed? The pressure to make the public sector more transparent came from all sides, including economists, who invoked the principal-agency theory to support full access to information. In its simplest terms, the principal-agency theory suggests that the principal does not know as much as the agent, even on the most important issues, and that the interests of the principal and the agent are often in conflict.[26] Transparency is crucial so that principals can see both how agents behave and the consequences of the agents' behaviour, thus ensuring accountability. Transparency thus leads to better accountability, and accountability can more easily align the interests of the agent with those of the principal.

The theory has been applied to both the private and the public sector. Neither has been warm to the theory, and the private sector in particular has long resisted applying it. Here, I can do no better than quote Russell Stevenson:

> Corporations – even the largest among them – have always been treated by the legal system as "private" institutions. When questions about the availability of corporate information have arisen, the inquiry has typically begun from the premise that corporations, like individuals, are entitled to keep secret all information they are able to secure physically unless some particular reason for disclosure could be adduced in support of a contrary rule. So deeply embedded in our world view is this principle that it is not at all uncommon to hear serious discussions of a corporate "right to privacy."[27]

To be sure, the private sector has had to adjust its ways in recent years, especially publicly traded companies, but the tendency is still to hold meetings and make decisions behind closed doors, ostensibly to protect commercial interests.

Things have been different in the public sector. Here, the pressure to open up government and make the principal-agency theory work in practice is strong, even though many in government are probably unaware of the theory's existence. In fact, governments have made great strides in opening up government. The underlying premise is that the more closely we are watched, the better we behave.[28] There is no need to go over in any detail here all the transparency measures introduced to governments in Anglo-American democracies since 1984. Suffice to note that many of these measures are now present in governments throughout the Western world, and they take various forms: access to information to those outside government, right to protection for whistle-blowers, a multiplication of oversight bodies, and newly written codes of ethics, values, and conduct.

The Canadian government broke new ground when in 1985 it proclaimed into law its access to information legislation. The legislation was labelled the gift Trudeau gave to Mulroney; that is, Trudeau would not have to live with the consequences of the legislation produced by his government, but his successor, Mulroney, would. Trudeau, who by then had been prime minister for nearly sixteen years, knew a thing or two about exercising power and could appreciate that the legislation was not without important implications.

The central purpose of the Access to Information Act is to provide a right of access for Canadians to information under the control of any government institution. It adds that exceptions to the right of access should be both limited and specific and, further, that decisions on disclosure "should be reviewed independently of government."[29] When the legislation was first introduced, it was envisaged that it would be "first and foremost" for citizens. Today, the media are the "major users." It was also envisaged that citizens would turn to the legislation only as a last resort, since government departments would be expected to respect the intent of the legislation and share accessible information freely. This, too, has not turned out as envisaged.

Canada has also introduced measures to protect whistle-blowers. There is a growing body of literature on the topic, reflecting a strong interest among governments in strengthening their disclosure processes. One definition of whistle-blowing reads: "the disclosure by organization members (former or current) of illegal, immoral, or illegitimate practices under the control of their employers, to persons or organizations (internal or external) that may be able to take action to stop the wrongdoing."[30]

Paul Thomas maintains that whistle-blowing has become more respected within society. Certainly, there are a number of signs suggesting that today whistle-blowers are more admired than ever. For example, *Time* magazine awarded its Person of the Year award in 2002 to whistle-blowers. It was not always so. As Thomas points out, "In earlier decades society looked less favourably on persons who revealed the wrongdoing of other individuals or organizations. Loyalty to employers and respect for authority were more strongly held values within society than is true today. Pejorative labels like 'finks,' 'squealers,' 'informers,' and 'rats' were applied to people who blew the whistle. Their motives were assumed to be suspect – they were acting out of bitterness or revenge, for personal gain or simply to pass judgement and claim moral superiority."[31] But here, too, things have changed. Aggressive media coverage of wrongdoing, campaigns by public service unions in favour of whistle-blowing legislation, and access to information legislation have all contributed to the notion that employees have rights that should be respected, including blowing the whistle on those with power.

The whistle-blowing legislation in Canada went through several twists and turns before it emerged in Harper's accountability package in 2006. The idea first surfaced within government in a task force led by a deputy minister, and it was subsequently pursued by a working group of senior officials who came up with a series of recommendations.[32] Bills were introduced in Parliament and later revised. Some felt that the proposed legislation contained "no framework of ethics and values" and that those responsible for overseeing its legislation should be truly independent of government.[33] Harper met these criticisms head-on in his legislation. He made the Public Sector Integrity Commission an agent of Parliament; gave employees direct access to the commission; created an independent Public Servant Disclosure Protection Tribunal, with the power to decide whether reprisals have occurred and to order action to remedy the situation and ensure that those who took reprisals are disciplined; and introduced specific penalties for offences under the Public Servant Disclosure Protection Act, including tougher penalties for those who wilfully impede investigations of wrongdoing.[34]

All Anglo-American democracies have since introduced similar legislation, and some have gone further than Canada. In Britain, the Civil Service Code and the Public Interest Disclosure Act (PIDA) deal with the disclosure of wrongdoing. The PIDA covers both public-sector (except in such areas as security services) and private-sector employees. There are a number of categories of wrongdoing that "qualify" for protection, including, a criminal offence, a miscarriage of justice, and damage to the environment. The Civil Service Code, meanwhile, calls on employees to report any instances in which they are required to act in a manner that is illegal, improper, or unethical; that are in breach of constitutional convention or of a professional code; and that may involve possible maladministration. The code also provides that employees who believe that their department has not given them a reasonable response to their disclosures may appeal to the Civil Service Commissioners, an independent body. If the commissioners' investigation leads them to uphold the appeal, they will "make recommendations" for remedial action to the discloser's department.[35]

Access to information and whistle-blowing legislation are not the only transparency requirements government officials have to deal with. The size of central agencies has grown in recent years, not only to assist prime ministers to govern from the centre but also to monitor the work of line departments and agencies to ensure that they run on track.[36] The Harper government added yet another level of oversight in its 2006 accountability action plan – the establishment of departmental and agency external audit committees (DAAC).

These committees report directly to deputy ministers (initially, they were to report to ministers, but the reaction among senior public servants was such that the prime minister decided to retreat), and they have a mandate to "provide objective advice on and oversight of their department's management control and accountability processes."[37] Specifically, the committees are asked to provide oversight and advice on values and ethics; risk management; management control framework; internal audit function; relations with the Office of the Auditor General and central agencies; follow-up on management action plans; financial statements and public accounts of Canada reporting; and risk and accountability reporting. In short, they can roam pretty well where they want in the name of transparency and good management. Committee members are all drawn from outside government, mostly from the private sector and from the ranks of recently retired senior public servants.

The transparency fad has hit the United States, Britain, Australia, and New Zealand. All have introduced access or right to information and whistle-blowing legislation and strengthened their audit processes.[38] The questions for our purpose are: How has transparency affected the location of power? And how have those with power dealt with the various measures to promote transparency?

Dealing with Transparency

People on the outside see every reason for organizations to open their books, processes, and decisions for all to see. The thinking goes that the more information we have about political, administrative, or business actors, the more it will make the individual accountable and thus more likely to work for the common good.[39] Things, however, look very different for those with power on the inside.

First, the call for greater transparency runs up against a long-standing view in the private sector that firms have every right to keep their business private. I asked a leading Canadian businessman about the matter. He was blunt and to the point: "My business is no one else's business. Talk to me about results, everything else is my business." However, transparency is about process, not results. Nevertheless, he added, "We are in the game of results, that's how we survive. Process is for government bureaucrats to worry about." Things, of course, are no longer that simple, and whether he likes it or not he has to make more and more information available to shareholders, securities commissions, and banking or lending institutions. When pressed, he acknowledged that his position "may not be as tenable today as it was when I first entered the business world nearly forty years ago."[40]

His point, however, is that when one reveals information it all too often lands in the hands of individuals who are not able to evaluate it properly or who may use it to gain an economic advantage. They may not be able to evaluate the information properly because they view things from a different perspective, in a different light, without the proper background and training to understand it fully. He had in mind environmental and consumer advocacy groups and a variety of what he described as "so-called public interest" groups.

There are a number of ways for private-sector executives to sidestep transparency requirements. They know what information is sensitive and where it is located. The media are less informed about what is going on inside a private firm than in government, where the opposition and disgruntled public servants will happily report rumours or give inside information to journalists. Politics and government are everybody's business, and there is always a ready market for inside information. This is not always the case for private firms.

Private-sector executives can put off a request for information on the grounds that releasing it might jeopardize their firm's commercial interests. If all else fails, a publicly traded company can go private. This frees it from the demanding transparency requirements flowing out of the Sarbanes-Oxley Act in the United States and similar reforms elsewhere. Those on the inside also maintain that full disclosure is not without cost. Hostile firms may make use of the information to inflict damage or gain an unfair advantage in the market. Much as a country's military wants to protect its strategies and plans, private-sector firms do not want to share much information, even with their shareholders, for fear that it will make its way to competitors.

It is one thing for a senior private-sector executive to suggest that individuals or groups would not be able to evaluate information from a proper perspective, but it is quite another for politicians to say that voters would not understand. They may think it, but they can hardly say it. However, politicians and senior public servants can find any number of ways to limit access to inside information. John Crosbie, a former cabinet minister, writes that the access to information legislation has added to the "woes of politicians on the government side. It gives the media and other mischief-makers the ability to ferret out snippets of information with which to embarrass political leaders and to titillate the public. In the vast majority of instances, embarrassment and titillation are the only objects of access to information requests."[41] The same appears to be the case in other jurisdictions. Trivia, for example, matters to the British press no less than it does to the Canadian. At the beginning of the Iraq war, a keen observer of British politics wrote, "With a few notable exceptions, the newspapers have lost their critical faculties to consider the difference between a looming war, that could kill huge numbers of people and destabilize the world's most sensitive region, and the question of the PM's wife's beautician's boyfriend's involvement in buying a couple of flats in Bristol."[42]

The media happily make full use of access to information laws to secure information from government departments and agencies that suits their agenda. But things are different when the tables are turned. After journalists with the CBC, a Crown corporation, decided to press a municipality to release the individual salaries of its employees with names attached, a journalist with an independent newspaper turned to access to information legislation to obtain a detailed breakdown of the CBC's budget, including individual salaries for its journalists. After more than a year, the journalist is still waiting for a reply. The CBC's chairman wrote a letter complaining that the organization was receiving far too many access to information requests. The Office of the Information Commissioner, meanwhile, reported that it had received 536 complaints about the CBC in 2007–08, more than any other government agency or Crown corporation, and that more than 90 percent of the complaints were valid.[43] The merit of transparency, it seems, is in the eye of the beholder.

There is some evidence that the emphasis on transparency has discouraged aspiring politicians from seeking electoral office. Leading business executives, community leaders, and prominent figures in their respective fields may well decide that entering the political arena is not worth it, given the disclosure requirements, which would entail their entire lives being the subject of close public scrutiny. Indeed, data exist showing that an increase in transparency requirements have reduced the "average quality of the politicians" a party has been able to recruit.[44]

There is also plenty of evidence that senior public servants do not see transparency as a good in itself. They fear that their views may appear in the media and force officials to support or defend them in public, a responsibility, they insist, that should belong exclusively to politicians. As one senior official at the Canadian Treasury Board Secretariat observed, "We are now all sitting ducks. I cringe when I write an email because I never know whether it will appear on the front page of a newspaper six months down the road. It is possible now for someone to ask for all exchanges, including emails, between senior official X and senior official Y. We can no longer blue sky or have a playful mind. We no longer have the luxury of engaging in a frank and honest debate. It is now very difficult to put down on paper – be careful, minister, there are problems with your ideas and what you want to do."[45] The fear is that anyone outside government could discover what public servants have said or written and make it public.

Politicians may find themselves in hot water if a project or decision goes bad after the press reports that public servants had expressed strong reservations while it was being developed. Public servants, particularly those operating under the Westminster-Whitehall model, will go to great lengths to avoid creating problems for their ministers, especially for their prime minister. It explains, at least in part, why there is a growing reluctance to commit views to paper. One can assume that this in turn leads to less disciplined thinking as strong memoranda give way to PowerPoint presentations. One can also assume that there is less room for critical thinking. Ironically, because advice along the lines of "be careful" is no longer committed to paper, in some instances the process has become less transparent than it once was. One can appreciate that this work environment flies in the face of the traditional bargain that has guided relations between politicians and public servants for years under the Westminster-Whitehall model. Under this model, there is an ingrained culture of anonymity.[46] Being forced to provide information to ministers in private, for fear that otherwise it would be subject to public scrutiny, could well encourage public servants to leave the profession.

I met with several long-serving public servants responsible for access to information legislation in Ottawa to discuss its impact on government operations. They reported a "fear" on the part of public servants to commit things to paper. The problem, one explained, is that the sure measure of success in government is now based on "nothing hitting the headlines."[47] Although it is difficult to establish it as fact, one can speculate that some public servants may be leaving early or moving to the private sector because of access to information and whistle-blowing legislation. Indeed, consultations with senior government officials in Ottawa reveal that some mid-level public servants have left or are planning to leave the public service because of "growing transparency requirements."[48]

Senior public servants also maintain that ignorance can serve an important social function. They argue, for example, that Canada's regional tensions are such that it would not be wise to let everything out in the open or to have regional fights within the government played out for all to see.[49] This, they insist, would only fuel further regional conflicts and make the governing of Canada even more difficult. Here, one is reminded of Walter Bagehot's advice on understanding the monarchy: "Its mystery is its life. We must not let in daylight upon magic." Similarly, a number of senior government officials insist that transparency does not always build trust between government and citizens. They may have a point. A multitude of public opinion surveys reveal that citizens in Anglo-American democracies no longer trust their governments to the extent that they once did.[50]

Transparency is also not without important financial costs. We saw earlier that the post-Sarbanes-Oxley world has added considerably to the cost of operating a business because of the auditing and governance requirements for publicly traded companies. Transparency requirements are even more costly in government. Access to information and whistle-blowing legislation, together with external audit committees and the work of parliamentary officers, all require staff and resources to comply with the various expectations and demands. Andy Scott, the minister of Indian affairs and northern development in Paul Martin's government (2004–06), reports that the department's communications branch employed 118 officials and that 111 of them spent most of their time on work related to access to information requests.[51]

Hugh Winsor, a veteran member of the Parliamentary Press Gallery, claims that he has "never met a deputy minister who didn't hate the Access to Information Act." The act, he reports, "chews up resources," and senior government officials are "particularly leery" of "information fishermen," who file requests for thousands of pages of documents in the hope of discovering something "hot" that they can shop around to the media. He reported that MPs are now turning to the legislation to get information.[52]

This is not to suggest that the staff is always preoccupied with complying with the legislation. Government officials, particularly at the senior level, will go to some lengths to sidestep the legislation. In a detailed review of the application of the legislation, one student of public administration reports that "requests that were identified as sensitive, or that came from the media or political parties, were found to have longer processing time, even after other considerations were accounted for."[53]

The concern over media use of access to information has reached the point where the government is actually directing public servants not to commit anything to paper. As we noted earlier, the Department of Indian Affairs and Northern Development told consultants in a $132,000 contract not to leave "a paper trail in government offices" and insisted that they deliver their findings through oral briefings.[54] As well, several months after Harper came to power in January 2006, his government launched a program review designed to cut at least $2 billion from expenditures. Public servants were instructed to do everything "orally," including briefing their ministers, in identifying potential spending cuts, and to avoid putting anything down on paper.[55] Public servants did as they were told, and the approach worked, at least from Harper's perspective. His government was able to announce $2 billion in spending cuts on 25 September 2006, including cuts in politically sensitive programs, without media reports or leaks beforehand.[56]

Some twenty years after access to information legislation came into force, Canada's information commissioner wrote that he had witnessed the emergence of "a deeply entrenched oral culture, tolerated if not encouraged, at the most senior levels of government." He added that the government's policy on the management of government information holdings was now "largely ignored in practice and that accountability for its enforcement and implementation was so diffuse as to be non-existent." He pointed to the consequences. The quality of decision making in government was being undermined, and so was the effectiveness of internal and external audits and the country's historical records.[57] Canada amended its Access to Information Act in 1999 (section 67) to make it a criminal offence for anyone to destroy, alter, or conceal a record or direct anyone to do so with the intent of obstructing the right of access under the act. No one to date, however, has been charged under section 67. In 2009 the information commissioner once again spoke about the government's oral culture and the unwillingness of government departments to respect the spirit of the Access to Information Act.[58]

As in other things, Canada's approach to transparency requirements is echoed elsewhere. Nicholas Barrington, a recently retired British public servant, maintains that "people are terrified of keeping records which may cast aspersions on people. The Freedom of Information Act is affecting the way the Government works ... In the old days the mandarins wrote things down, that was part of their skills. I think the fact of this fear of the Freedom of Information Act, people's reluctance to put things down frankly on paper is encouraging sofa government, wrong decisions, and is damaging to the government's decision-making process."[59] Those who wield power in government see that, bit by bit and precedent by precedent, their control over information and what they think about policy issues is becoming public knowledge.

Chewing up resources is hardly the only problem deputy ministers have with transparency, and one can doubt whether it is the most important problem. There is evidence that transparency has altered their behaviour in a number of areas. It will be recalled that in 2004 the

Canadian government directed all senior managers to post their travel expenses on their departmental websites. As a result, two of Ottawa's most renowned restaurants – Café Henry Burger and Clair de Lune – closed their doors. The owner of one said that the moment hospitality claims had to be disclosed on the Internet, "they simply didn't come anymore." Another reported, "It wasn't necessarily the politicians, but it was the top civil servants that stopped coming."[60]

The work of the Gomery Commission, charged with looking into Chrétien's sponsorship scandal, was revealing on several fronts. One point that became clear was that resistance to transparency requirements grew as one went up the departmental hierarchies. Indeed, the Gomery Commission discovered that some front-line workers had shown courage in insisting that the access to information legislation be respected.[61] Thus, the more one goes up the influence and power ladder, the greater the resistance to transparency requirements.

There are many ways for the more powerful bureaucrats to sidestep the spirit of transparency legislation. We have already seen some, but there are still more. It will be recalled that Stephen Harper had a very different take on access to information legislation before he came to power. While leader of the opposition, Harper pledged:

> to implement the Information Commissioner's recommendations for reform of the Access to Information Act; to give the Information Commissioner the power to order the release of information; to expand the coverage of the act to all Crown corporations, Officers of Parliament, foundations and organizations that spend taxpayers' money or perform public functions; to subject the exclusion of Cabinet confidences to review by the Information Commissioner; to oblige public officials to create the records necessary to document their actions and decisions; to provide a general public interest override for all exemptions, so that the public interest is put before the secrecy of the government; to ensure that all exemptions from the disclosure of government information are justified only on the basis of the harm or injury that would result from disclosure, not blanket exemption rules and to ensure that the disclosure requirements of the Access to Information Act cannot be circumvented by secrecy provisions in other federal acts.[62]

Harper's intention was to include all these measures with his overhaul of the government's accountability regime. In the end, he decided to leave well alone, and he has yet to make good on these promises. Harper's perspective on transparency took an about-turn not long after he sat in the prime minister's chair. Suddenly, the world looked different once he had access to the levers of power.[63] The Information commissioner Robert Marleau declared in early 2009 that "a lack of political leadership" explains why there is now "a stranglehold on communications" flowing out to the media and to citizens. He added, "Six out of ten government departments reviewed this year received a failing grade for their response to access-to-information requests."[64]

Harper also backtracked on his commitment to introduce the British accounting officer model to the Government of Canada. Accounting officers occupy a key position in the system of financial control and accountability in Britain; they hold responsibility in their own right and are the responsible witnesses before the Public Accounts Committee. As the Treasury explains, "The essence of an Accounting Officer's role is a personal responsibility for the propriety and regularity of the public finances for which he or she is answerable."[65] The responsibilities of an accounting officer are laid down in a memorandum that is sent to every new accounting officer on appointment. The memorandum establishes the procedure to be followed when a minister overrules an accounting officer's advice on an issue of propriety and regularity. In the interest of greater transparency, it also makes it clear that the accounting officer is responsible for delivering departmental objectives in the most economic, efficient, and effective manner.

There is every indication that the Privy Council Office had serious reservations about Harper's proposal, and this may well explain his decision to change his position on the issue once he was in power. For instance, the PCO produced a document for the use of deputy ministers on the accounting officer concept that did not square with Harper's original position. In the end, the accounting concept in Canada became a watered-down version of the British model. The British model includes the responsibility to ensure value for money, while the Canadian model does not. The scope of issues for dispute resolution is much narrower in Canada, and the Canadian method refers the matter to other ministers for decision, which is not the case in Britain. The British model makes it quite clear that the responsibilities of the accounting officer are held personally, but this is much less clear in Canada.

Transparency has also run up against another fashion in governance: privacy laws. Anglo-American democracies enacted privacy legislation at about the same time, or shortly after, they introduced access or right to information. As Christopher Hood writes, "There is no doctrine of government without its counter-doctrines and, unexceptionable though it may seem at first sight, transparency is not an exception to that rule."[66] It will come as no surprise to readers that I have always sensed among senior government officials more enthusiasm for privacy than for transparency legislation.

But there are other less subtle ways for those with power to work around transparency requirements. There is such a thing as "idiot transparency" – that is, when senior managers provide a surplus of information. Transparency is or should be a "function of communication, not a function of the quantity of information technically disclosed."[67] One can assume that the government engages in idiot transparency when one looks at the material it sends to Parliament every year. It takes a brave soul with patience and plenty of time to go through the government's parts I, II, and III spending estimates. All in all, parliamentarians in Canada now receive – among other documents – more than ninety reports on plans and priorities, a similar number of departmental performance reports, and various reports from some forty Crown corporations. We know that MPs, or anyone else in Parliament for that matter, spend precious little time going over them.[68]

We also know that governments have introduced changes in record keeping, making it difficult to pinpoint where information may be located. No access to information legislation can generate information if records have not been kept or are incomplete. As Paul Thomas writes, "Politically savvy aides have learned the lessons from cases in Canada, and even more prominently from the White House case, that keeping careful records of interactions can be politically hazardous for their bosses. Solidarity and loyalty are emphasized."[69] In addition, governments have established a process to segregate and manage politically sensitive information requests. Lastly, governments have introduced changes for gathering information and restructuring the delivery of government services, making it difficult to determine where the requested information is located.[70]

It will be recalled that the goal of all Western governments was to promote an "open government" culture and an environment in which government officials would not ask why citizens should have access to government information but, rather, why not. The transition to open government remains a work in progress, and there are precious few observers making the case that open government is just around the corner. Alasdair Roberts, arguably the leading student of access or right to information legislation in Anglo-American democracies, recently came to a blunt conclusion. He writes that freedom of information legislation "will not produce a culture of openness." Nor, he adds, is it clear that the legislation "will improve trust in government."[71] Why, then, have senior government officials been unwilling to embrace a culture of open government?

It is important to remember that secrecy is deeply ingrained in bureaucratic culture. The father of twentieth-century bureaucracy, Max Weber, wrote that a high degree of secrecy is characteristic of all bureaucracy.[72] Peter Hennessy wrote in his *Whitehall* that secrecy is "Whitehall's cardinal virtue and dominant characteristic"; it is "the bonding material which holds the rambling structure of government together." He concluded with the observation that "of all the rules of government, secrecy is the most sacred."[73] But another defining characteristic of the traditional bureaucratic model is the need to keep records and files and to obey rules.

Old habits die hard, particularly those that go to the heart of an institution's culture. Here we are referring in fact to two institutions – Parliament and bureaucracy. Secrecy is important for the prime minister and ministers because of Parliament's highly competitive and partisan nature. Secrecy is no less important for bureaucracy because of the nature of the relationship between politicians on the government side and public servants, with their ability to influence public policy and speak truth to political power. Secrecy is sacred for bureaucrats in the sense that their advice to ministers needs to be confidential. Bureaucracy without secrecy and hierarchy is an institution that has been stripped of its most basic defining characteristics. Transparency requirements also invite the powerful to bypass institutions and organizations if they wish to get things done or to pursue their agenda. It is in this sense that transparency at times makes it difficult to locate power.

When Power Confronts Transparency, Those with Power Win

Much as tigers do not easily part with their stripes, those with power will not easily part with it, nor will they willingly accommodate measures designed to shed light on how they manage their power. Transparency requirements, from Sarbanes-Oxley in the private sector to access to information legislation in the public sector, have altered power relationships. In the face of new transparency requirements, those with access to the levers of power have circled the wagon, protecting their organization from outsiders and strengthening their hold within it, with varying degrees of success. As a result, the emphasis has shifted from organizations to individuals, because it is powerful individuals, not organizations, that are more often the target of access to information requests.

Those with power insist that, to be effective, they need to narrow the decision-making process, not enlarge it. Prime ministers wield considerable power within the government not only because they are the boss but also because they are able to restrict the number of hands involved in making a decision. Transparency tends to add to the number of hands, and this makes things more complex and difficult at a time when instant communication requires quick decisions. The same can be said about the private sector. Transparency slows down decision making and makes management more cautious and operations thicker.

Power is far more fluid today than in years past. Richard Wilson, as already noted, went to the heart of the issue when he wrote that power is "never constant, it moves around from day to day and somebody who was powerful last week is less powerful this week ... Reputations rise and fall like a stock exchange."[74] This poses a problem for those with power and those who aspire to power.

Transparency can and often does reveal the strengths and weaknesses of individuals as well as their views on key issues. Individuals can only see negative consequences resulting from transparency because they can no longer predict who will have political or bureaucratic power next month, let alone next year. Transparency stands a much better chance of taking root in a stable environment where one can predict with some assurance who will wield power in the years ahead. If power frequently changes hands, one will want to be careful in expressing strongly held views openly for fear that they will come back to haunt one. Best to keep such views private if the objective is survival in the political, bureaucratic, and business worlds.

Yet transparency can also strengthen the hand of those who have power. One of Canada's leading private-sector executives insists that transparency requirements of the kind promoted by Sarbanes-Oxley encourages a "command and control" management style. "Who else," he asked, "can protect his own business? We have to be on top of everything and we need a constant flow of information to ensure that what is made publicly available does not hurt the business or at least can be properly managed."[75] Being on top of things requires subordinates to constantly feed information up the line. This, of course, is even more important for political leaders and their senior public servants.

All of the above is to make the point that the new transparency requirements have had a considerable impact on the location of power. Contrary to expectations, on the one hand, transparency makes it more difficult to locate power and, on the other, it has strengthened the hand of those who hold power, even if only temporarily. Transparency, particularly in the public sector, has become a hurdle that powerful individuals must deal with or sidestep at a considerable cost to taxpayers. This in turn has forced individuals down the organization to deal with a very demanding level of public scrutiny, which make decisions very difficult, again, particularly in the public sector. It has also pushed more and more decisions up the ladder, given the need to deal with public controversies that may flow out of the decisions, thus creating a log jam at the top.

One always has to keep an eye on what the public, the stakeholders, and the shareholders may think, not only about results but also about who was involved in taking decisions. In government, things slow down to a crawl unless the national media and the prime minister decide to make them an issue to be resolved. This may well explain why citizens are lashing out at politicians and public servants, because they cannot seem to influence the government decision-making process. Transparency and its inability to promote open government has come with a price: an apparent inability, even for many inside government, to influence policy and decision making – unless one is able to give the policy and decision-making process a powerful wrench of the wheel. Only the very powerful can do this.

Transparency has forced the hand of powerful individuals to come up with a means of circumventing its requirements. Transparency has not made government better or fixed the problem, however defined; if anything, it has revealed how serious the problem is.

6 REVISITING GOVERNING FROM THE CENTRE

Brian Laghi and Jeffrey Simpson wrote in the *Globe and Mail* that Prime Minister Stephen Harper "liked having his hands on the levers of power."[1] What levers of power are these? In 1999 my book *Governing from the Centre: The Concentration of Power in Canadian Politics* received wide media attention. The book argued that prime ministers, starting with Pierre Trudeau in 1968, introduced various reforms and processes designed to telescope power into their own hands and those of their immediate offices and weaken the power and influence of ministers, traditional line departments, and even Parliament. The book made the front page of the *Globe and Mail* and other national and regional newspapers, as well as news magazines. The timing of its publication, probably more than anything else, explains why an academic book came to enjoy such wide media interest. It hit a sensitive chord, since the country at that time was dealing with the political fallout from a high-profile public inquiry into allegations of political interference by the Prime Minister's Office (PMO) into the actions of the RCMP in its dealings with protesters at the Asia-Pacific Economic Cooperation (APEC) summit that had been held in Vancouver in 1997.

I was soon to discover that the book also had hit a sensitive chord in Ottawa. Opposition MPs praised it and often quoted from it in debates and speeches. Some political observers used it to make the case that Prime Minister Chrétien ran Ottawa like a "friendly dictator."[2] Many senior politicians and their advisers on the government side, as well as some senior public servants, however, were less enthusiastic. One senior official in the PMO challenged my findings by insisting that there is no other way than "to govern from the centre" and that "the alternative to governing from the centre is not governing effectively at all."[3] A former adviser to Prime Minister Chrétien told me over lunch, "You know, my boss never believed that he had too much power. He actually felt that he could do a better job if he had more power."[4] To be sure, one can easily imagine that there were moments when Chrétien could feel nostalgic over Henry II's power. He had simply to say, "Will no one rid me of this meddlesome priest?" to see the matter resolved.

I later discovered that the book also sparked interest in Britain. Robert Hazell of University College, London, told a round table in London in 2002 that "every page of Savoie's *Governing from the Centre* now resonates in Britain."[5] Both Margaret Thatcher and Tony Blair, like their Canadian counterparts, stood accused of concentrating more and more power in their own offices. Thatcher liked to say, "I don't mind how much my ministers talk as long as they do what I say."[6] Blair, for his part, actually broke with constitutional convention when he empowered partisan advisers, including his principal adviser on media and communications, to give instructions to permanent public servants.[7]

I was, however, hardly the first to write about this matter. As far back as 1975, W.A. Matheson wrote about the prime minister's gaining power at the expense of cabinet ministers, as did Denis Smith in 1977.[8] But the issue continued to gain traction, and by the late 1990s there was a *prise de conscience* in both Canada and Britain that more power was shifting to prime ministers and their offices, and the same could be said about other prime ministers operating under the Westminster-Whitehall parliamentary model.

There are precious few voices today denying that Canadian prime ministers have been grabbing more and more power from their ministers since Trudeau's time. Prime ministers currently dominate the machinery of government to an extent that was not possible forty years ago. In hindsight, however, I have come to recognize that the issue is much more complex. What about forces operating outside government? Is power now leaking from the machinery of government itself that restricts prime ministerial power? Is prime ministerial power now constrained by forces that did not exist forty years ago? Why do prime ministers want to concentrate more power in their own offices? This chapter seeks to answer these questions by revisiting the prime minister's role in government.

Parliament Still Matters, At Times

Parliament retains all the constitutional powers that it had in its golden years in eighteenth- and nineteenth-century Britain. These powers are particularly evident in a minority Parliament. The self-inflicted government crisis in December 2008 saw the Canadian House of Commons bring the Harper government to heel and threaten its very survival.

Harper decided, as part of his government's November 2008 economic update, to scrap the $28 million in public subsidies that political parties receive for votes they garner in federal elections and to impose a ban on public-service strikes. It will be recalled that the October 2008 general election gave the Harper government a stronger parliamentary mandate, but still left it twelve seats short of a majority. Harper's decision was completely unexpected. His party had held a policy convention a few weeks earlier, and neither issue was raised, let alone debated, which again speaks to the growing irrelevance of political parties in shaping policy.[9]

The opposition parties reacted strongly to Harper's decision, with three of them (the Liberals, Bloc Québécois, and Green Party) worried about their very survival, given their precarious financial position. It forced opposition MPs to decide between voting for the demise of their own political party or voting to defeat the government. They opted for the latter. All opposition parties agreed to support a vote of no confidence in the government, and two of them (the Liberal and the New Democratic parties) agreed to form a coalition to replace the Harper government, assuming that the governor general would invite the leader of the opposition to meet the House to see if he could secure support for the coalition.

Harper, sensing the danger, decided to scrap both the plan to eliminate public financing for political parties and the proposed ban on public-service strikes. A government spokesperson declared, "We do not think it's in the interests of Canadians to have an election over this issue."[10] Harper thus came face to face with the reality that the prime minister's power has limits, particularly when the government does not enjoy a majority of seats in the Commons.

In the process, Canadians received a crash course on their parliamentary system of government. They came to appreciate that, unlike the Americans, they do not choose a prime minister: that responsibility belongs to the House of Commons. In addition, albeit on rare occasions, the governor general has the power to say no to the prime minister. They also learned that the prime minister has many cards to play when his power is threatened. For instance, he can request that Parliament be prorogued, which gives him a tactical advantage and unleashes the government's communication resources to spin a message to Canadians. Canadians, in turn, came to appreciate that constitutional requirements are one thing, but politics and political strategies matter a great deal when deciding who should have political power.[11] Harper's decision to scrap public subsidies to political parties was extremely ill timed, if not ill informed. He would pay a high political price. His reputation and, by ricochet, his power with his Cabinet and caucus would suffer.

Word soon circulated around Ottawa and in the media that the decision to eliminate public financing for political parties was Harper's alone. His Cabinet was not consulted, nor obviously was his caucus. He simply sent, at the last minute, a directive to the minister of finance to include it in his economic update statement, "without ministers or deputy ministers knowing." This, the media argued, demonstrated that he was a "ferociously partisan leader" with a profound desire to centralize "everything in his own hands."[12] The national media were quick to point out that the prime minister could hardly fire the finance minister for the miscalculations. One leading journalist wrote, "Jim Flaherty isn't really the Finance Minister. The miscalculations originated in the Prime Minister's Office, how could the Prime Minister fire Mr. Flaherty when it was the PM who ordered up the stuff in the first place?"[13]

Centralizing everything in one's own hands is not without drawbacks. The prime minister has to wear the decision and any political fallout. With the media, political observers, and even some Conservative Party officials suggesting that Harper had committed a major political blunder, the focus of the media and Canadians turned on him rather than on Cabinet or even the minister of finance, who actually delivered the message in Parliament. A Conservative Party official argued, "This was a big whopper and it was his whopper. It wasn't anybody else's." He added, "Certainly, people are less willing to defer to his strategic brilliance."[14] The point is that when it comes to political power, the individual who has it matters, as does his or her ability to manage it. If a prime minister knows how to handle the available levers, he can dominate government in a way that was not possible forty years ago. But if he missteps, he has to bear the consequences.

The Boss Is Still the Boss

Jean Chrétien called Pierre Trudeau *le boss* when he served in his Cabinet. He himself later became the boss and was also called so by many of his Cabinet colleagues when he became prime minister in 1993.[15] Trudeau became *le boss* in a way that his predecessor, Lester B. Pearson, never was. He brought to his office and to central agencies the instruments and resources required to govern from the centre. The prime ministers who followed, from Mulroney to Harper, have not turned back the clock to Cabinet government as Pearson and his ministers knew it.[16]

Anyone seeking to locate political power should still start by looking at the prime minister – there is plenty of political power there. Within the federal government, the prime minister is king, especially when holding a majority of seats in Parliament. Consider the following: prime ministers chair Cabinet meetings, establish Cabinet processes and procedures, set the Cabinet agenda, establish the consensus for Cabinet decisions, appoint and fire ministers and deputy ministers, establish Cabinet committees and decide on their membership; they exercise virtually all the powers of patronage and act as personnel manager for thousands of government and patronage jobs; they articulate the government's strategic direction as outlined in the Speech from the Throne; they dictate the pace of change and are the main salespersons promoting the achievements of their government; they have a direct hand in establishing the government's fiscal framework; they represent Canada abroad; they establish the proper mandate of individual ministers and decide all machinery of government issues; and they are the final arbiter in interdepartmental conflicts. The prime minister is the only politician with a national constituency and, unlike members of Parliament and even cabinet ministers, has no need to search out publicity or national media attention, since attention is invariably focused on his or her office and residence, 24 Sussex Drive. In short, the prime minister is head of government with limited checks on his or her power inside government or in Parliament if the PM's party holds a majority of seats. However, the prime minister is not head of state, a role still played by the governor general as representative of the monarch. This is just as well, since that role is now largely ceremonial.

Each of the above levers of power taken separately is a powerful instrument of public policy and public administration in its own right, but when you add them all up and place them in the hands of one individual, they constitute a veritable juggernaut. Other than going down to defeat in a general election, it can be stopped or slowed only by the force of public opinion or by a Cabinet or caucus revolt. Even then, public opinion may not be much of a force if the prime minister has already decided not to run again in the next general election. One only has to think back to Trudeau's, Mulroney's, and Chrétien's final years in office to appreciate this. History also tells us that a caucus or Cabinet revolt, or even the threat of a revolt, is extremely rare in Ottawa.

The power of prime ministers and presidents has grabbed the attention of political scientists and journalists in recent years. We now have a spate of books and journal articles on the topic, and the great majority of them report on the efforts of both prime ministers and presidents to shift still more power to their own hands and offices. Recent books with titles such as *The Return of the Imperial Presidency*, which reported on the George W. Bush years, make the case that US presidents will push the envelope as much as they can to bring more power to their offices.[17] Barack Obama served notice early in his administration that he would be governing from the centre.[18] To be sure, individuals who make it to the top of the political ladder in whatever jurisdiction have no shortage of ambition, pride, and ego. We noted earlier that James Madison recognized this and argued in the *Federalist Papers* that "ambition must be made to counteract ambition."[19]

American presidents have been able to build a case to draw still more power away from Congress by insisting that such developments as the Cold War, the War on Terror, and managing the economy have made it necessary.[20] We know that presidents, for example, in more recent years, have been transformed into "commanders-in-chief." We also know that the US Supreme Court has recently tilted towards a sympathetic view of executive power. As a result, the system of checks and balances that the Founding Fathers designed is, by many accounts, under severe strain and has been for some time.[21] Students of American politics argue that, leaving aside the Watergate years, US presidents since Franklin D. Roosevelt have successfully brought more and more power to their offices.[22] Jack Balkin, a constitutional law professor at Yale, maintains that Barack Obama "will enter office as the most powerful president who has ever sat in the White House." The power of the president, he maintains, soared under George W. Bush, in part because of "Congress's recent history of complacency."[23]

Eoin O'Malley carried out an extensive survey to test the power of prime ministers in twenty-two countries. The results varied from country to country, but the fact that the survey was even undertaken is telling. O'Malley provided the usual caveat – "power, though essentially contested and difficult to define or measure," could be "assessed in a more objective way."[24] His objective assessment was that Canadian prime ministers ranked at the very top of the twenty-two countries surveyed for the years 1980 to 2000 in terms of the level of their power and influence; but also that prime ministers everywhere have sought, with varying degrees of success, to concentrate more power in their own offices.[25]

However, power is not purely institutionally based. What about forces outside the internal machinery of government? And what about forces that may inhibit the ability of prime ministers to do as they wish?

Some Power Drifting Down and Out

Canada's federal system means that the prime minister does not have much power in some key policy areas. In Canada, as is well known, the provinces hold jurisdiction over important sectors, from health care and education to social services. The prime minister may have strong views on what ought to be done in these sectors but must employ soft power or the power of persuasion, together with the hard power of cash in the form of transfer payments, to influence provincial policies and programs. But one can never be certain to obtain the policy objectives one seeks when things are turned over to federal-provincial negotiations. Compromises have to be made, and there are many federal and provincial actors involved, each with a position to promote. Things can also break down in the implementation stages when policy objectives are altered to correspond to changing circumstances, so what the prime minister had in mind when he agreed to support an initiative may look very different when it is finally delivered.

There is also pressure to decentralize still more power to the provinces in areas that in the past either belonged to Ottawa or were shared responsibilities between the federal and provincial governments. I do not recall an instance when the provinces urged the federal government to assume more power or responsibility over jurisdictions that traditionally belong to them. It will be recalled, for example, that in December 2006 Ottawa signed an agreement establishing a formal role for the Province of Quebec in the United Nations Educational, Scientific, and Cultural Organization (UNESCO). UNESCO exists to promote peace, security, and cultural diversity through education, science, and the arts. Membership in UNESCO has traditionally been limited to nation-states, and Canada has been a member since 1946. The Harper government's decision meant that henceforth Quebec would be an associate member of UNESCO and would have an official representative inside Canada's UNESCO office in Paris.[26] The deal was not extended to the other provinces. Canadian citizens wishing to establish where power is now located need to understand the asymmetrical nature of Canada's federal system. They will discover that who has power in one province does not always have it in another.

Shared-cost agreements between Ottawa and the provinces have been in vogue since the 1960s. It is now difficult, if at all possible, to identify a single policy sector that belongs unambiguously either to the federal government or to provincial governments. It seems that everything in public policy in Canada is now interconnected. Indeed, if anything, the interconnection between federal and provincial policies and programs has intensified in recent years; there are well-staffed units in all governments whose only responsibility is to monitor federal-provincial relations and agreements. For example, Ottawa recently signed a series of labour market and immigration agreements with the provincial governments that allow provinces to assume responsibility to plan and deliver initiatives to promote job creation and skills development and to fast-track the citizenship applications of skilled workers.[27] The Harper government even announced its intention in the summer of 2008 to let Quebec negotiate a unilateral labour mobility deal with another country, France.[28]

Experience shows that once Ottawa turns over power or decides to share power with provincial governments, it is extremely difficult to backtrack.[29] What Ottawa can do and has done, particularly in the economic development field, is to turn off the funding tap and not share the costs of certain initiatives. But this hardly strengthens the prime minister's hand in shaping new measures. It simply means that the provinces are on their own in funding initiatives and Ottawa is left with little influence in these sectors.

As Ottawa transfers more power to the provinces or decides to cut funding for certain sectors, the prime minister has less control over the making and implementation of public policy. But this is part of a broader trend – prime ministers have become more powerful within their own cabinets and inside the machinery of government but have seen their control over the implementation of public policy decline.

If New Public Management (NPM) and its accompanying reform measures (which were designed to empower front-line managers and their employees) mean anything, then prime ministers have had to relinquish some management control. Privatization, deregulation, public-private partnerships, delegation of responsibility for human and financial resources, and contracting-out have all played havoc with the government hierarchy. The logic behind NPM and its accompanying measures was that front-line government managers were or should be better at running things than politicians, hence the need to turn more power over management issues to them. Everyone cannot be empowered at the same time, so if front-line managers are delegated greater power, someone up the hierarchy must lose power. This has proved to be true in financial and human resources management.

Front-line managers have been told, time and again, to imitate their private-sector counterparts and take charge of their operations. NPM's central message is to instill a bias for action in government operations, to get things done, and to eliminate, to the extent possible, red tape and centrally prescribed rules. New management development programs and performance bonuses were introduced to encourage this. A prime minister's political power, which is based on hierarchy and command and control, does not apply as easily under this new model, and the PM's ability to steer the system is somewhat compromised. The problem for political leaders, however, is that the media and voters do not absolve politicians of the responsibility for problems when things go wrong. They assume that political leaders still have the power and responsibility to make things right and will continue to look to them for answers.[30] This adds to the confusion over who actually has power in government.

Power Drifting Outward

Political authority has not only drifted downward, but it has also moved outward to international organizations and regional and international trade agreements. Prime ministers, presidents, and finance ministers meet at G7, G8, and G20 gatherings, and Canadian prime ministers and American presidents meet or talk by telephone from time to time. They meet to resolve issues and strike decisions, as G20 leaders did in November 2008 and April 2009 to map out a plan to deal with the world's financial and credit crisis.

Prime ministers and presidents can influence policy prescriptions at these sessions, but they cannot dictate them. Some, notably US presidents, have more influence than others by virtue of the country they represent. But even here their power is not static. George W. Bush in late 2008 had less power and less political capital than Barack Obama had in early 2009. Power not only shifts outward from government, it also shifts from individual to individual.

It will be recalled that the leaders of the G20 met in Washington on 15 November 2008 to identify measures to stabilize the global financial system. A number of decisions were taken at the meeting, including initiatives to subject rating agencies to more oversight and regulation. They also agreed to begin work on crafting "a new financial order" and that such institutions as "the World Bank must be comprehensively reformed." They decided to put in place initiatives to "strengthen transparency," including "enhancing required disclosure on complex financial products."[31] Accordingly, if one looked to national capitals to locate political power, one would not be looking at the right place. However, in this instance at least, power was shared between twenty powerful individuals and their key advisers. Unless one had a ringside seat at the gathering, one would be hard pressed to identify who specifically had power over which issue. The one thing we do know is that for brief periods at least, political power is concentrated in the hands of seven, eight, or twenty powerful individuals.

Leaving aside the role individuals play at international gatherings, it is also true that an increasing number of policy instruments are leaking out of national governments. As already noted, free trade agreements, by definition, limit the power of national governments. Power transferred to international trade organizations such as the WTO is power lost to presidents and prime ministers. Angelo Persichilli pointed to power drifting out of the hands of national governments when he wrote that the federal government had to resort to "begging" Nortel to "at least" consider a Canadian offer in the course of selling its assets. He explained, "The reality now is that power has escaped the hands of any national government and lies in the boardrooms of international business organizations. Politicians used to have real power when major corporations had a national scope."[32]

There is also a growing number of issues, ranging from the environment and global warming to terrorism and financial markets, that call out for international action, and here again presidents and prime ministers must share power with one another to get things done. This speaks to the multilevel model of governance which has become an important part of the global economy and the modern nation-state. The model, however, serves to separate power from responsibility. One could, at the national level, turn to advisory or sectoral committees to lend a hand, but this only serves to complicate matters by further muddying the location of power. However, it strengthens the hands of prime ministers and presidents within their own governments. They require the necessary flexibility to strike a position or agree to deals at international gatherings. Prime ministers invariably compare their ability to get things done with that of their counterparts. They do not want to be seen as weak or unable to deliver a decision as quickly as their counterparts. If ministers or senior public servants are not happy with what the prime minister agrees to at these gatherings, they are of course free to resign. Few ever do, which further strengthens the hand of prime ministers.

Governing by Announcements

Prime ministers, probably better than anyone else, understand how some political power has drifted downward and outward and that there is less "loose" power around national governments than, say, thirty years ago. As a result, power inside government is not as evident as it once was. This may explain, at least in part, why even prime ministers have come to believe that the levers of political power do not work as well as they would like or as they once did. It may also explain why they want to centralize power in their own hands. In any event, they reason that it is the only way to get things done in modern government. It may also explain why Canadian prime ministers since the latter days of the Trudeau government have put in place two policy processes – one for themselves and one for everybody else.

When Canadian prime ministers and their advisers wish to approve a new initiative, they move everything out of the reach of ministers, departments, and career officials and simply get it done. This approach can be described as policy making by announcement. The prime ministers will deliver a major speech to unveil a new policy and then let the government decision-making process pick up the pieces as best it can. Given that the prime minister has a direct say in the career prospects of ministers, aspiring ministers, heads of departments, and aspiring heads of departments, as well as heads of Crown corporations and aspiring heads of Crown corporations, everyone has an interest in seeing the prime minister's initiative come to a successful conclusion.

Prime ministers invariably come to power with some pet projects to pursue, and they pick up a few more while in office. Think of Trudeau and the constitution, Mulroney and free trade, Chrétien and arresting the deficit. We could add Trudeau and official languages policy, Mulroney and regional development agencies, and Chrétien and the Millennium Scholarship Foundation. Unlike his predecessors, Harper has not enjoyed a majority mandate, so he could not pursue his pet projects, such as Senate reform, to the extent he had hoped.

When prime ministers make an issue a priority, there is no stopping them. At the risk of sounding repetitive, if one wants to locate power inside the Government of Canada, one need look no further than to prime ministers and their advisers. On issues that truly matter to them, Ottawa's formal policy-making process is pushed aside and their priorities or pet projects will be approved as first envisaged or, in the words of a former Chrétien minister, "with the bark still on."[33] It will be recalled that Chrétien bypassed the cabinet process in launching the Canada Millennium Scholarship Foundation. He feared that his idea would look different by the time it reached the other end if it had to go through Ottawa's formal decision-making process. He simply ignored it and decided to establish the initiative after speaking to his minister of finance.

It will also be recalled that Stephen Harper tabled a motion in Parliament in 2006 that read, "This House recognizes that the Québécois form a nation within a united Canada" after consulting only a handful of his closest advisers. Cabinet was left outside the loop.[34] Even the minister responsible for intergovernmental affairs was not informed, let alone consulted, before the decision was made and before the full caucus was told. The minister subsequently resigned, not because he felt slighted but because he is opposed to special status for any particular ethnic group, even when that group is one of the country's two founding peoples.[35] It is not difficult to locate who had power in this situation.

Once again we emphasize that prime ministers have tremendous power in their own hands. They have built up a strong capacity in the Prime Minister's Office (PMO) and in the key central agency, the Privy Council Office (PCO). On the changing role of the PMO, I can do no better than quote Tom Kent, principal secretary to Prime Minister Pearson: "The PMO was then utterly different from what it became in the Trudeau era and has since remained. There was no bevy of deputies and assistants and principal this-and-that, with crowds of support staff."[36]

The PCO also has grown so much that Pearson would not recognize it today. In Pearson's days, it had a staff of less than two hundred people. Today, it employs about a thousand.[37] It is important to stress that the PCO does not deliver programs or services to Canadians; in the past it existed to serve the prime minister and the Cabinet, whereas today it exists largely to serve the prime minister. It has the resources as well as the time to manage the prime minister's priorities. The clerk of the privy council and secretary to the cabinet is the most powerful public servant, if only because the person holding this position is the prime minister's deputy, and the other deputy ministers and aspiring deputy ministers (there is never a shortage of the latter) know that the clerk can promote them or play havoc with their careers at the stroke of the pen.

Retired senior public servants report that before Michael Pitfield (clerk under Trudeau between 1975 and 1982), clerks would never recommend a deputy minister appointment without consulting widely and would ensure that the chair of the Public Service Commission would be supportive. Things no longer work this way. The prime minister and the clerk of the privy council make the appointments with or without consulting others if they so decide.

One should never underestimate the power of appointment. Few people in government have such power. Ministers do not appoint their deputy ministers, and appointments below that level are, or should be, based on competition. MPs wishing to become ministers and assistant and associate deputy ministers wishing to become deputy ministers are not short on ambition. They keep an eye on what the prime minister and the clerk of the privy council desire, and they attempt to deliver the goods. The point is that the current system and the machinery of government are designed to serve prime ministers, which enables them to have their way on issues they identify as a priority.

There Are Constraints

There are, however, constraints within the federal government that inhibit prime ministers from always getting their way. The first is time. Prime ministerial time is the rarest of commodities in Ottawa. The flip side to having most key areas of public policy channelled to the prime minister is that the PM can hardly find time to give each the attention it deserves. Unless prime ministers pick policy areas and issues they want to concentrate on, they may be rendered ineffective by trying to shape too many activities and decisions in too many areas. In brief, prime ministers only have time to drive a limited number of issues.

There are always telephone calls to return, correspondence to deal with, government and patronage appointments to make, documents to read, meetings to attend, party functions to support, and ministers and members of Parliament to meet. The prime minister will also want to be available to meet foreign heads of government, provincial premiers, and important members of the business community. Parliament, Cabinet, and caucus meetings eat into the PM's agenda. The prime minister must also make time available for senior PMO staff. When in Ottawa, a PM meets four and sometimes five times a week first thing in the morning with the chief of staff and the clerk of the privy council. Trudeau met with his two senior officials every morning, Monday to Friday.

Senior policy advisers and the head of appointments also need to see the prime minister from time to time if they are to do their jobs well. Making patronage appointments often requires consultation with the relevant ministers and other senior party members, including provincial premiers from the same party. The prime minister needs to be briefed on potential appointments, and some of the briefings are better done face to face. Meanwhile, policy advisers need access to the prime minister to gain an understanding of the PM's views and to bounce ideas around to make sure that they can successfully pursue the PM's agenda.

Prime ministers are also members of Parliament and need to devote time to their constituency, to maintain personal contact with constituents, and to meet with riding association and local opinion leaders. As Marc Lalonde wrote, "The prime minister, like all other MPs, represents a particular electoral riding. The prime minister's responsibility to his constituents is the same as that for any other member of Parliament. Residents of his constituency expect the prime minister to provide them with the same services as are provided by all other MPs."[38] One president of a federal Crown corporation reports that he was "startled one day to have Prime Minister Chrétien on the phone inquiring about a relatively minor issue involving his constituency."[39]

Prime ministers read or should read about 300-plus pages of briefing material and correspondence every week. Unless they read at least some of the more important briefing documents and correspondence, they will go into meetings unprepared and perhaps not as able to influence the outcome of a discussion as they would like. The 300 pages of material, Cabinet documents, correspondence, press clippings, and briefing notes cover any number of policy issues, from international security matters to the government's fiscal health. Some will require a decision from the PM; others are for information only. But they should all be attended to because a careful prescreening will have already taken place. Officials in both the PMO and the PCO are all too aware of the pressure on the prime minister's time and will be careful to weed out the less urgent material.

A great deal of planning goes into putting together the prime minister's agenda. Clearly, there are many more demands on a PM's time than can possibly be accommodated, and the staff will juggle several possibilities for most time slots that are available. For example, Cabinet and caucus meetings are always blocked off when the prime minister is in Ottawa, and time is also made available to ensure that the PM meets a cross-section of people and can focus on his or her priorities.

About twenty-five years ago, Prime Minister Pierre Trudeau's agenda was described as follows: "In an average month, he works about 250 hours. Roughly 90 of them, or 36 percent of his working time, are spent on government business, including Cabinet and its committees, the House of Commons, the governor general and other government officials, foreign visitors and ambassadors, outside groups, and foreign travel. Political activities involving ministers, MPs, senators, or Liberal Party officials account for 50 hours, or 20 percent of his time. He spends 12.5 hours, or 5 percent, in press conferences or other forms of contact with the news media; 30 hours, or 12 percent, with staff in the PMO and PCO; and 67.2 hours, or 27 percent of his time, on paperwork, correspondence, and telephone calls. On a typical day, his activities as prime minister have spanned 11 hours."[40]

I was shown a typical weekly agenda prepared for Prime Minister Chrétien. There was not an empty spot anywhere on it. A prime minister's agenda is always subject to last-minute changes to accommodate new political developments that must be attended to. The agenda, however, hardly tells the full story. It does not include more important matters, such as quick exchanges with key staff members, a private word with a senior minister in between meetings, and, more crucially, many important telephone calls.[41] Prime ministers must also make time to deal with real, perceived, or emerging political crises. These might include a ministerial resignation, a political scandal, or a high-profile bureaucratic blunder. If nothing else, it is clear that prime ministers need to be able to manage their time very well in order to influence more than a handful of public policy issues of direct interest to them, because they cannot influence everything at once.

Tom Axworthy, former chief of staff to Pierre Trudeau, has advice for prime ministers. He writes: "Only with maximum prime ministerial involvement could the host of obstacles that stand in the way of reform be overcome." A strategic prime ministership, he writes, "must choose relatively few central themes, not only because of the time demands on the prime minister, but also because it takes a herculean effort to coordinate the government machine."[42] Unless prime ministers decide to concentrate on a handful of issues and then manage them outside the formal decision process, it is unlikely that they will be successful.[43] Paul Martin's tenure as prime minister was short-lived, and few would describe it as successful. He sought to reshape many policies, from health care and foreign policy to Aboriginal development, but in the end he was able to influence very little.

Political scientists have for some time been focusing on what they have labelled the "overload problem." James Douglas writes: "Modern democratic governments are overwhelmed by the load of responsibilities they are called upon … to shoulder."[44] The term "political overload" describes the sense of urgency in government matters and of being overwhelmed both by events and by things to do. Hardly a week goes by without the prime minister having to manage a political crisis, a new development at the international level with national implications, a major firm encountering economic problems, a provincial premier hurling accusations at the federal government, a leaked memo that reveals a problem in the bureaucracy … and so on.

The overload problem and other developments have, as already noted, led prime ministers to establish two policy-making processes: one for themselves and another for the rest. The process that applies to everyone else is much more complex and less decisive. In fact, it is not an exaggeration to write that this process can hardly generate meaningful decisions, if any at all. It deals with issues that have not made it to the front pages of newspapers or to TV screens and that are not of sufficient interest to grab the attention of prime ministers and their overloaded agendas. For example, no less than twenty federal departments were directly involved in planning new measures to promote development in Canada's North.[45] It took two years for the process to run its course, and it involved extensive consultations with stakeholders and a number of consultants' reports. The end product had all the bark taken off from the initial proposal and left no one satisfied. Indeed, the two-year effort had little to offer in terms of a final product. This is how the bulk of major policy issues are now handled in Ottawa. Any proposed policy not co-opted by the prime minister, and at times by the minister of finance, invariably brings together several federal departments or agencies, along with provincial departments, interest groups, consultants, lobbyists, think tanks, and pollsters. It is a process by osmosis, in which the original idea becomes so watered down by the time the process has dealt with it that it is hardly recognizable.[46]

This process has no stomach for bold attempts or bold failures. It is a product of many hands, with no one having the power to deliver anything other than, at best, a package of compromises, and only if the prime minister and the minister of finance agree to fund the package. Meeting after meeting are held within and between departments as departments and agencies sharpen their arguments to influence the package to accommodate their interests.

Gordon Robertson, who was once described as the gold standard by which other clerks of the privy council and secretaries to the cabinet are judged, warned governments that they could make it very difficult to produce innovative decisions if they increased the number of public servants at the centre of government. He wrote that the Privy Council Office, for example, should operate on the basis of a few principles, notably, that "the office should be kept deliberately small" and "should stay off the field" of line departments and agencies.[47] Prime ministers since Trudeau have rejected his advice. In a similar vein, Colin Campbell wrote of "a law of diminishing returns" when more and more staff are added to a public policy issue, because this can "cut down on the amount of diversity and criticism in the system." The result is "a relatively harmonious, but unimaginative administration in which a chief executive accepts non-creativity in most policy actors."[48] It is revealing to note that "network building" is now regarded as one of the key skills a clerk of the privy council can possess.[49]

Central agency officials have certainly demonstrated deftness at diverting ministers from bold measures, unless of course this is what the prime minister wishes. Paul Thomas writes that the "job of central agencies is to make a mush of things."[50] At the risk of overgeneralizing, when it comes to policy issues outside the prime minister's immediate interest, central agencies perform two major functions. They play a *coordinator* role by ensuring that an initiative of a minister and his department does not conflict with the interest of other ministers and their departments. If it does, which is very often the case, they outline a compromise solution. This speaks to their second role – as *arbitrator*. Not only do they sort out the cause of the dispute but they make a recommendation to the chair of the Cabinet committee as to its resolution. Meanwhile, the PM and the PMO are kept informed of significant developments.

Central agency officials in Ottawa attach a great deal of importance to their coordinator and arbitrator roles and to their capacity to iron out the wrinkles in proposed initiatives. A student of government from Australia visiting Canada compared decision making in both countries and recorded his views as follows: "Canadian bureaucratic and political culture places great emphasis on consultations to avoid conflict between ministers. In Australia, there is a greater tolerance for robust debate and perhaps a greater unwillingness to allow officials to decide the details of policy. A consequence is that the nature of bureaucratic consultation differs – in Canada, it is typically an attempt to secure agreement and in Australia it is more about defining the outstanding issues."[51] It will be recalled that Paul Martin expressed his impatience with the "process-oriented" nature of government policy making, saying, "Everybody in the system is happy ... as long as the meeting breaks up with nobody throwing a punch."[52] The problem is that prime ministers are able to throw punches successfully only when the target is within the jurisdiction of the federal government and when the topic does not compromise regional or international trade agreements.

One federal public servant, reflecting on his role and responsibilities in a line department, said that he was paid to "keep turning a crank that is not attached to anything."[53] The former chair of the Public Service Commission of Canada recently teamed up with a well-known student of public policy to carry out an extensive survey with federal government executives, and they described a public service that values "self-censorship as a survival instinct in a world where critical thinking and sharp exchanges are no longer valued as they used to be." They discovered a world where senior executives are not – and do not want to be – in charge: "When faced with the hypothesis that they have to take charge, because nobody is truly and completely in charge, there was a forceful reaction of disbelief."[54] It may well be that Ottawa is now home to a very large bureaucratic machine in which no one is in charge or has power unless the prime minister decides to make it an issue.

Power, then, is increasingly tied to an issue, to an individual, and not to an organization. When, for example, Trudeau decided to patriate the Canadian constitution, he appointed Mike Kirby – a senior public servant, a trusted lieutenant, and a Liberal partisan – to take charge of the initiative. Ministers and the public service may have had other interests, but Trudeau put everything on autopilot so that he could concentrate on the constitution and the National Energy Policy (NEP).

Putting issues on autopilot means that line departments and agencies are expected to run on their tracks, turning cranks not attached to anything, while a number of federal departments, interest groups, lobbyists, and perhaps provincial governments participate in meeting after meeting. There is no political power to drive the process, so it is left on its own to make a "mush" of things. This is deliberate. It is often said that power abhors a vacuum. Here, political power deliberately creates and manages the vacuum.

A Thick Government

Governments have become "thicker" in many jurisdictions, and Canada is no exception.[55] Governments in Canada, in particular the federal government, have grown considerably in size in recent years. It will be recalled that Ottawa maintained that in 1995 it had eliminated 50,000 positions from the public service in its attempt to deal with a growing deficit and debt problem. Observers, however, argued that the number was misleading because some responsibilities were devolved to the provinces and territories, together with cash, while a number of public servants were given a golden handshake to retire but came back to work a few weeks later as consultants.[56] Whatever the number actually was, the public service is now bigger than its pre-1995 size.

The Glassco Commission calculated in the early 1960s that there were 216,000 employees in the Canadian public service, employed in 80 federal departments and agencies. During the Trudeau years alone, 117 new departments, agencies, and Crown corporations were established.[57] Today, there are about 460,000 public servants, employed in 150 federal organizations covered by the Financial Administration Act (FAA), including 43 parent Crown corporations, another 140 that fall outside the FAA, 17 special operating agencies, about 200 semi-autonomous organizations housed within federal departments and agencies, 143 mixed, joined, or shared governance entities, and 26 foundations.[58] One only has to unleash this massive bureaucratic machine to come up with a word of caution here and a concern there and to point to potential difficulties, to make sure that many hands are kept busy turning cranks attached to nothing.

Size tells only part of the story. Oversight bodies, the push to have error-free government, and the need to promote horizontality at every turn have also made government thicker. Public servants in search of promotion or a performance bonus must embrace horizontality with enthusiasm, however defined. For example, public servants are now told that if they fail to meet environmental targets they will lose at least part of their performance pay.[59] All government managers must now take environmental concerns into consideration as they plan new initiatives in whatever sector they are employed – from transport, industry, and fisheries to finance. But that is not all. Apart from their department's immediate interest, they must also consider regional development, rural development, Aboriginal matters, minority language rights ... and the list goes on.

Departments have expanded, adding a large number of new units that have little to do with delivering services to Canadians. All too often, the purpose of these units is to participate in or monitor the interdepartmental policy process, the work of provincial governments, and the work of parliamentary officers. Going through departmental organizational charts, one is struck by the growing number of overhead or coordinating units of one kind or another. One is also left wondering how the people employed in these units pass the time. A cursory look reveals that some directors are responsible for such things as "accountability," "policy coordination," "program coordination," "regional affairs," "program integration," "interdepartmental co-operation," and so on.[60] All these directors have staff, and all have to work at somehow promoting "accountability," "program integration," or "the interdepartmental process."

Public servants in these units talk to one another as they go about their work. The federal public service today is far more concentrated in Ottawa than it has ever been, and public servants have less and less contact with non-public servants in their work.[61] In Canada in the past, something like 30 percent of federal public servants were employed in Ottawa and 70 percent in regional offices. In more recent years, the percentage has shifted considerably, with close to 40 percent now working in the National Capital Region.[62] A government survey of 221,434 positions was carried out nearly twenty years ago to identify all jobs that had at least some responsibility for dealing with the general public, even if that "some" amounted to only 10 percent. The survey found only 92,481 such positions, or 41.8 percent of the total number of positions.[63] I asked a senior Treasury Board Secretariat official in November 2008 if a more recent survey had been carried out. He said no, but added that the percentage has probably gone down still more in recent years. He explained why: "It is the changing nature of our work. We manage networks, partnerships, and we now get things done through others."[64]

Past efforts to "de-layer" management levels in the Government of Canada have failed. In the 1990s, the government announced that all departments were to de-layer their management levels so that there would be only four levels of manager between the working level and the deputy minister. No one in Ottawa now talks about de-layering the public service. The number of layers has actually gone up in recent years, to the point that in some departments there are eight layers between the deputy minister and the working level.[65] Not only have existing units expanded and new ones been created to manage or monitor various processes, but there are now more management layers between front-line employees and the department's deputy minister.

Prime ministers, as well as pursuing their favoured initiatives, have to manage cabinet, the government caucus, and their political interests. Recent prime ministers have taken great pride in saying that they were able to leave line departments to their own devices in managing ongoing programs and maintaining the status quo. There is evidence that they have been able to do just that by pushing decisions down to line departments. In 1983, for example, the Treasury Board issued 6,000 decisions; in 1987 the number had dropped to 3,500; by 1997 it had fallen still further, to 1,100; today it is less than 1,000.[66] Prime ministers are quite happy to see line departments manage continuing programs, but for other things they prefer to see line departments at rest. They do not want departments and agencies to create political problems for the government by becoming embroiled in controversies, especially if the media gets wind of it.

Prime ministers are quite happy to have no one with any substantial power in the policy-making process that is designed to take care of things that do not matter to them. It is much easier for them to manage a process where the location of its power is unclear, if only because it avoids bold moves or decisions. Bold moves require political power to see them come to fruition. In addition, bold moves initiated by anyone other than the prime minister can create political problems. The process also enables the prime minister's advisers to monitor developments carefully and keep potential rogue politicians and bureaucrats under watch.

The government is made thicker by the multitude of oversight bodies constantly looking over the shoulders of managers. Managers may have more authority to make decisions in financial and human resources issues, but the level of oversight has increased tenfold from thirty years ago. The Treasury Board may not make as many decisions as it once did, but the Treasury Board Secretariat employs more people than ever.[67] In 1969 it employed 414 people;[68] today it employs 1,455 people.[69] Again, these people are employed to manage processes, not to deliver services, and to oversee the work of departments and agencies, not to deal directly with Canadians. They, too, make it more difficult to locate where power now resides in government.

The Office of the Comptroller, which is part of the Treasury Board Secretariat, has had several lives since it was established in 1978. It was at one time a stand-alone agency but later was put on life support as it was integrated fully in the Treasury Board Secretariat.[70] It was, however, given a new lease on life in the aftermath of Canada's sponsorship scandal. It will be recalled that the federal government unveiled a new policy in April 2006 to strengthen "accountability and good governance." A reconstituted Office of the Comptroller General was given the lead role in establishing independent external audit advisory committees for every department and agency. These committees consist of at least three outside members with a mandate to review internal audit reports and management action plans as they are submitted to the deputy minister. The committees are also asked to "ensure that management takes the necessary steps to support the Office of the Auditor General (OAG) and central agencies in doing audit work in the department."[71]

Where does power lie in this potpourri of organizational units, processes, and activities? It is hard to tell even for public servants inside the machinery, let alone for the general public. Those who have power – the prime minister and the clerk of the privy council – are well served by this state of affairs. It is an ideal system to keep things running on their tracks and to avoid controversy. It poses, however, a daunting challenge to those outside government who are trying to understand both how government decides and who has the power to make decisions. It also makes it very difficult for Parliament to get to the bottom of things, to grasp why and how decisions were taken, and to hold anyone accountable for the management of the government's financial resources.

The two parallel processes also make it difficult for the government to manage financial resources efficiently. We have seen government after government, year after year, make firm commitments to manage expenditures better. We have heard the Trudeau, Mulroney, Chrétien, Martin, and Harper governments announce, always with great fanfare, that they have plans to carry out a meaningful program review, reduce red tape, fix procurement, and improve management. Perhaps leaving aside the Chrétien 1995–97 program review, the efforts have never lived up to expectations. Indeed, nothing much ever changes. Years after the arrival of New Public Management in Canada and several program reviews, the Harper government pledged in its 2008 Speech from the Throne, to "make government more effective by reducing red tape, fixing procurement, improving program and service delivery, and improving the management of federal agencies, boards, commissions and Crown corporations."[72] The problem is that the policy process designed for the prime minister and his advisers does not have time to focus on such issues, yet the one designed for everyone else does not have the power to deal with them.

This explains why to this day Parliament and Canadians have never been able to get to the bottom of the gun registry financial fiasco to determine the exact level of its cost overrun, the reasons for the overrun, and why Parliament was kept in the dark.[73] In short, we could never fully deconstruct an issue that dominated the media for months. The problem has everything to do with elaborate bureaucratic processes, and no one could point to an individual or individuals to establish what went wrong, why, how, and to what extent.

7 THE NEW BUREAUCRATS: SHORT-ORDER COOKS

The machinery of government in Anglo-American democracies has been subjected to a veritable orgy of reform measures over the past thirty years. Some of these have served to empower front-line managers and their employees, others were designed to insulate government programs and decision making from politicians, and still others were introduced to make the public sector look like the private sector. The appetite for change remains strong to this day, as governments recognize that public policy issues can no longer be the responsibility of a single department. Call it what you will – horizontality in Canada, joined-up government in Britain, or collaborative government in the United States – the object-ive is the same: to promote an interdepartmental perspective to deal with increasingly complex public policy issues. This suggests that both policy makers and citizens should view government as a collectivity, an organization able to transcend boundaries and hierarchies when devis-ing policies and delivering public services. In addition, the pressure to do more with less (government officials insist that this has been the case for about thirty years, but it is virtually impossible to know if they are correct) and the public sector's search for greater credibility have led government to introduce still more reforms.

While the machinery of government has undergone some change, pol-itical institutions have remained largely intact, as have the basic rules and processes of accountability. Parliament, the doctrine of ministerial responsibility, and relations between politicians and public servants still operate much as they did forty years ago, when hierarchy mattered a great deal more than it does now.

Politicians, through various means, have been trying their best to wrestle from public servants the power and influence over policy making. This alone has made it considerably more difficult for citizens to establish who in government has power, especially who is responsible for what. Indeed, government reforms since the early 1980s have muddied the waters to the point that experts on the machinery of government and even those inside government have great difficulty establishing, with any degree of clarity, who in government, other than prime ministers and their courtiers, have power.

There is no need to review in any detail the public-sector reforms introduced in Anglo-American democracies since Margaret Thatcher came to power in Britain in 1979. The Thatcher revolution in Britain and subsequent reforms in Canada, the United States, Australia, and New Zealand have already been well documented.[1] This chapter examines changes to the machinery of government from the perspective of who now holds power and responsibility. By "machinery of government," I refer to the way the government is structured to generate policy advice, shape policy, promote program coordination, and deliver public services.

There are essentially two reasons behind the attempts of politicians to overhaul the machinery of government. One was to promote efficiency in delivering public services by borrowing a page from the private sector, and the other was to establish that it was politicians, not bureaucrats, who should have power. Thatcher's main message to bureaucrats could not have been clearer: politicians will both shape and decide policy, while public servants should manage government operations more efficiently.

By the early 1980s, politicians had become convinced that public servants had too much power and that they were poor managers; an overhaul was urgently needed. They were not alone in this conclusion. Herbert Kaufman wrote in 1981 that "antibureaucratic sentiment had taken hold like an epidemic." Another scholar wrote that "bureaucracy is a word with a bad reputation," and yet another insisted that "government functionaries work hard and accomplish little. Many people would question the first part of that statement."[2] The politicians of the day were no less critical: Ronald Reagan said that he went to Washington to drain the swamp, Margaret Thatcher admitted that she disliked bureaucrats as a breed, and Brian Mulroney talked about giving bureaucrats pink slips and running shoes if he was elected to power.[3]

The criticism did not stop there. In introducing his running mate in the US 2008 presidential election campaign, John McCain said that Sarah Palin had "fought do-nothing bureaucrats in Alaska."[4] Senior public servants in Ottawa report that they have heard first-hand that Harper and some of his key advisers have made disparaging comments about the public service and the bureaucracy.[5]

The Scene

Public servants were not prepared for the wave of bureaucracy bashing that arose. It came from the media, from citizens, and especially from political leaders. Bureaucrats expected business as usual – that politicians elected to office would have some pet projects flowing out of campaign commitments and a pledge to do better than the political crowd they were replacing. Little did they expect that the newly elected politicians would lay at least some of the blame for their country's poor economic performance at their feet and then actually implement plans to do something about it.

It will be recalled that a dreaded new word, "stagflation," made its way into our economic vocabulary in the 1970s. The economies of Anglo-American democracies were all experiencing a slowdown, coupled with rising inflation. There was double-digit inflation, and the growth in the costs of government outstripped growth in the economy. Political parties promoting a greater role for government in society and increased government spending were losing support. In California, for example, a grassroots movement successfully championed in 1978 a measure designed to limit taxation and, by extension, government spending.[6] If bureaucrats and politicians were not able to control government spending, then citizens would have to get involved.

Many politicians became convinced that the only way forward was to confront their bureaucrats. Criticism came from everywhere, even from former politicians who traditionally had been supportive of public servants. One of the most stinging criticisms came from a left-leaning former British cabinet minister, Labour MP Richard Crossman. In his widely read diaries, published in 1975, he took aim at the civil service as a powerful bureaucratic machine that had taken on a life of its own. He insisted that "whenever one relaxes one's guard the Civil Service in one's Department quietly asserts itself ... Just as the Cabinet Secretariat constantly transforms the actual proceedings of Cabinet into the form of the Cabinet minutes (i.e., it substitutes what we should have said if we had done as they wished for what we actually did say), so here in my Department the civil servants are always putting in what they think I should have said and not what I actually decided."[7]

The Crossman diaries opened a floodgate of criticism against bureaucracy throughout all Anglo-American democracies. Even the Fabian Society, a British left-of-centre think tank and a strong advocate of government intervention, joined the debate. It put together a study group in 1979 to look at government operations in the aftermath of Labour's electoral defeat. Its membership included former ministers, political advisers, academics, and even former civil servants. The group reached several conclusions: that the civil service has "distinct ideologies of its own"; that the "nature of departments limits a minister's capacity to produce a long-term and radical approach"; and that "civil service advice needs to be augmented by alternative sources of ideas and analysis."[8] In Canada, left-leaning politicians such as Allan MacEachen and Lloyd Axworthy, who had once been supportive both of government intervention in the economy and of the bureaucracy, became openly critical of the public service. MacEachen reported that if Liberals had learned anything during their brief stint in opposition, it was that his party would no longer rely as much as they had on the advice of senior public servants.[9] The point was not lost on anyone, including bureaucrats: public servants had too much influence, and something had to be done to curtail it.

Thatcher's diagnosis of the problem was straightforward: the state was too interventionist and the bureaucracy too privileged.[10] Accordingly, she saw no need to ponder possible solutions for very long; the answer was simply to roll back the state by privatizing state enterprises, to cut government spending or slow down the rate of its growth, and to contract out to the private sector the responsibility for delivering services. However, Thatcher's diagnosis and Mulroney's pledge to give pink slips and running shoes to bureaucrats could hardly constitute the full solution. Not everyone could be given pink slips, and indeed at the end of Mulroney's two mandates, very few bureaucrats had been fired. In fact, the federal public service had actually grown during Mulroney's nine years in power.

Bureaucrats were well aware of the vendetta against them. But there was no one onto whom they could divert the criticism, at least publicly, and some even began to bad-mouth the bureaucracy themselves. Politicians had no overall plan to offer, other than reiterating that bureaucrats had to accept a major part of the responsibility for the state of affairs.

Bureaucrats had little to offer in the way of policy prescriptions. To be sure, they understood that they could no longer be trusted on policy and that they should become better managers, but it was not at all clear what exactly needed fixing. More importantly, most were not convinced that they were responsible for the problem, however defined. If anything, bureaucrats came to believe that if there was a problem, it was politicians and their political institutions that should be held responsible. Though they could not engage in a public debate with their political masters, they were saying, at least amongst their own ranks, "heal thyself" – that politicians should fix their political institutions before setting out to fix the public service.[11] The solution for many bureaucrats was to do what they had done in the past: batten down the hatches and wait for the latest political storm to pass. This time, however, the storm would not pass.

What to Do?

Thatcher's first few weeks in power were revealing. She declared a freeze on hiring the day she came to office and scrapped civil service plans to add new positions. She ignored the claim in the civil service briefing books that the 733,000-strong civil service was already stretched to the limit. The books argued that there was no fat in the system and that "even modest" cuts in staff would inhibit departments from functioning effectively. She announced a series of cuts early in her first mandate, and she directed that the civil service be reduced in size by nearly 15 percent. By the time she left office, it had been cut by more than 22 percent, down to 569,000. Richard Wilson, former cabinet secretary, pointed out in March 2006 that the size of the civil service had been reduced further in recent years, to 460,000. Thatcher imposed cuts by simply outlining targets. It can hardly be described as a sophisticated approach, but it worked. Convinced that more could be done without a reduction in services, she insisted that cuts could be absorbed through superior management practices.[12] She had the power to issue a command to cut the public service, and she was all too willing to exercise it.

I asked one of the authors of the briefing books if Thatcher had it right when she ignored their claim and imposed cuts by picking a number out of the air. Yes, was the answer. Why, then, I asked, did you attempt to persuade her to hire more civil servants? The answer: "Permanent secretaries made their claim, and we simply packaged the various requests and made the case for more resources."[13] If nothing else, this served to confirm in the eyes of politicians that the advice, influence, and ultimately the power of senior public servants could not be fully trusted, at least when it came to managing their departments.

Although it was a step in the right direction for Thatcher and those of like mind, cutting the public service down to size could never be a complete solution. The search was on for ways to improve management practices and to operate government departments and programs more efficiently. If bureaucrats could not offer solutions, politicians could always look to the private sector for inspiration, and they did. Again, Margaret Thatcher led the way. She invited Derek Rayner, chief executive officer at Marks and Spencer, to lead an efficiency exercise in government. Rayner established a small seven-person office within the Prime Minister's Office to "scrutinize" government spending. Thatcher considered the exercise a success, suggesting that if cuts in government spending were needed, the power and influence had to be turned over to people from the private sector who knew how to manage and had no vested interest in the status quo.[14] Before long, other politicians adopted much the same strategy, albeit with varying degrees of success (for example, Ronald Reagan with Peter J. Grace and Brian Mulroney with Erik Nielsen).

At the end of his work in government, Rayner spoke about the "superiority of the business-management model" and used the phrase "Whitehall culture" to describe management practices in government that were inferior to those in the private sector. He reported at some length on "the inbuilt limitations of the civil service to think about management."[15] He concluded that the problem was that senior civil servants were mainly interested in shaping policy, not in management. Responsibility for management, he felt, was placed in the hands of second-class bureaucrats, while policy skills were the road to the top of the organization.

Politicians in all Anglo-American democracies accepted that the traditional bureaucratic model was no longer up to the task and that the private-sector model held considerable promise for government. No one, however, has been able to duplicate market forces in the public sector. The result is that bureaucrats have been trying to adapt the business-management model to their operations without changing traditional accountability requirements or finding ways to duplicate market forces. This alone has led to confusion about who actually holds power and responsibility inside the machinery of government.

The business-management model has made its way inside government operations through several initiatives since the early 1980s. State corporations have been sold to the private sector, make-or-buy policies (a test to determine whether the public or private sector is best able to deliver the service) have been introduced, and new public-private partnerships have been put in place to build roads and schools and deliver various public services. In addition, senior public servants have been told time and again to emulate their private-sector counterparts, and they have introduced management development programs and courses largely inspired by the private sector.[16]

It is no exaggeration to write that there is now a widely held consensus among politicians of *all* political persuasions that government operations would be much better run if they were guided by the private-sector model. President Bill Clinton and Prime Ministers Tony Blair and Jean Chrétien – all left-of-centre politicians – were as enthusiastic about the idea as Margaret Thatcher was. Tony Blair, on coming to office, declared that "some parts of the public sector were not as efficient, dynamic and effective as the private sector" and that things had to change.[17] In the private sector, market forces and a firm's competitiveness dictate success and, ultimately, who has power. Though politicians have sought to make the public sector look like the private sector, government bureaucrats play by vastly different rules, and success is determined in ways that do not resonate in the private sector.

Sharing Responsibilities and Power

The widespread belief that government operations were not as well managed as private-sector activities and that the market was key to identifying economic winners led many to conclude that there was a need to thwart the concentration of governmental power. Country after country, and Canada was no exception, decided to rely more on the market to produce goods and services rather than having traditional government departments do so.

The past thirty years or so have demonstrated what political scientists have known for years – that the structure and machinery of government are not static, but any change requires a powerful wrench of the wheel. Political scientists have produced a rich literature on "path dependency," arguing that initial choices about institutional and administrative arrangements in government become deeply entrenched and are difficult to reverse.[18] Encouraged by politicians leaving office at the end of the 1970s, by political ideology that came in fashion in the early 1980s, and by demanding fiscal circumstances throughout much of the Western world, the political leadership has ever since sought to break away from path dependency.

The solution: force government bureaucracies to share their responsibilities with others for generating policy advice and delivering public services. The power of public bureaucracies in Western democracies has historically been built on its ability to hold a relative monopoly over information, to provide policy advice to politicians on the government side, and to possess a well-honed capacity to shape and control the government's expenditure budget.[19]

A number of changes have recently been introduced to involve non-governmental actors in virtually every facet of public administration. The effect has been to disperse power both within and outside government. Politicians set out to reassert power over their bureaucrats by creating new policy advisory capacities outside the bureaucracy. Prime ministers and ministerial offices have been overhauled and expanded. The politicians have turned to consultants, established outside task forces, and called in independent advisers and lobbyists for advice to a far greater extent than in years past. The goal is to create a more responsive policy advisory capacity, one that can easily identify with the political ideology and objectives of the party in power. A number of politicians, including those reared on the Westminster-Whitehall model, no longer accept that the "neutral competence" of public servants is viable as they set out to change policy direction.

As far back as 1956, Herbert Kaufman defined neutral competence as the "ability of career officials to do the work of government expertly, and to do it according to explicit, objective standards rather than to personal or party or other obligations and loyalties."[20] This model was no longer acceptable because it was considered insufficiently responsive to politicians, to public opinion, and to market forces. A number of politicians in Western democracies came to believe that neutral competence gave too much influence to career officials or drained away their commitment to political and even policy objectives.

Politicians began to insist on responsive competence, or at least on a proper blend of neutral and responsive competence. The academic literature began to suggest that career officials were not value-free in their behaviour and that their influence in making policy should not go unchecked.[21] Career officials were left to square this development with the basic values of their Whitehall-inspired institutions, which entailed an anonymous, neutral, and merit-based career service designed to promote detached, non-partisan, and objective policy advice. For some, these values would die hard, if at all. In Canada as recently as 1996, a federal task force on values and ethics, chaired by a former deputy minister of justice and inspired by the work of Aaron Wildavsky, stressed the need for career officials to provide non-partisan advice and to "speak truth to power."[22]

Just as some politicians were seeking to make policy advice more responsive to their views and their policy agenda, policy making became more complex. Think tanks and research institutes began to break the monopoly that career officials held on the provision of advice (more is said about this later). Modern technology also served to make information on virtually any public issue more accessible; think tanks, lobbyists, consultants, communication specialists, and interest groups are now all able to obtain information quickly, and many can analyze it as well as anyone in government. As Patrick Weller argues, "Policy advice, once an effective monopoly of public servants, is now contestable and contested."[23] A large number of organizations became involved in governing, which increased both the cost and the complexity of public administration.

Public servants were being challenged by other developments: the shift towards more collective policy making and the growing dominance of prime ministers and their offices in that process; the pervasiveness of public opinion polling to provide policy answers; the need to make policy on the run to accommodate "news breaks" from aggressive media; and policy overload and the interconnected nature of public policies.

A new model would emerge that asked career officials to look outside their departments to shape new policy measures. By choice or not, politicians would henceforth turn to several sources for policy advice, not just to their senior departmental officials. Career officials would no longer be allowed to offer policy advice by themselves. The process would become "porous" and involve many actors, so one must now look to multiple centres to see who has influence and to a more limited number of individuals to see who has power.

Politicians have always been free to seek policy advice from wherever they wish. The difference today is that there are many more highly qualified sources always at the ready to offer advice on virtually any policy issue. Gone also are the days when senior public servants worked in relative isolation, developing policies, while the role of ministers was to decide what was politically salable and what was not. Today, a majority of Cabinet documents in the Government of Canada are produced by consultants, rather than by public servants, something that would have been unthinkable thirty or forty years ago.[24]

A good number of independent observers and public servants are now reporting that outside advisory groups have "fundamentally altered public policy-making in Ottawa."[25] No one knows for certain how many such advisory groups exist, but one "conservative estimate" suggests that there are five hundred in Ottawa. Parliament has never sorted out how it should deal with these government-funded groups or how it should hold them to account. Ken Beeson maintains, however, that some groups can be helpful to government ministers because they provide a level of experience and expertise that lies outside the public service, but he adds that at times these groups "take on the role of politicians in forging common ground on policies and finding compromises."[26] They also make it more difficult to establish who has power and influence.

But that is hardly the only factor that has muddied the waters. The rise of horizontal government and governing by network requires public servants to develop different skills. As Christopher Pollitt explains, "Public servants need to acquire new skills. Different professional practices must be aligned. Mutual trust between different stakeholders must be built. Citizens must have the opportunity to exercise their diverse voices and themselves learn the value of participation."[27] Clearly, none of these things can be accomplished in weeks or even months. Senior officials increasingly speak about "networking skills" and the "capacity for teamwork," of "reaching out and building strategic alliances," and of a capacity to "lead or follow the lead of others, depending on the needs of the time at hand."[28] *Government of the Future*, a report of the Organization for Economic Co-operation and Development (OECD) based on the experience of its member countries, gives a strong endorsement of the new approach in the name of public participation. It states, "Policymaking is influenced by a wide variety of players, ranging from interest and lobby groups to think tanks and other policy entrepreneurs. Increased participation by these groups reinforces the democratic process and helps government to better anticipate citizen desires."[29]

In addition, hand in hand with the emergence of horizontal government, there has been the growth of a host of new movements giving voice to dissatisfaction with government policies and operations. A number of single-issue movements, albeit some with a broad policy agenda, came into their own in the 1970s: women, peace, environment, minority languages, Aboriginal rights, gay rights, and visible minorities. Canada in the early 1980s and Britain more recently have joined the United States in becoming "rights-oriented" societies.[30] The new movements have been able to attract both funding and members, and many of them have carved out a presence in the public policy-making process. They want a straight answer and quick action, and are prepared to talk to the media to put pressure on politicians, and this, if nothing else, has narrowed the role of career bureaucrats in the policy process.[31]

When you turn over policy making and decisions to a horizontal process, it becomes not only interdepartmental but also extends to outside players. Again, gone is the minister working with a line department to bring forward proposals to Cabinet. The relationship between the government and citizens is also redefined. Influence is divided and dispersed, and managing some of the bargaining and accommodation processes becomes the responsibility of public servants. However, citizens who are not engaged or represented by stakeholders may well come to view government as slow moving and unresponsive, and individual public servants as incapable of acting responsibly. They may also come to the conclusion that the policy process is designed only for those with sufficient resources to hire the expertise required to participate in an elaborate, complex, and porous policy-making process. They have a point.

Public Servants Losing Their Administrative Space

In Canada and in other parliamentary systems, senior officials no longer have a monopoly on policy advice to ministers and no longer dominate their policy sectors. Deputy ministers in Canada, permanent secretaries in Britain, and heads of departments in Australia and New Zealand were for a long time largely recruited from within their departments. They knew their departments well – the policies, the programs, the staff, and outside groups with a strong interest in the department. It was an ideal setting to practise "stove-pipe" management and to protect one's turf. Today, senior officials are hired on the basis of their ability to navigate the policy process, to network, to make things happen, and to manage. If senior government officials have a comparative advantage over policy specialists operating on the periphery or outside government, it is their knowledge of key players in government, an intimate knowledge of how the policy process now works, and an ability to keep their ministers out of trouble – or keep them from their propensity "to fall on hand grenades," as one senior Canadian official put it.[32]

Those with strong networking skills and with a well-honed ability to sense a political crisis in the making will very often rise to the top. They may not be as politically partisan or as politically responsive as their

American counterparts, but they are far more tuned in to the realities of their political masters than was the case forty years ago, because it has become increasingly difficult to locate the line separating the political from the bureaucratic worlds. This in turn has made it harder in some instances to locate where political power ends and bureaucratic influence begins.

Politicians today are much less willing to respect that the bureaucratic world differs from their own. Nowhere was this more evident than when Prime Minister Harper took dead aim at the head of the country's nuclear regulatory commission in January 2008. The commission, a quasi-judiciary agency, regulates the use of nuclear energy and materials to protect the health, safety, and security of Canadians and the environment. The commission decided to shut down the Chalk River reactor for safety reasons. However, the reactor produces two-thirds of the radioisotopes used around the world in medical tests, and closing it down would result in a shortage of radioisotopes.

Harper went on the offensive, telling Parliament that Linda Keen, the head of the commission, was a Liberal appointee and was politically partisan. There was in fact little evidence that Ms Keen was a partisan Liberal, and she insisted that she was a career public servant and simply doing her job. Harper responded by saying that he was "very troubled by the response of the president of the nuclear commission."[33]

The matter did not end there. Under the careful eye of the prime minister and the Privy Council Office, the minister responsible for the commission initiated a process to fire Keen. In the end, he was successful, saying that she had demonstrated a "lack of leadership."[34] The message was not lost on public servants. If Harper could do this to the head of a quasi-judicial commission, there was no place for them to run. One senior public servant at the time lamented, "It's open season on bureaucrats."[35]

It is becoming clear that public servants are losing the fairly distinct administrative space that they once occupied. They are no longer anonymous, operating under the radar screen, discreetly advising their political masters and delivering public services. For this reason alone, public servants must now shed their anonymity as they "network" to shape new policy initiatives. Networking requires them to become political actors in their own right, able to present and defend policy positions outside government circles.

The world of networks has blurred the lines between the public and private sectors and between the political and bureaucratic arenas. It plays to the advantage of the political, intellectual, and economic elites. The instruments of governance and their accompanying power and influence are now distributed across certain segments of society and the economy. Relationships are now more horizontal than hierarchical, so one can no longer expect to locate power within departmental hierarchies. It takes a deep knowledge not only of the relevant policy issue but also of the ways of the machinery of government and the key actors if one sets out to influence public policies and government decisions. However, with sufficient financial resources, one can hire both the knowledge and the contacts inside government to get things done. This is what many private firms now do. "Have knowledge and political connections, will travel" provides lucrative business opportunities for those who know their way around government and public policy issues.

Both politicians and public servants have also had to learn to live with access or freedom to information legislation. The legislation has enabled the media, the opposition parties, interested parties, and lobbyists to pin down what issue particular public servants are working on, what policy positions they may support, and even with whom they had lunch, if taxpayers paid for it. The only way for senior public servants to remain anonymous is to avoid expense accounts and refrain from putting their views on paper or on their computers, since e-mails are accessible under many right to information laws. But even these precautions may not be sufficient to maintain anonymity, since many politicians are no longer reluctant to name individual public servants in order to deflect criticism directed against themselves in the media.

To avoid being drawn into political controversies, senior public servants now avoid putting things down on paper. As already noted, oral briefings, powerpoint presentations, and telephone conversations have in many instances and in many governments replaced the written document. In this sense, and as we have already noted, legislation designed to promote greater transparency has had an unintended consequence: it has made it more difficult for those outside government to determine who inside government holds power and influence.

Adjusting the Machinery for Multilevel Governance

There is hardly a public policy issue left that is the preserve of a single government. Governments in a federal system came to terms with the fact that K.C. Wheare's classic definition of federalism no longer applied as easily as it once did. Wheare wrote, "By the federal principle, I mean the method of dividing powers so that the general and regional governments are each within a sphere, co-ordinate and independent."[36] We can no longer talk of the autonomy of each government: "co-operation" and "collaboration" define present-day federalism. A.H. Birch put it succinctly when he wrote as far back as fifty years ago that "the guiding principle of mid-twentieth century federalism is the need for co-operation."[37]

Large bureaucracies have grown over the years in the two senior orders of government in federal states, simply to manage federal-state or federal-provincial relations. These units do not deliver programs or services to citizens. They exist to monitor, to brief politicians, and to participate in intergovernmental negotiations. They too have contributed to thicker government, and again thicker government makes it more difficult for citizens to identify who in government has power and responsibility.

Blurring constitutional responsibilities through intergovernmental or shared-cost agreements may provide the necessary flexibility to operate in the modern economy, but there is a price to pay. As long as thirty years ago, we reached the point where, for example, some provincial governments in Canada could no longer "point to a single policy area for which it was unambiguously and solely responsible."[38] In addition, in many instances, intergovernmental agreements are deliberately broadly defined to give officials greater flexibility in implementing them. It is now very difficult, even for public servants in government departments, to establish who is responsible for what, given the flexibility inherent in many intergovernmental agreements. Many of these agreements provide ample opportunities to pass the buck, to blame officials in other departments or, better yet, in other governments. One can imagine what it is like for politicians with limited knowledge of the machinery of government or the finer points of intergovernmental negotiations trying to hold public servants accountable for their decisions or activities. Think again about citizens with no expertise on the workings of the machinery of government, let alone intergovernmental agreements. They also have no time or interest in gaining the necessary knowledge to understand how these agreements work and who has the power to make decisions.

Creating Agencies

The political leadership that came into office in the 1980s wanted not only to reclaim the upper hand from bureaucrats in shaping public policies but also to force managers to manage better, to emulate private-sector managers. Things were no different in Canada with the election of the Mulroney government in 1984. Margaret Thatcher again showed the way by moving the machinery of government away from the traditional form of public organization. By "traditional form," in the Westminster parliamentary model we mean government departments headed by ministers, using taxes to pay for the services they deliver, and staffed by public servants who pursue long careers in the public service and are organized in a hierarchical manner operating under the minister, who monitors and commands action. The departments operate under centrally prescribed rules that rely on input controls on activities, notably on budget and staffing activities.[39]

Thatcher decided to break with the traditional model so that the job to be done would receive a higher priority than centrally conceived rules and controls could ever provide. Today, more than three-quarters of British public servants work in executive agencies.[40] Other countries, including Japan, the United States, Australia, New Zealand, and Canada, sought to reform the traditional bureaucratic model, but had varying degrees of success. As in so many other things, when it comes to the machinery of government, Canadian officials looked to Britain for inspiration when they created the Special Operating Agencies (SOAs). However, SOAs are only a pale imitation of British executive agencies. There are only a handful of them in Canada (17) and the agencies remain subordinate to their parent departments.[41]

There has been some confusion about the nature of the Canadian model. One deputy minister described it simply as "a bureaucratic version of a halfway house. It is neither a jail, nor is it total freedom. It is part of a department, yet separate from it." He added that SOAs "are still very much part of the federal family. Staff in agencies are still public servants. SOAs still report to the department, to the minister, and to the Treasury Board."[42] The secretary of Treasury Board wrote: "SOAs are not quasi-Crown corporations. They remain a distinct part of the home department, albeit with enhanced operational authority."[43] Thus, some administrative power was shifted from line departments to the newly created agencies.

It remains unclear how to evaluate them, and it is not clear why they were established in the first place. It appears that the government itself was not at all certain why. One government official wrote: "Several different perspectives inspired the establishment of the initial five SOAs. Some viewed the initiative as a way of delaying pressure to privatize or as a halfway station to privatization. Others view SOAs as a pilot project or laboratories for public sector reforms ... Yet another perspective is that the SOA concept offered a prototype for the public service (similar to Executive Agencies) in the United Kingdom ... Over time the rationale for the initiative became even more cloudy."[44] We do not know if programs under SOAs are better managed than they were in traditional government departments.[45]

Government officials report that establishing SOAs was to provide the first clear break with the traditional control-and-command model and to initiate a culture that emphasizes management practices rather than program administration. In brief, the objective was to increase managerial flexibility and efficiency by shifting some power to them. The Treasury Board Secretariat made it clear that SOAs should be "business units oriented to good management" and should promote more "business-like services, improve service to the customer and demonstrate concern for efficient management."[46]

In more recent years, two high-profile new agencies have brought related activities under one roof. The Canadian Food Inspection Agency (CFIA) deals with the regulation of animal, food, and plant health and with consumer safety vis-à-vis the labelling and packaging of food products. The Canada Customs and Revenue Agency (CCRA) replaced Revenue Canada. The new agencies, unlike the SOAs, enjoy separate employer status under the Public Service Staff Relations Act, although employees remain federal public servants. This change and other financial changes are designed to give the agencies more power in personnel and financial management.[47] The government never explained why it was more appropriate to give these newly created agencies more power than other departments, whether citizens should relate differently to them, or how elected politicians would hold them to account, given their new authority.

Creating new agencies and permitting them to break from the traditional organizational model is not without implications for the location of power. Centrally prescribed policies, rules, and regulations constitute power in their own right as they dictate how decisions are to be made. Removing them will invariably shift power – indeed, that is precisely why they were removed, so that some public servants would be empowered on some financial and human resources issues. Put differently, it moves the locus of power or influence on management matters away from processes and towards individual managers.

Adjusting the Machinery for Networked Governance

Intergovernmental relations and agreements have, if anything, increased in importance in recent years. But there have been other important developments that have made it even more difficult to locate power and responsibility inside governments. Much has been said and written of late about post-sovereign, networked, and "hybrid" governments.[48]

Global or international organizations have also looked to partnership arrangements with national governments to pursue their missions. National governments have responded by adding new units to their bureaucracy to deal with international and regional organizations. There is hardly a government department in Anglo-American democracies that does not have a unit or units with a mandate to deal with regional or international issues.

The great majority of public policy issues now have a regional (e.g., trade agreements) or international (e.g., the environment) component. Intergovernmental forces at home, combined with regional or international forces, provide an ideal setting for both public servants and politicians to argue that "the devil made me do it," as they define their position or explain why things have gone wrong or why they arrived at a particular decision on a controversial issue.

Units in national governments established to look after regional and international issues also make government thicker. They operate under different circumstances from traditional units, and they do not provide a link between citizens and politicians. They, too, have no clients and deal only with issues or with officials in other governments. The units are part of an emerging networked governance where hierarchical accountability does not easily apply. One can legitimately ask where power and responsibility lie in government units that have competing and overlapping mandates dealing with forces that flow out of other countries or multisectoral networks. The answer is not obvious.

Looking Back

The orgy of bureaucratic reforms first launched by Margaret Thatcher and the need to adjust the machinery of government to accommodate intergovernmental negotiations, combined with sustained efforts by politicians to gain the upper hand in their dealings with bureaucrats, have had a profound impact on the location of political and administrative power in government. Power has shifted, between politicians and bureaucrats, between political advisers and bureaucrats, and between government officials and lobbyists, but also within the bureaucracy itself. Power and influence have moved away from centrally prescribed processes for human and financial management to individual managers.

If power has shifted, presumably so has responsibility. Yet political institutions and accountability requirements have scarcely evolved in recent years. This development may entail political and management benefits, but it runs the risk of having different actors holding the same position in different departments, and agencies having different levels of authority and power.

8   SOFT POWER: WHO HAS IT?

Power today is not only fluid, it also takes different forms. The international relations field, for example, distinguishes "soft" from "hard" power. Joseph Nye coined the term "soft power" in his work on American foreign policy to deal with the predicted decline of the United States as a superpower because of the perceived diminishing importance of the military in world affairs and the high cost of maintaining a large sophisticated military.[1] Nye later applied the distinction to national politics. He wrote: "The basic concept of power is the ability to influence others to get them to do what you want. There are three major ways to do that: one is to threaten them with sticks; the second is to pay them with carrots; the third is to attract them or co-opt them, so that they want what you want. If you can get others to be attracted, to want what you want, it costs you much less in carrots and sticks."[2] He said that a proper combination of both soft and hard power leads to "smart power."[3] Smart power is neither hierarchical nor static.

Where, then, does soft or smart power fit in the new scheme of things? Who has it? Where is it? This chapter explores the question. It argues that one now has to look more and more to individuals rather than to institutions or organizations to locate power. Institutions, and organizations in particular, depend on hierarchy to exert power. Individuals, meanwhile, are free to roam wherever they can to exert influence or even power whenever an opportunity surfaces.

Soft power takes many forms and is in the hands of many individuals. Some journalists have it, as do some lobbyists, some religious leaders, some business people (in their dealings with their communities and governments), and some academics. Information obtained through Ottawa's access to information legislation reveals that Department of Defence officials expressed deep concern that the media and others were "more inclined to trust outside experts than inside experts."[4] The work of outside experts speaks to soft power. Such people are, however, more difficult to identify and hold to account than officials properly lodged in a departmental or business hierarchy. Indeed, individuals with influence are not held to account in the same manner as those who hold power, but they can exert considerable influence on public policy and government operations.

The hierarchy identifies where one sits, who does what, what one's responsibility is, and to whom one is accountable. In a hierarchy, one can employ sticks or carrots or a combination of both to get things done. Hierarchies also have processes that shape how decisions are made. The same is not true with outside experts. They move around from issue to issue, from contract to contract, and from organization to organization. In many instances, they are not part of an organization or even work for one. They are hired hands, high-priced temporary help, whose job it is to come up with fresh thinking or to move a file forward.

In this chapter, we review the growth of soft power and its impact on politics and public administration. We focus on the work of those who do not work in a structured organization with access to carrots and sticks to influence others. They include consultants, research institutes, think tanks, communication specialists, lobbyists, and journalists. Their role has expanded considerably in recent years, particularly in Canada, to the point that it is not possible to write about locating power without considering their growing influence.

The World of Ideas Merchants

Jack Welch, Tom Peters, and Robert Waterman, among many others, have had a profound impact on many business organizations and business strategies without having set foot in the business or, in many cases, even being aware that the business exists. Many businesses sought to emulate Welch's leadership style because it exemplified sure ways of achieving great success in the business world. Welch had plenty of advice for the business community and became one of the most "widely emulated managers in business history."[5] When he became CEO at General Electric, he tore down its management structure, streamlined it, and focused its efforts on building shareholder value.[6] Executives around the world emulated his approach, not solely because Welch was highly successful at GE, but because he enjoyed a high profile in the media. Welch's opinions became popular, and subscribing to them meant that one was in step with modern management practices, whether or not they applied well to one's business.[7]

Peters and Waterman, meanwhile, co-authored a bestseller book, *In Search of Excellence*, which argued that the key to business success was to do away with overhead processes as much as possible and empower front-line managers and decision makers. The book came into fashion throughout the business world, and many businesses in North America and Europe embraced its ideas without much reflection on its application to local circumstances.[8]

Peters and Waterman's influence did not stop with the private sector. Their ideas were also taken up by governments throughout much of the Western world. Government was to be reinvented, and politicians were told that they would be much better at "steering" while leaving the "rowing" to somebody else. David Osborne and Ted Gaebler essentially reformulated these ideas to apply to the public sector.[9] The arrival of Margaret Thatcher, combined with the rise of New Public Management, all sought, albeit with varying degrees of success, to shift decision-making power over management matters to front-line managers or private-sector partners.

The writings of Peters, Waterman, Osborne, and Gaebler gained traction in all Anglo-American democracies so that the governments that did not subscribe to them were regarded as not keeping up with the times. For example, in their review of public-sector reforms in France, Philippe Bezes and Patrick Le Lidec wrote about their country being "out of step" with public-sector management reforms introduced in other jurisdictions, particularly in Anglo-American democracies.[10]

Canada's private and public sectors have both imported ideas from the United States and Britain to modernize their operations. Ideas move around more quickly than in years past, given developments in technology and modern means of communication. Senior business executives and government officials do not want to miss out on the latest management fashions and fads for fear of being left behind or being seen to be out of touch with new management thinking.

The search for a competitive edge fuels the adoption of new ideas, whether they apply to local circumstances or not. The former New Brunswick premier Frank McKenna, for example, directed his senior public servants to read Osborne and Gaebler and apply its findings to the provincial government. New Brunswick is a small province with a population of 730,000 and a provincial bureaucracy that is no bigger than a typical federal government department, so the distinction between steering and rowing in this case applies with great difficulty, if at all. No matter, senior public servants were asked to make sense of it all and launch measures to divide responsibilities between those tasked with steering from those asked to do the rowing.

There is no evidence that Osborne and Gaebler ever set foot in New Brunswick or were remotely aware of the size of the provincial bureaucracy, its history, hierarchy, and organizational culture. Always the energetic politician looking to introduce "transformative change" in his province, McKenna had heard about Osborne and Gaebler from other political leaders, and he would not allow his province to be left behind.[11] Although McKenna was more dynamic than most politicians, he was, like many present-day politicians, constantly on the lookout for transformative change, which explains in large part his impatience with the public service as an institution.

A subsequent New Brunswick premier, Shawn Graham, turned to Jack Mintz in 2008 to review his province's tax structure. Like McKenna, Graham wanted to champion change and transform the New Brunswick economy by making it "a magnet for outside investment." Mintz, a Calgary-based academic-consultant, has been described as "one of the country's leading tax experts," and we are told that he is "frequently sought by government and industry to provide advice and insight."[12] His ideas carry weight in financial and business circles. Not only would Graham obtain the advice of a leading expert, he could also tell Ottawa, other provincial governments and, more importantly, the investment community that he was able to get Mintz to give New Brunswick his seal of approval on its new taxation structure.

The world is now full of experts in every sector of the economy and for every management challenge. They sell their ideas to those willing to pay. Their names, their presence, and their opinions can have a profound influence on an organization, public or private. The organization's hierarchy is then left to figure out how best to implement these ideas.

Today, no one in the Government of New Brunswick refers to the work of Osborne and Gaebler, but there are still signs that their presence was felt at one time (for example, a reduction of overhead processes, some efforts to empower managers, and public-private partnership arrangements that date back to the McKenna years are still evident). Welch, Peters, Waterman, Mintz et al. all share something in common – their ideas gained currency in the media and in discussions in business circles. Once their ideas were taken up by opinion leaders, there was no stopping them. They were the new fashion, and their label came to matter as much as the content of their ideas. Their advice also came to matter more than that of long-serving business executives or government officials down the hierarchy.

Research Institutes and Think Tanks

As already noted, there is now tremendous appetite on the part of top executives in both the public and private sectors to look outside their organizations for innovative ideas. This has given rise to a new class of ideas merchants associated with research institutes or think tanks who can wield a great deal of influence.

Think tanks and research institutes have added to the cacophony of forces trying to shape public policies and government decisions. They too have muddied the waters in locating power and influence. Think tanks and research institutes have long enjoyed an important place in the public policy process in Washington. Other Anglo-American democracies, including Canada, have made up for lost time since the 1980s.[13] Today, we have think tanks and research institutes covering virtually every area of public policy, and it seems that new ones are continually being created, many through government funding.

No major public policy development is the product of a single linear progression of events and ideas. There are many rivulets of thought. What is beyond dispute, however, is that research institutes and think tanks have become a significant part of the public policy architecture. Some are paid for their input, and their success is measured by their perceived influence on government and by the attention given to them by the media.

The result is that power in government has become increasingly diffuse. We bring to your attention once again the words of Richard Wilson, former cabinet secretary under Tony Blair. He said, power is "never constant ... it moves around from day to day and somebody who was powerful last week is less powerful this ... reputations rise and fall like a stock exchange."[14] It is no small task to keep track of where power has moved to, and there are now specialists who are making a handsome living by keeping tabs on who is up and who is down in government and selling this information to those with the necessary financial resources to influence government.

It is not always possible to establish clearly who influenced whom or what, which makes the location of power and influence more difficult. In the past, research institutes were often associated with left-of-centre politics and policy preferences, but this is much less true today. We saw a growth in the number of conservative think tanks at about the same time as we saw a shift in society favouring the attributes of individuals over those of the community. The point here is that political leaders and the media are free to shop around and consult individuals who suit their policy bias.

It will be recalled that leading conservatives from the business community in the United States decided in the 1970s that the time had come for a conservative alternative to the left-leaning Brookings Institution. As is well known, Adolph Coors agreed to provide the American Enterprise Association with $250,000 in 1972 to research and analyze a number of issues going before Congress. In the early 1980s, Coors gave another $300,000 to the right-leaning Heritage Foundation. By the late 1980s and 1990s, there were several right-of-centre think tanks in Washington capable of challenging the left-leaning research institutes or think tanks and promoting right-of-centre policies.[15] They made a point of publicly promoting their research findings and then trying as best they could to influence public opinion and policy makers.

Other Anglo-American countries were quick to follow. The Fraser Institute set up shop in Vancouver in 1974 and has since expanded to Calgary, Toronto, Montreal, and the United States. The institute sponsors research on a variety of public policy issues, from health care to taxation, all from a distinctly conservative perspective. It takes great pride in reporting that it does not accept government funding to support its research activities. The Fraser Institute receives wide media coverage. It reports that it now receives over 3,300 media mentions a year, suggesting that its findings are both accessible and widely reported. Much of the media attention early on centred around Michael Walker and his work. He founded the institute and became highly visible in both print and electronic media.

The *Globe and Mail* carried out a review of fifteen public policy research institutes across Canada from different perspectives, including the number of mentions an institute received in the newspaper. It reported that over a two-year period, the Fraser Institute received more mentions than all of the others combined.[16] One can assume that it met with some success in influencing public opinion and, by ricochet, public policy, given its high media profile.

Like the Fraser Institute, the C.D. Howe Institute and the Atlantic Institute for Market Studies (AIMS) regularly publish research findings on a variety of public policy issues, also from a conservative perspective. Established in 1994, AIMS has challenged government intervention in virtually every sector in Atlantic Canada, and its research has received wide media attention. It points out that it "promotes practical research" and makes a point of being present and highly visible in the media.[17] Staff members often write op-ed pieces for daily newspapers and willingly make presentations before parliamentary committees and other public bodies. It is funded by private foundations, individuals, and corporations, the bulk coming from foundations and individuals.[18] Much of the media attention has centred around Brian Crowley, AIMS's founder. He has been highly visible in the media, sharing his views on any number of public policy issues, again from a conservative perspective.

There are institutes that purport to have no policy bias. Montreal's Institute for Research on Public Policy (IRPP) was established in 1972 with government funding and given a broad mandate to undertake research on public policy. Its mission is to "improve public policy in Canada by promoting and contributing to a policy process that is more broadly based, informed and effective."[19] The institute prides itself on being non-partisan and objective. Its role is to speak truth on major policy issues to whoever wants to listen. No sooner was IRPP set up than other such institutes followed to deal with a wide number of economic and social-policy fields.[20]

The 1980s and 1990s brought a plethora of new creations, including the Caledon Institute for Social Policy, the Canadian Centre for Policy Alternatives, the Canadian Centre for Arms Control and Disarmament, the Canadian Energy Research Institute, the Canadian Institute for Research on Regional Development, and the Canadian Institute of Health Research. Paul Martin's federal budget of December 2001 unveiled new funding for such groups, including a $10-million endowment for a research institute on minority official language communities.[21] Canada may well have too much of a good thing. Indeed, as far back as twenty years ago, two political scientists expressed concern about an overload of papers and publications from such institutions.[22]

Research institutes in Canada perform various functions and roles. Leslie Pal maintains that they do not formally engage in "making specific recommendations" so much as stimulating debate, but he doubts that many of them have had a "discernible impact" on the policy process.[23] Bruce Doern and Richard Phidd argue that, if nothing else, they challenge the "earlier bureaucratic monopoly of research and information."[24] Some institutes, such as the IRPP, make every effort to influence public policy and government officials by producing non-partisan objective research, which is what the bureaucracy is supposed to be doing. Institutes like IRPP have become part of Canada's "public policy architecture."[25] Some observers suggest that their rise "is a consequence, and yet another cause, of the decline of political parties as forces in Canadian politics."[26] If influence has shifted away from political parties, some of it has probably moved to research institutes and think tanks.

Research institutes and others have made ambitious claims about their impact. Thomas D'Aquino, head of the Canadian Council of Chief Executives (CCCE), reports: "Look at what we stand for and look at what all the governments, all the major parties have done and what we want them to do. They have adopted the agendas we've been fighting for in the past two decades."[27] Michael Walker of the Fraser Institute is no less boastful: "The Fraser Institute has played a central role in most policy developments during the past decade and it is simply too onerous a task to specify."[28] Apparently the C.D. Howe Institute helped convince Prime Minister Mulroney to pursue a free trade agreement with the United States.[29]

There are research institutes and think tanks that are particularly responsive to the government of the day and will try to accommodate the government's policy agenda as best they can. They seek influence through their close ties with key policy makers inside governments. The Ottawa-based Public Policy Forum (PPF), funded at least partly by the federal government, seeks to act as a "trusted facilitator." It maintains that its purpose is not to "sit in judgement of what government does, but to look at how public policy is developed."[30] David Zussman, its former head, had close political ties to the Liberal Party and Jean Chrétien, and the organization was particularly useful to Chrétien's government in reviewing a number of sensitive policy issues.[31] Ministers and senior bureaucrats knew, or at least believed, that Zussman could get to Chrétien if necessary, and this alone gave him and the forum influence. Zussman was later replaced by Jody White who, in turn, had close political ties to right-of-centre politicians, having served as a partisan adviser in the short-lived Joe Clark government in 1979.

The Conservatives, like the Liberals, have their favourite research institutes and think tanks. It will be recalled that shortly after Stephen Harper came to power, Brian Crowley, the head of AIMS, was invited to Ottawa to serve for two years as a senior visiting economist with the

Department of Finance.[32] The point here is that governments have their favourite individuals outside government to turn to for advice, even when this involves a research institute. The critical factor for the government of the day is often the individual who leads it.

There are now a number of research groups in Ottawa heavily dependent on government funding and still others that are in fact part of the federal government. The Policy Research Initiative (PRI), for example, is a federal government organization that brings together researchers from both inside and outside government to work on policy issues. It claims that its researchers come from "over 30 federal departments and agencies, other governments, think tanks and universities." The PRI reports that it "was launched by and remains a priority of the Clerk of the Privy Council."[33] The group still employs about forty people and performs a number of tasks, including the "sharing and use of policy research knowledge" and the building of a "policy research community through networks, vehicles and venues."[34] It operates through networks of outside experts and public servants, bringing together task forces and ad hoc groups to work on specific public policy issues.

The Chrétien government was the key player in the establishment of the Canadian Policy Research Networks (CPRN). It is Ottawa-based and employs about twenty-five full-time people. One would be hard pressed to explain any substantial difference between the PRI and CPRN, given that both are essentially networking policy groups. The CPRN reports that during 1999 it received "a long-term unrestricted grant of $9,000,000 from the Government of Canada."[35] It also obtained project funding from seventeen federal departments and agencies. Its web page reports that it has received funding from numerous federal and provincial government departments and agencies and has worked with hundreds of researchers from government and universities. This, it points out, "is what networking is all about."[36] The CPRN claims that it encourages government departments to look outside their own organizations for new ideas or research findings, and academics to look to government departments to tailor or shape their research interests, suggesting that they could not do this on their own. In effect, it has received funding for taking networking in the public policy process to new heights. Judith Maxwell founded the CPRN. She was a participant and presented a paper at the Aylmer conference that Jean Chrétien organized when in opposition to plan a platform for the 1993 election and was highly regarded by the Chrétien Liberals.[37] One can assume that the CPRN has taken networking to new heights only because the federal government saw a need for it to do so.

The federal government decided to finance yet another research group in 2006, the Canadian Academies of Science (CAS). The chair of the board announced with considerable fanfare that Peter J. Nicholson would serve as the group's first president. Nicholson had previously served as deputy chief of staff for policy in the Prime Minister's Office under Paul Martin. Ottawa now turns to the CAS "to provide a source of credible, independent, expert assessment" on a number of policy issues, particularly as they relate to "science in the public interest."[38]

Leaving aside some notable exceptions (such as the Fraser Institute and AIMS), federal funding has played a major role in both launching and sustaining these institutions hovering around the Ottawa policy process. Indeed, without federal funding, the CPRN, the Institute on Governance, the North-South Institute, IRPP, PPF, and many more either would not exist or would have to curtail their activities.

Why did the federal government decide to fund these research groups, and what has been the impact? The IRPP was established in 1972 after a commissioned consultant's report concluded that there was insufficient multidisciplinary and policy-oriented research being conducted in Canada.[39] Federal government thinking, as Les Pal explained in his *Interests of State*, was to create advocacy groups to promote the federal policy agenda.[40] In brief, the government decided that it needed voices outside government to help it gain visibility and credibility by applying pressure to promote a given public policy initiative or perspective. The government got more than it bargained for.

The growth of research institutes and think tanks has given a high public profile to non-elected individuals and has forced governments to establish units in their central agencies and line departments to deal with these voices and to brief their superiors and ministers. This in turn has contributed to thicker or bigger government, which in turn has made the government policy process slower and more difficult to manage. It has also made government operations more expensive.

To be sure, outside experts can provide fresh insight on a public policy issue or can challenge the traditional views of a government department. As a rule, politicians tend to welcome outside views more than public servants do. Politicians are traditionally far more open to change, however defined, than public servants, who will welcome outside reports that support their views but obviously not those that challenge department policies. Welcomed or not, many links with outside experts have been established between the executive and the research institutes and relevant stakeholders. The prime minister and the PMO can easily obtain the work of outside experts. The great majority of research institutes and think tanks, if not all of them, would consider it a measure of success if the prime minister were to be seen asking for their advice. The same can be said about cabinet ministers and senior officials, particularly deputy ministers.

At the risk of sounding repetitive, career officials value anonymity, but many research institutes and think tanks do not: the more public their profile, the greater the indication of their success. According to Donald Abelson, "there is a tendency among some journalists and scholars to equate media visibility with policy influence."[41] Abelson looked to the media to determine the visibility of 22 bodies. His ranking, in descending order: the Conference Board, the C.D. Howe Institute, the Fraser Institute, the Canadian Tax Foundation, the National Council of Welfare, the Canadian Council on Social Development (CCSD), and the IRPP. At the bottom were the PPF (16th), the Caledon Institute (18th), and the CPRN (21st). It is interesting to note that several top-ranked institutes operate outside Ottawa and enjoy considerable independence from government funding (C.D. Howe, Fraser, and the Canadian Tax Foundation), while those at the bottom are Ottawa-based and depend on government money (PPF and CPRN). One has to be a great deal more careful in dealing with the media if one is dependent on government funding to survive.

In any event, gaining a media profile tells only part of the story. Ivan Fellegi asked senior public servants to list policy research institutes that had helped them. The Conference Board, the CPRN, the CCSD, the Caledon Institute, and the C.D. Howe Institute topped the list. Abelson suggests that "think tanks that have received little media attention have been actively involved in consulting government departments."[42] Some institutes may wish to avoid media attention and public controversy in order to have better access to career officials and the policy process, and thus influence government from within rather than through public opinion. A high public profile can cut both ways: if research findings cast a minister or a government department in a bad light, there is a risk that the institute's continued funding from government may be compromised.

However, from whatever place on the political spectrum they come, the influence of research institutes, think tanks, and high-profile individuals associated with them is "soft" in that they are in no position to offer carrots or sticks to shape public policies. They offer advice, and governments are free to accept or reject it. Some will make every effort to gain positive visibility in the media in order to exert pressure on government to embrace a policy they favour, a form of soft power. Since research institutes and think tanks are not part of government, they need not worry about access to information legislation or embarrassing their ministers. They are free to explore all policy options and to establish a preference, and can time the release of their research findings to gain maximum media attention.

In addition to all of the above, we have royal commissions and commissions of inquiry offering advice on policy and the machinery of government. Some, notably the Lambert and Gomery commissions, did not hesitate to offer sweeping recommendations on how to fix relations between politicians and bureaucrats. It will be recalled that Justice Gomery became a media star. He did not hesitate to turn to the media to challenge how government bureaucracy operated and to sell his prescriptions for better government.[43]

To a senior career official of forty years ago, the current process must appear as a kind of free-for-all, an undisciplined process where individuals matter and the process is ignored. Well-known researchers and career officials, not only politicians, have become key players in building consensus. This has more to do with identifying trade-offs and finding some common ground, an essentially political exercise, than with facts. However, as James A. Smith argues, "All research begins to look like advocacy, all experts begin to look like hired guns, and all think tanks seem to use their institutional resources to advance a point of view."[44]

Hired guns now matter as never before. The federal government has been party to this development by making full use of its own resources to fuel selected research bodies. Research institutes and think tanks have thus contributed to the rise of high-profile but unelected policy actors. Politicians and public servants have learned never to underestimate the influence of high-profile policy actors speaking from the pulpit of a research institute. Links to outside experts have also opened up the policy process to the influence of many hands operating outside a command-and-control hierarchy. Consequently, politics enters the policy process much earlier than in the past, and career officials must now share the space with a variety of actors. Indeed, the consent if not the direct participation of stakeholders is now required even at the data-gathering stage.[45] Many voices and thicker government, however, makes it difficult to establish who has power, who has influence, and who is responsible for what. It also requires powerful personalities to be able to drive through initiatives of any significance, if only because all those outside centres and voices are rarely in agreement. This has also made consensus building a more complex process, involving many actors from both inside and outside government.

Consultants: Have a Per Diem, Will Travel

Consulting firms have also grown in number and size over the past forty years. There are now hundreds in Ottawa, covering economics, program evaluation, and various aspects of public policy. Many of them employ former federal officials and perform tasks once done by public servants. A number of government departments today turn to consultants even to prepare Cabinet and Treasury Board submissions – unthinkable forty years ago. Indeed, public servants of yesteryear would be alarmed to discover that a majority of Cabinet documents and Treasury Board submissions are now produced by consultants rather than by career public servants.

Consultants do not have to live with the requirements of the traditional relationship that has over the years shaped relations between politicians and public servants. They lack the security of tenure and have an economic interest to promote. They are individuals out to secure a contract, and the next contract may well depend on how they perform on the current one, so they want to present what they think the client wants to hear. They "speak truth to power" at their peril and at a potential economic cost to themselves.

Can consultants, keen to secure new contracts, say no to power? One former senior official explained the importance of truth speakers: "No one enjoys being a nay-sayer, constantly pointing out difficulties. But when the difficulties are real, and important, you have no choice; to express unwarranted optimism, or to just keep quiet and let your minister discover the hard way that a pet idea won't work, is an abdication of what you're paid to do."[46] Consultants do not have "a minister"; they have clients. Career officials not only have ministers, but they must live with the consequences of their policy advice.

Some consultants are experts in whatever issue may surface or, better yet, in whatever contract they can secure. I know one, a former public servant, who has worked on defence, foreign affairs, industry, regional economic development, Aboriginal affairs, immigration, and agricultural policies. He obviously has little sense of institutional memory in these areas. However, he is well known for bringing a quick pen and a sense of what sells in Ottawa and what does not – a highly valued skill for senior public servants to be able to turn to whenever the need arises.

In addition, because of his reputation, some deputy ministers will want to retain his services to gain his seal of approval.

Consultants are hired to produce a report and to give advice, and unlike public servants they have a limited interest in seeing their proposals properly implemented, because they are nowhere to be seen during the implementation stage. Their concern, for the most part, is serving their clients well and then securing the next contract. Accordingly, their relationship with political power is vastly different from that of public servants in that they can be highly responsive to politicians, particularly if they are clients.

Consultants are yet another cause of thicker government. It is no longer possible, for example, to establish the size of the public service simply by doing a body count. There are thousands of consultants in Ottawa, many of them former public servants, who have only one client – the Government of Canada. But that is not all. There are now a good number of public servants employed full time managing the relationship with consultants on behalf of their departments.

Consultants also increase the number and range of participants in the policy-making process. More participants from different organizations attenuate still further the importance of hierarchy in government. The prime minister, ministers, and senior public servants today have a multitude of centres and individuals always at the ready to provide advice. In addition, if they need to challenge the advice of some senior officials or a department, they can now call on a high-profile "authority" in every policy field to give them a hand. This in turn makes it more difficult to locate who has influence in government, if not responsibility, control, and accountability.

The above has changed the dynamics inside government between public servants and politicians, since public servants know full well that politicians can turn to any number of sources outside government for advice. This alone weakens their hand in providing policy advice. It has also made some senior public servants "excessively eager to please" their political masters in their search for promotion and influence.[47]

Lobbyists: Have Influence, Will Travel

Lobbyists, in the words of a leading Canadian journalist, have grown "like Topsy" in recent years in Ottawa. From a dead start thirty-five years ago, there are now some sixty lobbying firms listed in the Ottawa directory. This number does not include law firms, which now have "hired guns" to look after lobbying on behalf of customers. By one count, there are well over two thousand lobbyists in Ottawa. A number of them are highly paid and politically partisan; they could not easily survive a change of political power. However, those who are politically partisan have access to ministers and in some cases to the prime minister when their party is in power.

Lobbyists are always ready to offer advice. They are hired to promote the interests of their corporate customers and are paid to sell truth to politicians about government policy – truth as their customers see it. There are even lobbyists working to promote the interests of the tobacco industry. If truth is neither pure nor simple, elected politicians can turn to paid lobbyists to get a second opinion on a policy issue and eventually find someone with a highly articulate ability to speak the kind of truth they want to hear.

Britain has claimed that lobbying is an American phenomenon. But even in Britain things have changed. British lobbyists have increasingly been making their presence felt in recent years and have become an important part of the political process, both at home and abroad. British firms top all foreign spending on lobbyists in the United States.[48] There is now a spate of books in the United Kingdom on how to lobby, including advice on lobbying at intergovernmental meetings, organizing protest campaigns, and beating the system.[49]

In Washington, lobbyists are everywhere and have been for some time. They can be found at the executive branch, in the House of Representatives, in the Senate, and hovering around the West Wing. Their ability to influence policy and decision makers has been well established for some time. Their ubiquitous presence has motivated many aspiring to the presidency to claim that they would clean up the Washington lobby industry if elected. Similar claims have been heard in London and Ottawa, but the lobby industry keeps fighting back.

Lobbyists in Washington, London, and Ottawa are well paid, and the best of them have considerable influence. Some are experts in how government operates and decides. Others sell access because of their strong connections to the politicians in power. They are the ears and eyes inside government and will promote whatever message, interest, or point of view a company is willing to pay for. One thing most lobbyists share is a desire to operate below the radar. They seek influence but not visibility, for fear that it would inhibit their relations with senior politicians and government officials. Similarly, they know that many businesses do not wish to be seen using lobbyists in an attempt to influence politicians or government decisions.

Lobbyists constitute an influential voice among those trying to shape public policy and government decisions, but they have made it more difficult for those outside government to establish who in and around government has power and influence. Well-paid hired guns, they are able to make things happen but are nowhere to be seen if things turn sour. Their future prosperity depends on their ability to operate under the radar screen and to avoid being involved in public controversies. In brief, their purpose is to influence policy and decision makers and key political or bureaucratic actors on behalf of clients, but to do so without being seen or heard outside these circles. To retain their power and influence, they must not come under the media spotlight.

Successful lobbyists are particularly adroit at keeping their clients away from political controversies. To do otherwise is a sure way to lose the client. On the other hand, they will discreetly make known their close ties with current political power, especially with the prime minister. Examples include Bill Lee and Pierre Trudeau, Bill Neville and Joe Clark, Frank Moores and Brian Mulroney, Edmond Chiasson and Jean Chrétien, David Herle and Paul Martin, and Ian Brodie and Stephen Harper.[50] Access to key decision makers (and no one is more important than the prime minister) and discretion (so as to avoid media attention) are key attributes of successful lobbyists.

Lobbying has become an extremely lucrative business. The private sector is not in the business of throwing money around without seeing results. Lobbyists provide a variety of services: they are their customers' eyes and ears in Ottawa; they promote a firm's image and interests before policy makers; they seek business opportunities that may exist in government departments; and they can promote a specific project or develop a public-private partnership agreement.

Ottawa's decision to introduce the National Energy Program (NEP) in 1980 proved to be a seminal moment in the growth of Canada's lobby industry. It will be recalled that the NEP turned foreign-owned oil companies into takeover targets, and some firms in the sector went out of business. John Sawatsky writes that "the oil industry reacted with fury. Calgary wanted to know what had happened, which politicians and bureaucrats were the culprits and how to defeat them."[51] The fury generated a boom for the Ottawa lobby industry, and to this day, lobbyists are hired as an insurance policy to ensure that someone is in Ottawa to keep an eye on things and to talk sense to decision makers.

Not all lobbyists are created equal. Some are, as noted earlier, politically partisan. They support the party at election time to show their loyalty to the party leader. They play an active role in the party's war room, in drafting speeches and in putting together policy proposals for the party leader. To the extent it is permitted under current campaign financing laws, they make financial contributions to the campaign. In this sense, lobbyists employ carrots in their dealings with politicians. But they get something in return. Their telephone calls and e-mails will be returned if their party wins power. The ability to have one's telephone calls returned by those with power and influence in Ottawa can translate into handsome fees.

Every year, the *Hill Times*, an Ottawa publication dedicated to Canadian politics and Parliament, puts together a list of the top 100 most influential people in government and politics in Ottawa. The emphasis is on which individuals have power or influence rather than on institutions, government departments, or agencies. This is a sign of the times. The publication identified eight consultant lobbyists in its 2008 ranking, all of them with close ties to the ruling Conservative Party.[52] A change of government would obviously see these eight dropped, to be replaced by lobbyists politically tied to the next party in power.

Do lobbyists have influence? Yes. The politically connected consultant lobbyist can deliver a message to those in Ottawa who have power, open doors for business executives, employ this contact to identify business opportunities, and perhaps explain the finer points of a public policy. If required, they can also help politicians with material to challenge the advice of their public servants or to spin for the media developments in their departments.

Canadians and the media have recognized the growing influence of lobbyists for some time and have pushed governments to regulate their activities and promote greater transparency in their dealings with government officials. While in opposition, Stephen Harper promised to make Ottawa's lobbying industry much more transparent. True to his word, he made transparency in lobbying an important part of his government's legislative package on strengthening accountability which he introduced shortly after he came to power.

The Harper reforms were proclaimed into law on 2 July 2008. Among other things, it is now necessary for lobbyists to produce monthly reports detailing communications with designated public office holders (DPOHs) to a commissioner of lobbying, yet another newly created independent officer of Parliament. DPOHs include but are not limited to ministers, ministers of state and their exempt staff, deputy heads, associate deputy ministers, and any positions that have been designated by regulation, such as certain senior members of the Canadian Forces. Communications that need to be reported include telephone calls, meetings, and any other communications that are arranged in advance.[53] The requirements generate much paperwork, and the onus for compliance lies with the lobbyists.

Lobbyists have protested against some of the changes, especially the monthly reporting on their communications with DPOHs. They fear that the reports could allow competitors to gain knowledge of a company's lobbying activities and allow them to gain insights into a company's lobbying strategy.[54] However, the reforms have not prevented senior government officials and close associates of Harper himself from joining lobbying firms. Ian Brodie, Stephen Harper's chief of staff, raised more than a few eyebrows when he left the PMO to join the lobby firm Hill & Knowlton in June 2008. Opposition MPs charged that Brodie's switch to Hill & Knowlton broke "the spirit of the Harper government's past promises on the lobby industry."[55]

Having spent a few years in government as a partisan political adviser had made Brodie an expert on public policy, the machinery of government, and business-government relations, or so Hill & Knowlton reported on his appointment.[56] The *Hill Times* ranked him in its top 100 influential individuals in Ottawa because his "access and knowledge of the inner workings of government make him one of the most connected people in Ottawa."[57] Being connected means that you will be listened to by people with power in government. This is soft power, but it works. One can assume that because his soft power is based on being well connected, Brodie's currency will drop sharply when Harper loses power.

There are three types of lobbyists: consultant lobbyists, who are hired to lobby on behalf of a client; house lobbyists, who are employed by an entity on its behalf; and in-house lobbyists, employed by a non-profit entity, such as an association, to lobby on its behalf. Being well connected matters for all three types of lobbyists, no matter for whom they work. It will be recalled that former New Brunswick premier Bernard Lord co-chaired Stephen Harper's 2008 national election campaign. A few weeks after the election, the Canadian Wireless Telecommunications Association appointed Lord as its president and CEO – essentially to perform a lobbying function for the industry.[58] Though Lord played an important role in the campaign and presumably was close to Harper and his key advisers, he did not have to deal with any post-employment restrictions, because he was never a federal government official. He may not know his way around Ottawa's machinery of government, but he will have his phone calls returned from ministers and officials in the Prime Minister's Office. Lord is not part of the government's hierarchy, but presumably his views and advice will matter to key policy and decision makers. Accordingly, his value to wireless firms is his ability to deliver their messages to those who matter in government.

When Paul Martin became prime minister, the television cameras caught members of his transition team, a good number of whom were the Ottawa-based lobbyists who had helped him wrestle power from Jean Chrétien.[59] Norman Spector, former chief of staff to Brian Mulroney, explains: "Once, politics was about a clash of ideas and policies in furtherance of the public interest; now, it's increasingly a spin war among competing lobbyists seeking to cash in on access to power."[60]

Lobbying is the new form of patronage. High-profile partisans are now able to reap significant financial rewards for being well connected with the government's political elites. They are well remunerated because they have influence with key policy makers. They are well known in Ottawa political and bureaucratic circles and to business leaders, but not to average Canadians. Indeed, their success depends to some extent on their ability to be discreet while letting potential clients know that they have access to key policy makers.

Some Journalists Matter More than Others

Martin Linton, a former British journalist turned politician, reports that his former colleagues asked him, "Why on earth did you give up all the power and influence of a job on a national newspaper for a job that is notoriously devoid of any power, that of a backbencher?"[61] The place to look for influence and power among journalists, he argued, is with in-house columnists, outside contributors who are experts in their fields, and the editorial pages. He could have added those journalists who regularly produce front-page articles in national newspapers and well-known television political commentators.

The *Hill Times* named eighteen journalists among its top 100 most influential people in Ottawa. It is revealing that nearly 20 percent of the most influential individuals in Ottawa, according to the publication, are in the media. It is also interesting to note that the *Hill Times* did not rank news organizations, national newspapers, or television networks. Rather, it focused on individual journalists. The publication has a point. A leading Ottawa-based journalist explains, "When it comes to news,

Peter Mansbridge is larger than CBC, larger than the organization in which he works."[62]

Some journalists exert a great deal of influence on policy makers because of the influence they wield, real or perceived, in shaping public opinion. Senior policy makers will read or at least monitor what leading journalists, particularly columnists and hosts of television political talk shows, have to say about the government, the country's political leadership, and public policy issues. Some journalists have become celebrities, and what they write or say can have a profound impact on the government's agenda or on a politician's electoral prospects.

Politicians and senior bureaucrats know very well which journalists truly matter. The list is never static, but those who make it onto the list are sure to be quietly fed inside information. Lunches with important government officials are booked days if not weeks in advance, and they will have access to inside information. Politicians and, increasingly, bureaucrats know that a favourable mention by a leading journalist can make an important difference. A member of Parliament on the government side who catches the attention of a well-known national newspaper columnist or a political commentator on television will see his or her chances of making it to Cabinet considerably improved.

Individual bureaucrats who get an honourable mention by leading journalists for work on a policy initiative could also see their career prospects improve. Forty years ago, bureaucrats went to great lengths to avoid media attention. Times have changed, in part because it is no longer possible for a large number of public servants to remain anonymous. For example, David Dodge's work on labour markets received highly favourable reviews in the 1980s, as did his work in the Department of Finance – he subsequently became its deputy minister, where his work in arresting the government deficit was highlighted over and over in the media. He was later appointed governor of the Bank of Canada. This is not to suggest that Dodge's work was lacking in any way. It is simply to demonstrate once again that the days of the anonymous bureaucrat are over, and those who have good press have a better chance of being promoted.

Individual journalists are the influential players, not the newspapers or the networks they work for. When in Ottawa, I often hear references to the views of a print journalist, a columnist, and a television political commentator to support or oppose a proposed initiative. I very rarely hear references to CBC news, CTV, or the *Globe and Mail* versus the *Ottawa Citizen* or *Le Devoir*. The PMO, ministerial offices, and government departments all now have communications specialists on staff keeping an eye on what leading journalists are working on, trying as best they can to influence their work. The focus is on individual journalists, not on news organizations, because that is where the media's political influence now lies.

Not All Bureaucrats Are Created Equal

Anyone looking to locate power in the federal bureaucracy can start by looking at whoever occupies the position of clerk of the privy council and secretary to the cabinet. Indeed, there is no better place to look. This individual has easy access to both hard and soft power and can carry a big stick, but also has plenty of carrots to offer. A good word there or a bad note here from the clerk can make or break the career of an ambitious public servant, at least until a new clerk takes over.

To be sure, the prime minister's chief of staff can wield a great deal of influence in a prime minister's court. But he or she is only connected to the political executive, to the prime minister, ministers, and ministerial offices. However, the clerk of the privy council has even more influence – is connected to both the political executive, by virtue of being the prime minister's principal policy adviser, and to the vast bureaucratic machine. The clerk is by statute (circa 1992) head of the public service. But even this hardly tells the whole story.

The clerk, through the prime minister, has an important – if not the most important – say on who makes it to the very top of the public service, to the deputy and associate deputy levels, and also who gets promoted within these ranks and who gets shuttled aside. The clerk even briefs the prime minister on the merit of ministers and on how well departments, policies, and programs are performing. Together, the prime minister and the clerk shape the government's agenda and its priorities, have a direct hand in the budget, and look after senior appointments throughout government and Crown corporations.

Clerks of the privy council, much like prime ministers, presidents, and CEOs, are powerful because of the position they occupy. But even this appears less clear in recent years. It will be recalled that Kevin Lynch recommended some deputy minister appointments after he announced that he was retiring. A well-known journalist wrote that the move gave rise to "a big debate" in Ottawa circles over whether Lynch should have filled "the vacancies with his picks" knowing that he would soon be leaving government. The journalist quoted public policy experts saying that "it was inappropriate" for the outgoing clerk to make the appointments.[63] The underlying point here is that the office of the clerk of the privy council should not recommend appointments; rather, it is the individual who sits in the office who should do so.

I asked a deputy minister in Ottawa to help me locate where power currently lies inside government. Her answer: "Actually, you can find it most mornings when the Clerk and the Prime Minister meet. The Prime Minister has a list of things he wants the Clerk to look after and the Clerk has a series of recommendations for the Prime Minister to consider. In some ways, they trade power. If they decide something should happen in a department, it happens. If they decide that it should not happen, it will not happen. Look no further. Line departments have power in delivering their programs, but nothing compared to the PM-Clerk. I am not saying that this is not the way it should be. It may be the best way to get things done. What I am saying is that this is the way it is."[64] In other words, the prime minister needs the clerk in order to pursue his or her priority issues successfully, while the clerk needs the prime minister's approval on any number of questions, notably the appointment of deputy ministers, to pursue his or her agenda. Of course, other senior public servants also have influence, but nothing like the clerk's.

Personalities matter, not just the title. Clerks who are not able to gain the confidence of the prime minister or are unable to deliver the goods from the prime minister's list are quietly moved on to other positions. Plum foreign postings appear to be the solution of choice in moving the clerk out of the Privy Council Office.[65]

Deputy ministers of finance also have power and influence. Major spending decisions invariably go through their desks. Their advice on the budget, on proposed spending commitments, and on broad economic policy can be critical in a proposal being approved or rejected. That said, deputy ministers of finance have to establish a solid working relationship with the clerk of the privy council if they are to function effectively. If one or the other has to go, it will be the deputy minister, as Simon Reisman discovered.[66] In leaving the Department of Finance, he complained about a diminishing scope for people with "a certain independence of mind" in the federal public service.[67]

All deputy ministers have influence, and under certain statutes they actually have administrative power.[68] Some have more influence than others, but leaving aside the clerk, all of them have less influence than in years past.[69] Formerly, the departments they directed established their level of influence, but today it is much more a matter of who they are and of their relations with the clerk of the privy council.

Thirty years ago, deputy ministers who headed large spending departments or important policy-oriented departments (such as Industry) held a great deal of influence by virtue of their department. Things are different today. A deputy minister's standing in the court of the prime minister-clerk is the most important factor, not the department he or she heads. Indeed, departments, their size, and activities today matter much less in Ottawa's hierarchy of power and influence. Deputy ministers who are perceived to be the prime minister's favourites or who have a particularly close relationship with the clerk, now wield influence.

Sitting inside government, it is relatively easy to identify which deputy ministers are in the ascendancy in Ottawa's power structure. In recent years, clerks have relied on task forces or ad hoc committees to review policy issues. The horizontal nature of policy issues demands an interdepartmental perspective, and it is up to the clerk to establish the process and decide which actors should take the lead. Deputy ministers who are picked to lead the more high-profile efforts often become members of the court, if they are not so already. In any event, their work gives them access to the clerk, and this now matters a great deal more than having access to individual ministers, even senior ones.

Looking Back

In looking to locate power, one learns that hierarchy and organizations matter less than they once did, and soft power now accounts for a great deal. Departments and hierarchy, it seems, are no longer able to deal with present-day challenges.

What matters is the individual, the one who can power through and get things done: the clerk of the privy council, other courtiers, well-connected lobbyists, and influential journalists. Sticks and carrots are still important, but only for a minority of decision makers. Networking, an individual's credibility, and the opinion of experts have come to matter a great deal in both the public and private sectors. The rise of the individual and of soft power also speak to our time. They are a reaction against collectivism and elaborate but slow-moving institutions and processes.

9   OUR INSTITUTIONS ARE MELTING THE CANADIAN WAY: WITH A WHISPER, NOT A BANG

One needs to look no further than Parliament to see that not all is well with our institutions. Power today resides less in institutions, organizations, government departments, agencies, and formal decision-making processes than it once did. In Canada, at least, the Cabinet has been transformed into a focus group for the prime minister, and there is evidence that this is also increasingly true throughout Western Europe.[1] Large private-sector organizations, from General Motors to the world's largest banks, no longer hold the kind of power they once did. Power does not usually belong to organizations that have to go cap in hand to governments looking for help just to survive. But the issue is more complex than simply running out of cash. General Electric became, at least for a while, the darling of the business world because of Jack Welch and not the other way around. If success is to be ascribed, it is no longer given to organizations but to individuals.

Contacts and networks have replaced hierarchy, while personalities have gained power and influence at the expense of institutions, organizations, and processes, which have become too complex, too complicated, too porous, and too slow to get things done. In short, they are no longer up to the task and, as a result, we increasingly focus on the power of individuals because we value results.

We have become impatient with institutions and organizations but, at the same time, fascinated with individuals who wield power. *Newsweek* recently prepared a ranking of the top 50 powerful people in the world of the "Global Elite," who "will figure in the era over which Obama will preside."[2] It is now fashionable to produce lists and even books of the most powerful or influential individuals at the international and national levels. The purpose of this chapter is to review how institutions, organizations, and processes have adapted to the modern economy and the new media, and to incessant demands to respond quickly to fast-emerging circumstances.[3]

What Matters Is What Works

I participated in an international gathering of a small group of political scientists in Gothenburg, Sweden, in January 2009. The theme of the gathering was "Steering from the Centre," which essentially dealt with issues raised in one of my earlier books, *Governing from the Centre: The Concentration of Power in Canadian Politics*, but from a comparative perspective. Sweden's most senior career public servant and permanent secretary to the prime minister met with the group. In his brief presentation, he argued that "what is important for the Prime Minister is what works. The idea is not to ignore institutions but rather how to work around them."[4] I found his words very revealing, if only because a few years earlier Britain's top public servant and cabinet secretary under Tony Blair made an almost identical observation when he wrote about the need to promote "the philosophy of what matters is what works."[5]

This hardly tells the whole story. Two well-known French scholars reported on an important shift of power within government, with President Sarkozy described as the "hyper President." The prime minister, we were told, was increasingly playing the role of a "mere Principal Private Secretary or the Minister responsible for parliamentary relations." They also reported important changes to the French public service, in which the "ministries' grand corps" was replaced by a handful of "super senior civil servants who enjoy more direct relationships not only with their own minister but also the President."[6] Sarkozy is being accused of arrogating "almost every lever of power to himself and his advisers"; one keen observer of French politics states, "For all the authoritarian habits of General de Gaulle or François Mitterand, Sarkozy's personalization of the presidency is unprecedented in the history of the Fifth Republic."[7]

B. Guy Peters reported on recent developments in the two centres of government operating in the United States: the president and Congress. He commented on the rise of the imperial presidency and on the increasingly frequent use of "Policy Tsars" appointed to take charge and get things done on issues that matter to the president. Others have reported similar developments in countries as diverse as Germany, Australia, and Finland.

All the more remarkable is that despite substantially different political systems, histories, and institutional and bureaucratic structures, there is a clear convergence towards individuals at the centre of government and in other sectors as the focal point for power and for getting things done. Institutions and formal policy-making and even decision-making processes are no longer able to accommodate current political and economic circumstances, and the solution in many settings is to have individuals work around them to pursue the "what matters is what works" mantra. Not many people have the power to work around institutions and formal processes, and those who do have such power will not hesitate to use it to get the results they want.

We saw in an earlier chapter that many private-sector executives in the United States decided to sidestep the new transparency requirements from the Sarbanes-Oxley legislation. Some firms went private, while others decided to move their head offices to Britain, thus avoiding the legislation's provisions. We also saw that senior business executives turned to new information technologies to centralize decision making further in their own hands and to ignore hierarchy whenever possible or necessary. The changes have been even more pronounced in the public sector. Institutions, organizations, and formal processes are regularly short-circuited by those in government with power to pursue their favourite initiatives.

Parliament: An Institution in Decline

Canadians can take some small comfort in the knowledge that all Western parliamentary systems are in decline. The decline of Canada's Parliament appears to be beyond question or even debate: MPs from all parties have been critical of their institution since the 1970s.[8] Indeed, they have been ringing alarm bells for years. A bipartisan committee of MPs wrote in 2003 that Parliament "has, in a sense, lost its way, lost its forum quality, lost its ability to scrutinize government activity and Parliament no longer contributes meaningfully to policy debates."[9]

Parliament's decline is not a recent development; it can even be traced back to the rise of political parties in Britain. Adam Tomkins describes the period between 1832 and 1870 as "the golden age of genuinely parliamentary government." This was the era that followed government by the Crown but before government by parties.[10] Between the two Reform Acts of 1832 and 1872, no less than ten British governments lost power because they lost the confidence of the House of Commons. The House had the power both in theory and practice to decide who should govern. However, the arrival of the modern, centralized organization of the political party gave rise to the "greatest single challenge that the system of political accountability had yet to face."[11] Another major issue was the growth of government. Accountability, let alone exerting power, became considerably more difficult for Parliament as government assumed a greater role in society.

One can appreciate that it was easier for Parliament to perform its role in simpler times and with a smaller government. Parliament traditionally has played a variety of roles. It represents the country's leading and legitimate deliberative body; it establishes a legitimate government; it makes government work by allocating resources and adopting legislation; it makes the executive steamroller behave and holds it accountable; and it provides for an alternative government. It also functions to express the "mind of the people, teach society and inform both government and citizens of grievances and problems."[12] But today it is no longer able to perform its most important function: making the executive steamroller behave and holding it accountable. The best it can do is heckle the steamroller as it rolls by.

There are any number of reasons why it is increasingly difficult for Parliament to perform its several roles, ranging from the size and complexity of government departments and agencies to a better-informed public and the role of the new media. It was, however, the rise of political parties that transformed parliamentary politics into party politics.[13] Political parties were the vehicle by which political power was secured, and as these parties grew, the party leader and professional party officials began to exert considerable influence on them. The House of Commons divided and remains divided between the government party and opposition parties or between "them" and "us," making the institution partisan and adversarial.

Party discipline became the key to survival for the governing party, but also for the opposition parties, if only to present a united front leading up to the next general election campaign. There are any numbers of carrots that party leaders have in hand to induce party discipline: a cabinet appointment, a patronage appointment, and strong party support, including that of the leader at election time. It is this that prompted Tomkins to write about "the golden age of genuinely parliamentary government before the arrival of disciplined political parties."[14] Before parties came to dominate the House of Commons, the prime minister and ministers were accountable to Parliament but could not yet control it. Now, though they remain accountable to Parliament, they can and do control it whenever they have a majority mandate.

The above is not to suggest that the rise of political parties has been a completely negative force in parliamentary politics. Disciplined parties are necessary in the search for reliable legislative majorities. Question Period, the consideration of legislative proposals, the review of the expenditure budget, and parliamentary business in general are better suited to disciplined political parties than to undisciplined ones or independents. Jennifer Smith writes, "While responsible government does not necessarily require party government in theory, it has become party government in practice."[15]

The problem is that political parties in Canada have lost their way. Party leaders and their close advisers dominate their parties to the point that the latter have been turned into little more than election-day organizations and a means of raising cash. Parties have little power to shape public policies or even to influence their leaders once they are chosen.

All in all, there are few voices today claiming that power belongs with Parliament or with the Queen in Parliament. Its sovereignty is now relegated to a legal concept and is no longer a political reality, in that whenever there is a majority government, sovereignty in practice belongs to the prime minister and his or her close advisers. When it comes to power, Parliament is on the outside looking in. In short, in our search for the location of power, Parliament is no longer an actor of consequence. C.E.S. Franks, one of Canada's leading students of Parliament, claims that the decline of Parliament can be viewed from two perspectives: actual measures that indicate its decline, and the growing complexity of modern politics and government, which has made it much more difficult for Parliament to perform its role.[16] The first wound is largely self-inflicted; the second includes forces that are beyond its immediate control.

There is ample evidence to document the substantial decline in the quality of parliamentary debates and in their significance to Canadians and to the government.[17] The prime minister and ministers increasingly make major announcements outside the House. Interest groups or special gatherings of one kind or another provide an ideal backdrop and also guarantee favourable reactions on the national evening news, where representatives of opposition parties are often not in attendance to add a negative spin. Contrast this development with the days when announcements were made in the Commons, giving opposition parties the opportunity to react immediately and point to flaws, real or contrived. In short, the prime minister and his or her courtiers can now ignore Parliament, even when making important announcements.

In recent years, we have abandoned Parliament to professional politicians, those whose careers are limited to partisan politics. Many on the front benches on both sides of the House of Commons are career politicians. They have no reference point from past experience other than partisan politics. Scoring political points and positioning their party to win the next election are what truly matters. Their knowledge base is circumscribed, they have no experience outside politics to give them a wider perspective on policy options or to enable them to assess the work of government officials. What matters for them is what works, and what works is all about what works politically or how one is able to score political points. One long-serving MP compares the work of Parliament in the 1970s with today and insists that "the parties' daily strategy meetings were not as dominated back then by party spin doctors whose prime objective is to get MPs to produce a sound bite for TV." He adds, "It's much more staged being and heckling now and the questions are much more scripted – ministers don't even pretend to answer."[18]

Their policy preferences are based on what works politically, based on what their favourite pollster says should work politically. Their goal is to win political power. They insist that change is required because that is what Canadians tell public opinion surveys is needed. Without either a political ideology or a backdrop of non-political experience to draw upon from which to assess policy proposals, they become obsessed with change as an end in itself. Change is focused on what works politically and less on their party's ideology or roots. The objective is to replace those in power with a new crowd that includes them. Former British prime minister Tony Blair spoke the language of Canadian political leaders when he observed, "People have to know that we will run from the centre and govern from the centre."[19]

Leaders, not political parties or government departments, will be asked to lead the charge for change. The prime minister's court will be on the lookout for ambitious public servants out to make a name for themselves and also willing to pursue change as an end in itself. This explains the observation of a senior Ottawa-based public servant: "It seems that the Prime Minister likes us as individuals but he, some of his Ministers and his advisors do not much like us as a group or as a profession. They may like individual public servants, but they do not much like the public service."[20]

Massive documents that government departments send to Parliament on a regular basis remain unread for the most part. Spending estimates, the most important documents to be tabled in the Commons, are now approved by a certain date with very little debate and without the active involvement of parliamentarians.[21] The chair of Parliament's Public Accounts Committee met with senior financial officials, including Treasury Board Secretariat officials, at a retreat in 2008 and admitted that MPs were not doing their job of holding the government to account. But he told them that the massive piles of documents sent to Parliament are of no help. He even challenged them to put in a pile of blank pages to see if anyone would notice. He reminded them that in one year the Department of Justice simply forgot to include financial statements for the firearms registry, a controversial initiative widely reported in the media. No one even noticed. He concluded with the observation that what they were sending to Parliament was too complex, too voluminous, and too convoluted to be of any use to parliamentarians.[22]

We have reached the point where MPs are forced to use access to information legislation to secure information from the government. Information requests under the legislation are easily understood and are more difficult for ministers to sidestep in Question Period. History has revealed that such requests show promise in uncovering missteps that are embarrassing to the government.[23]

The relationship between government and Parliament has broken down. Parliament is now largely about political theatre – and not particularly good theatre at that. Politicians entertain Canadians with bombast, smart ten-second clips, and partisan posturing. Policy debates, it seems, are now better left to research institutes and think tanks, so they are very rarely heard in Parliament. In addition, as already noted, Parliament's ability to hold government to account – traditionally, its most important role – is virtually non-existent except for the search for scandals or gaffes. All too often in recent years, debates and Question Period have degenerated "into insults and accusations that would get MPs sued if uttered outside the Commons." Robert Sibley maintains that this is a result of "impotent frustrations" on the part of MPs. This, he adds, "is all the more troubling because at the heart of Canada's political history, until recently, we were a nation of institutions, not identity."[24]

Former prime minister John Turner recently expressed deep concern about the state of Canadian democracy and argued that "one of the reasons is that the role of the member of Parliament isn't what it used to be."[25] Turner is hardly alone in this view. Wayne Easter, a sixteen-year veteran of the Commons and a member of Chrétien's cabinet, reports that "MPs don't have as much power as they used to, certainly not on the government side anyway." Parliament, he added, is "not a fun place anymore. It's become bitter, vindictive and vicious, right through the whole system."[26] For whatever reason, then, Parliament has not been able to define for itself a more substantial role, given the changes to both society and the state in recent years.

Cabinet: A Focus Group

Two former clerks of the privy council have asked me to identify the minister in the Chrétien cabinet who described it as a "focus group for the prime minister."[27] They even suggested a few suspects. I have also heard from one clerk that several ministers have openly referred to Cabinet as a focus group in Cabinet deliberations and in their discussions with the clerks. I have not revealed his or her identity to them or to anyone else. If I ever did, I would not be able to gain access to people and information in Ottawa who have been so much a part of my research over the years.

If anything, Cabinet as a focus group is even more obvious today than it was when I wrote *Governing from the Centre* in 1999. Tony Blair once observed that one of the most frustrating things about coming into government is the time it takes to get stuff moving through the system.[28] Imagine the frustration if one is a line department minister who is not a member of the prime minister's inner court. Prime ministers have the required instruments of power in their hands to push through their favourite policies and projects and bypass the system. In doing so, they do not hesitate to turn to key political or bureaucratic actors, all members of their courts, to champion the proposal and to ensure that it gets done.

It is no exaggeration to write that Canadian prime ministers, particularly in recent years, have all but given up on Cabinet as an effective decision-making body. It is also no exaggeration to write that it is no longer clear, in Canada and now even in Britain, what is meant when we refer to Cabinet's collective decision-making role. We no longer know what decisions, if any, require some kind of collective deliberation. To be sure, Cabinet may come in handy, but it is clear that it no longer directs the work of the government.[29] If power no longer belongs to Cabinet, or if decisions are no longer made by a collective decision-making body, then someone or some other body now has that power.

There are other reasons why Cabinet is no longer very effective as a formal decision-making body. For one thing, there is less "loose power" available to governments, and prime ministers by virtue of their position are able to grab much of what is still available. As we saw earlier, trade agreements, intergovernmental policies and programs, officers of Parliament, research institutes, think tanks and the new media, access to information legislation, privatization, the rise of public-private partnerships, and increased delegated authority to front-line managers and bureaucrats have all moved some of the power away from the centre of government. Someone in government has had to lose power and influence because of these developments, and prime ministers have decided that it will not be them.

This is not to suggest that individual ministers have no power and influence. Some do, but as individuals, not as part of a collectivity. Eleven ministers in the Harper government, for example, made it on the top 100 most influential people in Ottawa in the *Hill Times* survey. All eleven are part of Harper's court. The minister of finance, by virtue of the position, is a member of the court. But others are there because of their close association with the prime minister. For example, John Baird is a member of the court at least in part, as anyone who has been in Ottawa for any length of time will discover, because he is a close friend of the prime minister.[30]

Members of the court can go directly to the prime minister and plead their case for a particular policy program or decision. Others, as already noted, have to go through the formal process, a process that is complicated, complex, and slow, which never generates the kind of decision, if it can actually deliver a decision, that one initially had hoped to secure. The formal process is for everybody who is not a member of the court. When one sees a proposal submitted through the formal decision-making process, one can be fairly certain that no decision will be made swiftly, if at all, and by the time it has been dealt with, the decision will be so watered down that it pleases no one. Indeed, prime ministers will ask their ministers to submit their proposals through the formal process if they have little interest in a project, knowing full well that this constitutes a highly effective delaying strategy. The interdepartmental consultative process and the need to consult interested parties outside government can kill the most deserving of proposals, and only prime ministers and members of court can rescue them.

Where does this leave Cabinet as a collective decision-making body? It leaves it as an adjunct to prime ministers and their courtiers, on the outside looking in at where the more important decisions are struck. Once again, power in government now belongs largely to prime ministers, their offices, the Privy Council Office, and individual cabinet ministers – those able to manoeuvre in the inner circle. One only has to look at what political leaders are saying to see evidence of this. Jean Chrétien wrote that a minister is "just another adviser to the prime minister. He can be told what to do and on important matters his only choice is to do it or resign."[31]

Ministers appear to confirm this view, and it is fascinating to see how they jockey for position to be close to the source of power, the prime minister. Stéphane Dion, for example, boasted before the Gomery Commission that "few ministers had the kind of direct relationship with the Prime Minister" that he had.[32] As already noted, it is well known in Ottawa that John Baird, the minister of transport in the Harper government, has a close personal relationship with the prime minister, a fact that serves him well in promoting his projects in the Ottawa system.[33]

In brief, Cabinet government has all but been destroyed in Canada.[34] To sum up thus far, if Parliament no longer enjoys the influence or credibility that it once had, if it has turned over at least some of its responsibility of holding the government to account to officers of Parliament and to the media, and if Cabinet no longer functions as a collective decision-making body, then Canada's institutions no longer work as they were designed to. Canadians now have to look elsewhere to sort out where power, influence, and responsibility for accountability reside.

Departments Matter Less

When I joined the Canadian public service on leaving university in the early 1970s, there were several departments that clearly stood out among the crowd. The Departments of Finance (where Bob Bryce was once its deputy minister), External Affairs (as it was then called and where Lester B. Pearson once served as its secretary), and Industry (where Jim Grandy once served as its deputy minister) had standing above the other departments. Indeed, a young ambitious public servant gained credibility simply by joining one of these departments.

This is no longer true. There is now little appreciable difference between departments, and all have lost power and influence to central agencies and powerful individuals. All departments may have more management authority than they once had, but even here there is a price to pay. Every department now houses a veritable army of bureaucrats to deal with a constant stream of "demands" from central agencies for performance reports, accountability requirements of one kind or another in the form of papers, briefing material, and reports for central agencies and ministers to arm them to meet the media and Parliament. In short, the power pecking order in Ottawa no longer belongs to departments. Rather, it belongs to central agencies, first with the Privy Council Office, then the Department of Finance and the Treasury Board Secretariat, and with powerful individuals. As for line departments, again, there is little appreciable difference between them in terms of power and influence.

Foreign Affairs is a case in point. Forty years ago, it held full responsibility for the sector, and what the department said and recommended mattered a great deal to everyone in government. The prime minister appointed ambassadors on its advice, often simply rubber-stamping departmental recommendations. It was clear to everyone that the department was the architect of Canada's foreign policy, and its minister and senior officials held special standing in Ottawa circles by virtue of where they worked.

Things are vastly different today. Prime ministers and their courtiers have access to several streams of advice on foreign affairs other than the department, including units in the PCO. There are any number of research institutes, think tanks, and former ambassadors always available to offer advice, solicited or not. Prime ministers have, since Trudeau, turned to units in the PCO and to advisers outside government, more often than to the department, to define their foreign affairs policy, to map out a strategy to deal with a foreign government, or to manage an international crisis.

The PCO units are close by, and their senior officials get to interact with the prime minister and his staff far more frequently than departmental officials do. It is interesting to note that the *Hill Times* ranked the prime minister's foreign and defence policy adviser in its top 100 most influential people in Ottawa. And so it should, because the PCO now has as much say, if not more, in foreign postings, particularly in the more senior postings, than the department does. This has not always been the case.[35]

When Paul Martin launched a foreign affairs policy review, he turned to Jennifer Welsh for help. Word spread around Ottawa that Martin had become frustrated with the "tone of the drafts emerging from the foreign affairs department that lacked strategic focus."[36] When Stephen Harper wanted advice on Canada's mission and future in Afghanistan, he ignored the department and established an independent panel made up of "five eminent Canadians" to advise him.[37]

There are still other signs that personalities now matter more than government organizations. Three out of the past four clerks of the privy council were able to secure Canada's best ambassadorial appointments – Paris, Rome, and London. None of the three had any previous foreign affairs experience. They simply struck a deal with the prime minister as they left the Privy Council Office.[38] The message could not have been lost on long-serving officials in Foreign Affairs. There is no intrinsic value to their work experience or their department, and clerks or heads of the public service will look after their own interests before those of government departments and institutions, no matter their traditions and standing in government, such as Foreign Affairs.

The above is true notwithstanding a highly generous pension scheme for deputy ministers. In Canada, deputy ministers, after ten years in that position, can enjoy an indexed pension set at 90 percent of their salaries based on the average of their best five years. Under the special retirement allowance, deputy ministers are credited with two years of service for every year worked, to a maximum of ten years. The special allowance was introduced in 1988 because deputy ministers had increasingly been working in "a volatile environment" that does not "allow most of them to continue to normal retirement age." This view, however, has been challenged. The head of a civil service union, for example, recently argued that while deputy ministers may get shuffled around, he had never "heard of a deputy minster getting fired."[39]

The demise of the Department of Foreign Affairs is increasingly being debated in the media and in bureaucratic circles in Ottawa. Former prime minister and foreign affairs minister Joe Clark recently said that the "erosion of Canada's diplomatic capacity may cost this country for years to come."[40] The *Globe and Mail* reported that the Department of Foreign Affairs "is in the grip of a kind of existential crisis," according to "a range of current and recently retired staff." It quoted an official as saying, "There is nothing worse than a scared, timid, reclusive, protective bureaucrat. It doesn't give you either good public policy or good service delivery."[41]

The Department of Finance still matters in Ottawa because it continues to shape the budget, the government's single most important document. It lays out in black and white who won and who lost in the battle for money – the lifeblood of departments, public policies, and programs. That said, the department matters less than previously. Without wanting to give undue influence to its findings, it is revealing to note that the deputy minister of finance never made it to the top 100 most influential individuals in Ottawa on the *Hill Times* list. This would have been unthinkable as recently as ten years ago.

The chapter heading for the department in my *Governing from the Centre* reads: "Finance – Let There Be No Light." The idea was that the Department of Finance wanted to be king in budgetary matters and in advising the government on economic issues. Today, the department is being challenged on many fronts, and politicians and Canadians in general have access to a multitude of views. There are several well-known research institutes and think tanks with a keen interest in fiscal issues (for example, the C.D. Howe and Fraser institutes) that are more than happy to share their work, findings, and advice with the media. The PCO also houses economic units that are all too willing to question the advice of Finance officials.

In addition, there is a new breed of commentators on budget issues who have gained both credibility and visibility in recent years. Chief economists at Canadian banks are now in strong demand by the media. Some have become media stars, and it seems that their views carry weight both in the media and amongst policy makers in Ottawa. Hardly a week goes by without Don Drummond, chief economist at the Toronto Dominion Bank and a former senior federal bureaucrat, making an appearance on national television, offering advice to governments or commenting on the country's economic circumstances. In the 2008 election campaign, Liberal leader Stéphane Dion often pointed to Drummond's views on taxation in support of his proposed tax policy.

The views of many other chief economists also are sought by the media, particularly by the twenty-four-hour television news channels. They all take turns. There is now an event, held every year, in which all chief economists from the banks participate in a round table at the Economic Club of Canada and share their thoughts and advice on the state of the Canadian economy. The event is widely reported in the media, and both federal and provincial governments take full note of the advice given, and in some cases senior ministers publicly respond to it.[42]

The Department of Finance now has to contend with a new voice that is perhaps even more challenging in the eyes of some than that of bank economists – the parliamentary budget officer. As we saw earlier, Harper made a commitment while in opposition to establish a parliamentary budget officer to ensure truth in budgeting. In introducing the legislation, the government declared that it sought to "ensure truth in budgeting by creating the position of Parliamentary Budget Officer to provide objective analysis to Members of Parliament and parliamentary committees concerning the state of the nation's finances, trends in the national economy, and the financial cost of proposals under consideration by either House."[43] The message could not have been lost on Finance officials – they are incapable of speaking truth in budget matters or at least need help to do so.

The idea of a parliamentary budget officer no doubt made sense while in opposition; it spoke to greater transparency and accountability. There is evidence, however, that Harper has had a change of mind since coming to power. Kevin Page, the newly appointed budget officer, was quick off the mark and received plenty of media coverage when he reported that the Afghan war would cost Canadians $18.1 billion by 2011 and projected substantial government deficits in the years ahead.[44] Harper probably now believes that while in government he does not need a parliamentary budget officer to ensure whatever truth in budgeting the government requires. Senator Noel Kinsella, a close ally of Harper, publicly argued that the budget officer was "exceeding his mandate" and called on the Library of Parliament "to rein him in with an appropriate accountability and operating framework." But Harper's decision while in opposition speaks to the philosophy of what matters is what works. He saw an opportunity to score political points at the time and paid little attention to the impact on the country's political and administrative institutions. Nor did he make any effort to clarify how the new office would fit in the existing constitutional framework.[45]

The Department of Industry used to be the "go to" department for anyone in government, including ministers, when seeking information on the state of the Canadian business community. This is no longer so. Industry Canada must now share the stage not only with a host of research institutes and think tanks but also with several government agencies. Every Canadian region, including southern Ontario since 2009, has its own federal regional economic development agency with its head office located at the regional level. When senior government officials want a sense of what the business community thinks, many now go to the regional agencies rather than to Industry Canada, with its very limited regional presence. The regional economic agencies must in turn share the stage with public opinion surveys, research institutes, and think tanks with close ties to the business world.

Industry Canada today is no different from other federal departments. Like Foreign Affairs, it has lost its standing and no longer speaks with its former authority. It is simply one of the many departments and agencies trying as best they can to influence Ottawa's elaborate formal policy and decision-making process.

The Privy Council Office dominates the Ottawa system in ways that would have been unthinkable forty years ago, and all departments follow its lead. It has become the "go to" agency for everything that truly matters. Gordon Robertson wrote in 1971 that sixty-eight officers worked with him in the PCO when he was the clerk. He said that the PCO should operate on the basis of a few important principles and that an important one was that the office should be kept deliberately small. One of the "other principles" Robertson cited was "staying off the field" by always remembering that "it is the minister who is responsible and his department that acts."[46] Robertson, like one of his predecessors, Arnold Heeney, saw the focus of his role and functions more properly tied to the Cabinet than to the prime minister. For Robertson, the job of clerk of the privy council and secretary to the cabinet was precisely as named – secretary to the cabinet – and not a "kind of political fixer for the prime minister."[47] One recently retired federal deputy minister explains, "Robertson would walk around with his letter of resignation if the Prime Minister or Cabinet pushed him too hard in a direction that was not acceptable. Now, the clerk walks around with every deputy minister's letter of resignation in his pocket."[48]

Today, there are about a thousand officials working in the PCO. Beginning with Michael Pitfield under Trudeau and gaining speed with Paul Tellier under Mulroney, the PCO made the transition from an office primarily concerned with the smooth running of cabinet government to one primarily concerned with supporting the prime minister. With the possible exception of Gordon Osbaldeston, no cabinet secretary since Robertson has sought to describe his or her job as secretary to the cabinet. As far back as 1987 the PCO produced a document on its role and structure, whose very first page makes it clear that the secretary's first responsibility is to the prime minister. It states that the clerk of the privy council and secretary to the cabinet has three primary responsibilities, the first being, "as the Prime Minister's Deputy Minister," to provide "advice and support to the Prime Minister on a full range of responsibilities as head of government, including management of the federation."[49]

Tellier's decision to add the title "Prime Minister's Deputy Minister" to his job and to declare that he was the prime minister's deputy minister simply reflected the reality of his day-to-day work. The secretary to the cabinet is accountable to the prime minister, not to Cabinet, and the great majority of his daily activities are now designed to support the prime minister, not the Cabinet. The prime minister, not the Cabinet, appoints the clerk of the privy council and secretary to the cabinet; the prime minister, not the Cabinet, evaluates the clerk's performance; the prime minister, not the Cabinet, will decide if he or she stays or should be replaced; and the prime minister, not the Cabinet, will decide if he or she will receive a plum foreign posting after serving as clerk. All this is to say that not only does the secretary to the cabinet wear the hat of deputy minister to the prime minister, but it is without doubt the hat that fits best and the one he or she wears nearly all the time. A former senior PCO official observed that "all clerks since Pitfield have done an excellent job at being deputy minister to the prime minister. As far as secretary to the Cabinet, the performance has been spotty."[50]

Officials who work in the PCO are now perceived as *la crème de la crème* of the Canadian public service, much as officials in the old Department of External Affairs were regarded some thirty years ago. Unleashing a thousand officials, with no program responsibility of their own to keep them busy, on the government's policy-making process and departments is not without far-reaching consequences. This thousand-strong group will want to stake a claim on power and influence, and there is only so much of it to go around within the federal government.

Many will be on the lookout to exert influence in the name of the clerk or the prime minister, hoping thereby to gain visibility in the system and make a name as a rising star. It is no coincidence that a great majority of appointments at the deputy minister level are now drawn from the PCO. It is difficult to become a star in a line department when all line departments and agencies look alike and all have lost standing in the system.[51]

The Public Service

It seems, as one senior public servant in Ottawa commented, that individual public servants have influence but the public service does not.[52] No one these days sings the praise of government bureaucracies. The Canadian public service has come under heavy criticism, even from quarters that in the past had been supportive.[53] Kevin Lynch, former clerk of the privy council and secretary to the cabinet under Stephen Harper, decided to speak out on the issue. He wrote, "Today, there seems to be increasing skepticism and negative rhetoric towards our public institutions in Canada, including the public service."[54] Canadian public servants can take some comfort in that this situation has been evident throughout the Western world for the past thirty years.

The Canadian public service has been torn off its moorings by several important developments. For one thing, there has been a significant loss in confidence. One can also detect major shifts in relations between politicians and public servants. The latter are less assertive in their dealings with politicians, notably ministers, than was the case thirty or forty years ago. Indeed, many senior officials have accepted as valid the criticism that they held too much influence over policy operations.[55]

There is also evidence that career officials are less assertive on the operations side. The presence of ministerial exempt staff is more tolerated in government operations than it was even twenty-five years ago. Access to information legislation and the media have made government operations and programs more sensitive to politics and political direction. Exempt staff want to get to the bottom of any potential news story so as to brief the minister and possibly the PMO on its development and political implications. Going up through the traditional bureaucratic channels to the deputy minister and then to the minister and the PMO will no longer do – that takes time, and the media won't wait.

Many officials have no objection to exempt staff being present in government operations because they agree that matters that have become issues of partisan controversy are not appropriate for formal briefings, and they welcome any opportunity to isolate themselves from the partisan political process. In any event, in many instances it is better for them to have exempt staffers brief the PMO than to do it themselves.

A senior Treasury Board Secretariat official reports that in the 2008 estimates, someone from a minister's office contacted him to have a graph removed from the departmental estimates. The graph, the ministerial staffer explained, showed that the department was receiving less funding than the previous year, which could suggest that the minister was not strong. The Treasury Board Secretariat responded, "It's your budget, we will take the graph out," though the relevant information would of course remain.[56]

Things were different twenty years ago. I put the above scenario to a retired deputy minister and former Treasury Board Secretariat official to see how he would have responded. He replied, "In those days, we would have told the staffer not to talk to us at the Board but to deal with his deputy minister. The deputy minister would have said no. If he did not say no, the Board would certainly have said no to the deputy minister, which would then have enabled him to say no." He added, "Things have changed for the worse."[57]

Notwithstanding their desire to avoid political controversies and to be anonymous, career officials have, as noted earlier, become more visible since the early 1980s. The *Globe and Mail*, the *National Post*, the *Toronto Star*, the *Ottawa Citizen*, and *La Presse*, as well as national television networks, all have staff members who report on major public service appointments and promotions. The clerk of the privy council now appears in public at least once a year to table the report on the state of the public service. The growing emphasis on consultation and partnerships in developing and implementing government programs also compels career officials to negotiate directly with interest groups and all types of "stakeholders." Paul Thomas maintains that "these trends have not brought us to the point where public servants are recognizable household names, but they are better known ... and interested members of the public are better able today to identify the occupants of important positions within the bureaucracy and may even feel confident in attributing certain policy perspectives to such individuals."[58]

Becoming better known outside government changes the nature of the work of senior public servants. The risk, of course, is that they will acquire a public personality and be dragged into political debates by the media and opposition parties, which can make public servants cautious in their work. This, combined with several other factors, explains why the public service's influence over policy has waned in recent years. Kevin Lynch acknowledged as much when he reported that governments have successfully used expert panels "on a wide variety of structural issues" and now increasingly look to "independent, non-governmental think tanks" for policy advice.[59]

There are still other factors at play. Bureaucracy bashing has taken a toll. Public servants have, to some extent, been deliberately pushed aside by politicians on policy issues. Quite apart from having access to many research institutes and think tanks, prime ministers and ministers have enlarged their own offices with partisan advisers while directing public servants to focus more and more on management. There are now more than five hundred politically partisan advisers and assistants in Ottawa, and some of them have more influence with their ministers than senior public servants.[60]

A number of public servants, particularly the ambitious ones, have acknowledged that they have not been sufficiently responsive in promoting the government's agenda for change. This has given rise to what Peter Aucoin calls "a promiscuously partisan public service" in Canada.[61] The point is that senior public servants have a choice – embrace the government's political and policy agenda or lose any influence in shaping policy. Jean Chrétien said as much in his memoirs when he wrote that he wanted to see deputy ministers as "allies" and that it was important to keep a tight control of the deputy ministerial appointment process because otherwise the "elected government would not be in charge of running anything."[62]

The Canadian public service, like other public services in the Western world, continues to suffer from a serious morale problem. Recent surveys reveal that morale is not improving, notwithstanding new reformed staffing initiatives.[63] Several reasons have been advanced to explain the problem. Some argue that governments have become "both highly centralized and highly politicized in their media management, which has left public servants on the outside looking in as key decisions are being made."[64] Others maintain that public servants have lost much of their policy advisory role and spend too much time searching for a new viable role.[65] Others argue that the traditional bargain, which in the past guided the relationship between politicians and public servants, has come unglued.[66] Still others maintain that bureaucracy bashing has forced public servants to circle the wagons and assume a defensive posture in relation to politicians, the media, and the public precisely at a time when they needed to be more aggressive.[67] Whatever the reason, the current Canadian public service as an institution pales in comparison to its glory days, when it held the respect of a great majority of Canadians from the Second World War to the early 1970s.[68] The solution, for senior bureaucrats at least, is to celebrate individualism over the institution. Jocelyne Bourgon, former clerk of the privy council and head of the public service, said as much when she wrote, "The only response to real change is – is it working for me, does it change my life, does it make me more effective, does it get the job done?"[69]

Governments have recognized the problem and have, over the past thirty years or so, introduced a variety of reform measures. Some have been high-profile initiatives, notably Public Service 2000 (PS 2000). The effort was highly ambitious and included 300 recommendations which sought to promote "trust and confidence in a non-partisan, objective and professional public service."[70] There have been other attempts at reform, including numerous external and internal exercises.[71] No one believes that any of these attempts, including PS 2000, have met with much success. Even Paul Tellier, the main architect of PS 2000, publicly "laments its failure and blames the bureaucracy."[72]

Looking Back

Parliament, the Cabinet, government departments, and the public service no longer enjoy the kind of support and credibility that they once did, and they are also less institutionalized. Where do loyalties now lie? The role of senior public servants increasingly consists of packaging for the prime minister and some ministers advice they receive from a variety of sources, including partisan advisers, consultants, research institutes, academics, and citizen groups. For public servants, loyalty is at best divided between government departments, policy networks, the government of the day, and their own career interests.

Bureaucracy has a bad name even in the eyes of those who lead it, such as Tellier. When generals start shooting at their own troops, people either run for cover or "look out for number one." There is evidence of both approaches in the federal public service. If loyalty is divided, the ability to influence government policy and program must be ad hoc. It always depends: on the individuals, on the circumstances, on the need to respond to media reports, on the wishes of prime ministers and their courtiers, and on one's ability to plough through what has become a cumbersome and slow government policy- and decision-making process. This suggests that power and influence are increasingly personalized. Personalization does not end there. We see it at the political level with party leaders dominating their parties. Parliament, political parties, government, and hierarchical departments have all lost standing at the expense of personalism. It seems that only individuals, not institutions or even organizations, can now drive change.

In brief, we have witnessed in recent years the fall of formal politics and the rise of informal politics. Informal politics enable privileged individuals to grab the levers of power all too often, leaving others, along with institutions, organizations, and formal processes, standing on the outside looking in.

10 LOOKING TO PERSONALISM FOR ANSWERS

The Bernie Madoff scandal on Wall Street speaks to our time. Madoff's reputation was such that individuals and foundations lined up to see if he would agree to invest their money. His strong personal reputation gave him the ability to pick and choose who was worthy of his knowledge and his ability to generate above average returns. The lucky ones got in, or so they thought. The Madoff name became synonymous with solid investments, and few it seems ever bothered to carry out due diligence. The Madoff name apparently was all that was needed, and if Madoff had your money, you could count on his personal reputation to generate a healthy return on your investment.

Institutions and organizations have processes, transparency, and re-porting requirements to respect, but individuals much less so. Madoff was able to get away with things that large commercial banks, for example, or even investment firms would not have been able to do because of transparency and reporting requirements to shareholders. Globalization, new transparency requirements, the need to network to operate in most sectors, and the interdependent nature of the public policy process, among other factors, have made many of our institutions and organizations, particularly in the public sector, much more cautious. They have also made them more cumbersome, complex, and slow at a time when we value quick responses and have a bias for action. In brief, it has become more difficult for large organizations, particularly in the public sector, to generate decisions. This has been true everywhere, and Canada is no exception.

The decline of deference in society has brought in its wake impatience with institutions and organizations. We want action, change, decisions, and above all success, however defined, and we want them quickly and with minimum fuss. A consensus has emerged that institutions, large businesses, government departments and agencies, and elaborate decision-making processes, overlaid with various transparency requirements, are no longer up to the task. The government bureaucracy had become too thick, too encumbered with reporting requirements and oversight bodies, and too dependent on networks of political and policy advisers, for it to be bold, to change course quickly, and to keep up with a fast-paced changing world. As a result, we concluded that what was needed were powerful individuals capable of introducing and driving change – this at a time when individual autonomy came into fashion as we began to favour the attributes of the individual over those of the community.

To be sure, organizations still matter a great deal as a source of power. Stephen Harper has power because he is the head of government in Canada. The day he returns to private life, his power will be transferred to someone else. But while he sits in the prime minister's chair, he – like his predecessors, from Trudeau to Martin, provided they had a majority mandate – can exercise power and all but ignore institutions, organizations, and processes. Organizations also have lost power and influence, as outlined in earlier chapters. In some ways, organizations, particularly public-sector ones but also some in the private sector, have essentially become long shadows of the powerful individuals who lead them.

There are, however, organizations that still exude power, if only because they have been more successful than others at retaining a coherent purpose and a hierarchy to deliver it. I am thinking of the military, and here the exception proves the rule. The internal structure of other organizations, from political parties to government departments and large corporations, lacks the kind of hierarchy, discipline, and cohesion found in the military, and as a result they have seen their influence and power wane.

This book makes the case that organizations are no longer the ultimate source of power, as Charles E. Lindblom once insisted.[1] What we now have is more of a movable feast linked to individuals rather than to institutions, organizations, and processes. Personalism is now the key to understanding where both power and influence are located and who has it. When things truly matter to those with political and economic power, they will push aside institutions, organizations, and formal processes to get the job done. As we noted earlier, Canada's central bank may well have violated its own act to put in place measures to deal with the 2008 financial crisis. It will also be recalled that Paul Volcker, former US Federal Reserve chairman, said that the Fed's decision to come to the rescue of Bear Stearns went to "the very edge of Fed's lawful and implied powers."[2]

The rise of personalism was brought home when President Obama appointed Richard Holbrooke his special representative to Afghanistan and Pakistan in early 2009. The two countries pose particularly difficult problems for the United States – both have unstable governments, highly effective insurgents, corruption, the Taliban, a deep resentment of the United States, and, presumably, Osama bin Laden. The inherent problems are much too important for the State Department to handle, hence the call to Holbrooke. Powerful individuals are needed to handle the most vexing problems because organizations are no longer up to the task. Holbrooke has been described by a colleague as "the diplomatic equivalent of a hydrogen bomb." General Wesley K. Clark claims that "Richard Holbrooke sees power the way an artist sees color."[3] This eloquently speaks to personalism. Imagine an abstract painting with powerful points of colour largely unrelated to one another and one can imagine where power now lies.

Government organizations no longer command the respect and influence they once did. They have been discredited as slow, costly, and ineffective, which explains the popularity in Western countries of public-private partnership arrangements, contracting-out, and privatization. No less revealing is the ability of individual public servants to shine, to be praised by the government of the day, and to go on to highly successful careers in the private sector.[4] In other words, while bureaucracy as an organization is no longer up to the task, some individual public servants are.

The widely held perception that Lee Iacocca single-handedly saved Chrysler from bankruptcy in the early 1980s also had a strong impact on the business community. Above all, it spoke to personalism in the private sector. If Iacocca could rescue Chrysler from certain bankruptcy, the solution for other firms experiencing economic difficulties was to find a leading executive, a star, to lead the way to recovery. Bill Gates, Warren Buffett, Steve Jobs, and Richard Branson, among many others, have since become household names and stars of the private sector. It seems that these individuals – not the organization's management teams – explain the success of their firms. Contrast this to the situation thirty or forty years ago when, in the eyes of the public at least, the pillars of the private sector were less personalities and more chief executive officers of management teams of large corporations, from General Motors to IBM. If the private sector could embrace personalism as a legitimate source of power, political leaders asked, why not government? Earlier chapters, as well as much of the public administrative literature over the past twenty years or so, have reported on the tendency of government to borrow and adapt management practices from the business community. It was in the interests of political leaders to have their governments emulate the private sector in this as in other things – get things done by having powerful individuals lead the way.

The military has been able to retain cohesion, hierarchy, and its internal power structure because it has retained clarity of purpose, for which submission from those in its ranks is obligatory. The structure of Canada's military mission in Afghanistan is clear, and there is no need for elaborate processes and networks of one kind or another to sort out who should do what. No one is suggesting that we should replace or even adjust hierarchy and the command-and-control model in the Canadian military. In addition, partisan political advisers are far more reluctant to interfere in military operations and even in the Department of National Defence than in other policy fields.[5] That said, General Rick Hillier exhibited signs of personalism as chief of staff between 2005 and 2008. The straight-talking soldier became a media star, often seen on the evening news pushing the government to give more resources to the military. The media reported that he "waged an all-out campaign" to win "the hearts and minds of Canadians."[6]

The more diverse the purpose or purposes of an organization, the less it can generate power and impose it externally and gain submission from within. Leaving aside the military, it is difficult to identify any government department that has clarity of purpose in a world of horizontal or joined-up government where a multitude of outside actors, from research institutes, think tanks, and consultants to a growing number of oversight bodies and partisan political advisers, have carved out a role for themselves. Internal discipline has also been made more difficult by various transparency measures. As many have already argued, networking has to some extent replaced hierarchy in both the public and the private sector.[7] The business model of large global firms now relies on elaborate networks to produce and market products.[8] This study has reported the extent to which networking has become an important part of governing. Networks, however, can never be as effective and decisive as hierarchy – hence the growing reliance on powerful individuals to get things done.

In this chapter, in looking for where power is located and who has it, we attempt to answer the questions posed in the introductory chapter. We argue that we now need to look to personalism to gain insight into the location of power. Personalism refers to loyalty to individuals rather than to institutions, organizations, processes, and rules.[9] To be sure, successful leaders throughout history have always commanded tremendous loyalty from their followers, and one could make the case that personalism is hardly a new development. The difference today is that personalism permeates institutions, organizations, and processes to the point that it has, to some degree, replaced hierarchy in the interest of getting things done and achieving the desired results sought by powerful personalities. In brief, loyalty today is to individuals more than to institutions, organizations, and formal processes.

Personalism

Evidence of personalism is everywhere in the private and public sectors. Henri-Paul Rousseau became a star in the private sector in the 1990s and was asked to lead Quebec's Caisse de dépôt et placement. His strong reputation and powerful personality were such that the organization cut him all the slack he wanted. He took counsel from statistical models and invested heavily in asset-backed commercial paper. The Caisse lost a considerable amount of money, at least $5 billion by one count, but by the time the losses rolled in, Rousseau had left the organization.[10]

In the public sector, Vladimir Putin has taken personalism to the extreme. Russia's President Dmitry Medvedev's constitutional supremacy means very little in reality because Putin continues to rule in the name of "directed democracy." Aurel Braun put it well when he wrote, "Far from institutionalizing decision-making and engendering a true succession, Mr. Putin seems bent on making himself the one indispensable ruler."[11]

We saw in earlier chapters that personalism is also evident in Canada's public sector. We can start at the very top in government, where everything revolves around the prime minister or the clerk of the privy council, particularly when it comes to loose power – power that has not drifted up to regional trade agreements or down to provincial governments and others. We also see evidence of personalism in Canada's business community, in the media, and in political parties. People have an increasing sense that they work more for an individual than for an organization. Deputy ministers in Ottawa, for example, have much stronger loyalty to the prime minister than to their own ministers and departments, and in turn ministers have far stronger loyalty to the prime minister than to one another.[12]

When leaders want advice or to have something accomplished, they often turn to a champion, a policy tsar or a high-profile consultant, a well-known academic, or a think tank. Organizations, particularly in the public sector, meanwhile, are allowed to run on their tracks, to deliver ongoing programs and services. Put differently, government departments and agencies can be trusted to collect taxes and deliver relatively routine programs and services such as transfer payments to individuals, or passports. However, for other initiatives – from shaping a new policy or developing a special initiative to delivering something new or different that truly matters to the powerful – things are turned over to a tsar, a champion, or an ad hoc group of one kind or another to get things done.

Shortly after Barack Obama was sworn in as the forty-fourth president of the United States, a debate surfaced in the media on the merits of his economic stimulus package. David Gergen, a well-known political commentator and adviser to former presidents, both Republican and Democratic, insisted that the package would not work unless Obama appointed a "tsar" to make certain that it was planned and delivered properly.[13] He, like many others, concluded that the relevant government department or agency was simply not up to the task.

Policy tsars are in vogue on both sides of the Atlantic Ocean. Among others, the United States government has a "drug tsar" and a "cyber security tsar," while the British government has a "behaviour tsar" and a "children's tsar." Tsars are high-profile individuals widely known for their ability to get things done. David Gergen suggested that Obama appoint Jack Welch as the economic stimulus tsar. Sir Alan Steer, who was appointed "the behaviour tsar" in Britain to combat antisocial behaviour in schools, is described as "the kind of man who, when he enters a room, everybody knows he is there."[14] When the US auto sector hit bottom in 2009, the media wondered why the president had "not yet appointed a car czar to oversee the sector's restructuring."[15] Obama later appointed Steven Rattner, a Wall Street veteran, as his auto tsar.[16]

Canada has "champions" rather than "tsars," but they perform the same role. The Canadian government has in recent years appointed "champions" inside government to promote "official languages," "values and ethics," "clean air," and so on. On 21 January 2009, the Harper government appointed yet another champion, this time to promote public-private partnerships in further developing the country's infrastructure. The government explained that it had decided to install a champion because it wanted to look for "innovative ways of doing public-private partnerships."[17] No government department, it seems, was up to the job.

One can only conclude that when things truly matter to the political leader or when the issue requires special attention because of its priority status, things have to be turned over to a tsar or a champion; that is, the attention of presidents and prime ministers, together with their designated tsars or champions, is required to make things happen. Failing that, experience tells them that things will all too often grind to a halt.

The private sector has, as already noted on several occasions, greatly influenced the behaviour of the public sector, particularly since the early 1980s. A widely held consensus emerged that the business community had a great deal to offer to governments – it knew how to move quickly in an increasingly fast-paced world, and its management techniques were far superior to those of government. Even left-of-centre politicians believed in the merits of the private sector over government. We noted earlier that Tony Blair, shortly after coming to power, tabled a major statement on modernizing government, lamenting the fact that some parts of the public sector were not as efficient and dynamic as the private sector – this after eleven years of Thatcher reforms designed to make the public sector look more like the private sector. Blair outlined the reasons for still more reforms, including departments and agencies that tended to look after their own interests, inertia, a focus on inputs rather than results, risk aversion, poor management, and low morale stemming from the denigration of public servants.[18] Blair made it clear, time and again, that the private sector was the key to improving management in government.

Personalism became the answer because political leaders gave up on a fundamental reform of political institutions and the machinery of government, a move that would entail plenty of risks. For one thing, there would have been no guarantee of success. For another, a fundamental rethink might have stripped them of some of their power. It is difficult to imagine a genuine shift that would leave their levers of power intact, let alone create new ones for them. For yet another reason, senior public servants were in no mood to overhaul the machinery in any basic fashion for fear that the change might be worse than the current arrangements and also might weaken the hand of the prime minister. It is in the interest of the clerk of the privy council to see that the prime minister firmly retains the key levers of power.

It will be recalled that Margaret Thatcher at first wanted to alter the doctrine of ministerial responsibility by introducing public-service reforms but then decided to leave things essentially intact. Though she was not known for turning once her mind was made up, she balked at the last minute on the advice of senior civil servants. Similarly, Stephen Harper attenuated some of his measures to strengthen accountability shortly after coming to power, also on the advice of senior public servants, those in the Privy Council Office. Jean Chrétien simply gave up on his efforts to introduce the accounting officer concept in Canada, again on the advice of senior public servants.[19] The result is that notions of ministerial and collective responsibility continue to cloud how decisions are really made in government, giving cover to both politicians and senior bureaucrats and allowing them to say, "I am responsible, but I am not to blame."[20]

In short, personalism enables political leaders to have their way without putting at risk their levers of power or those of their senior advisers. When there is the need to push aside thick bureaucratic requirements, policy networks, and interdepartmental considerations, they can designate someone close to them to take charge to ensure that things do not get bogged down. As for issues that do not hold much interest to prime ministers and their courtiers, the formal or traditional policy and decision-making process carries a number of advantages. It enables them to keep ministers and public servants busy turning cranks not attached to anything while they themselves pursue their policy agenda, deal with the pressures of the day, and manage the media and the permanent election campaign as best they can. It also ensures that only the powerful are permitted to take bold steps. As for the rest, the goal is to have departments, agencies, and programs run on their tracks.

What Matters Is What Works

Power brings its own rewards, and there is still never a shortage of people pursuing it. The difference is that institutions, organizations, and hierarchy now matter less in acquiring and exercising it. It appears that those who have it, those who pursue it, and those who exercise it subscribe to the view that "what matters is what works." It seems that institutions, organizations, and hierarchy can no longer deliver what those with power want. The powerful have concluded that they now need to overlay organizations with a regime of personalism, a regime that relies on creative personal interaction rather than on hierarchy.

Those with power turn to carrots and sticks, soft power, or whatever is required to deal with the situation at hand. Indeed, everything centres on the situation at hand. Again, what matters is what works. If institutions, organizations, and formal processes need to be put aside for any reason, so be it. The powerful will use the instruments of power that traditional processes offer if it suits them, but will just as easily put aside requirements that inhibit their ability to get things done. The powerful, having climbed to the top of their organizations, know that their time there is limited. During what could be a brief stay at the top, they want robust action on things that matter to them, and organizations are simply no longer able to respond adequately – hence the rise of personalism.

There are several other important factors that have given life to personalism. Modern communications, starting with television, invariably focus on the personal qualities of political or business leaders. It is very difficult for television cameras to give life to institutions or to formal decision-making processes. The main focus of election campaigns is selling party leaders before national television viewers and much less on local candidates and local events. Globalization also places a premium on the individual, on personalities and leadership, rather than on institutions and processes, if only because one has to respond quickly to rapidly changing circumstances and emerging opportunities. The dynamic element in the global economy is the individual, not countries, companies, or institutions.[21] In addition, as we saw in an earlier chapter, there are no global institutions or much in terms of formal processes to deal with global issues.

At the risk of sounding repetitive, political leaders, from both the right and the left, continue to look to the private sector for inspiration to modernize bureaucracy. The business world, which has long favoured individual efforts and the rugged adaptable entrepreneur, can show political leaders how to manage and to get things done. The bureaucracy, with its traditional reliance on hierarchy and formal processes, has never been able to duplicate how the private sector operates, despite the various reform measures of the past thirty years.

Attempts by all Anglo-American governments to introduce pay for performance for senior public servants speak to the desire to make the public sector look like the private sector. It also speaks to the inherent inability to make the public sector look like the private sector. No attempt to make pay for performance in government has been able to live up to expectations. The efforts have been described essentially as senior public servants writing letters to themselves or public servants marking their own exams.[22] The point is that the public sector can never look like the private sector unless one rips apart political institutions and the machinery of government and (assuming for a moment that this could ever be achieved), unleashes market forces in every corner of government to establish clearly who is good at doing what.

Political leaders for the most part continue to lament bureaucracy's inability to respond to their call for change. Bureaucracy bashing has not let up since the Thatcher days. In many ways, political leaders have given up on traditional institutions, organizations, and formal processes. They have turned to key individuals to implement the philosophy that what matters is what works to deal with a broad governance structure that is increasingly porous, slow, complex, and fragmented. As already noted, time is the rarest of commodities for prime ministers and the powerful, and they will always focus on issues that matter to them. Fixing bureaucracy does not rank high on their to-do list. Rather, they appoint partisan advisers to keep a careful eye on who makes it to the top of the public service, in order to ensure a degree of responsiveness to their agenda, and they leave much of the rest to the public service. The risk of leaving the public service to handle what does not rank at the top of their priority list is low because of bureaucracy's cautious nature.

Government bureaucracies have become too big to fail, so there is little political cost to the powerful in leaving well alone. Politicians and citizens know intuitively that the cost of government bureaucracy far exceeds its economic value. But trying to prove this is quite another matter, and doing something about it would divert political leaders from the issues and priorities that rank very high on their to-do list.

The public service has lost standing as an institution partly because public-service unions have made management much more difficult and government operations much too expensive. Students of government have not paid sufficient attention to the role unions have played in an organization that is not disciplined by market forces.[23] It is left to union representatives to push public servants as far as possible and for public servants and managers to push back as best they can. That said, public-service managers stand to gain when unions are able to secure more generous economic benefits in their negotiations with management. There is no economic discipline to establish clearly the optimal size of the public service, the social and pension benefits, the salary levels. It is simply left to a push-and-pull exercise, and all public servants have a vested interest in seeing more generous social benefits.

There is also plenty of evidence to suggest that public-sector managers are not able to deal with non-performers.[24] These public servants are left to their own devices, leaving managers with little choice but to ask for still more staff whenever new responsibilities or activities come their way.[25] Some large private-sector firms also may avoid dealing with non-performers. But there are limits – too many non-performers will inhibit a firm's ability to remain competitive in the global economy.

The above, together with the public service becoming just one voice among many in the policy advisory process, has enabled personalism to take root. Personalism holds considerable appeal for the powerful because it promises change, getting things done, and overcoming a lethargic bureaucratic machine. What matters is what works.

We saw personalism in full force in Canada between November 2008 and January 2009. It will be recalled that Harper's ill-timed economic statement, which called for doing away with public subsidies to political parties, led opposition parties to form a coalition in a minority Parliament and to try to defeat the government. Harper, sensing the danger, asked the governor general to prorogue Parliament, hoping that cooler heads on the opposition benches would prevail after several weeks away from Ottawa.

The media, some members of the academic community, and opposition parties questioned whether the governor general should have agreed to Harper's request to prorogue Parliament. Harper's inner circle, including John Baird, quickly swung into action. Baird mused publicly about bypassing the head of state if the governor general refused Harper's request. He said, "I think that what we want to do is basically take time out and go over the heads of the members of Parliament, go over the head, frankly of the Governor General, go right to the Canadian people."[26] Harper decided somehow that only voters could effect a change of government across party lines, a move that would take away Parliament's role in the formation of government. Harper never explained exactly how the electorate, rather than the governor general and the House of Commons, decides who governs.[27] For Baird and Harper, holding onto power was more important than respecting the constitutional power vested in the country's head of state. For

Harper and his courtiers, the governor general became little more than just another individual around whom one needed to work in order to hold onto political power.

They apparently saw no need to respect an institution that remains an important part of our constitution. They were also happy to ignore a fundamental constitutional principle in a Westminster-style parliamentary system: to govern, one needs the confidence of the House of Commons. Surely, they are well aware that there is no national vote for prime minister and one cannot simply sidestep the governor general and the House of Commons by appealing to public opinion. A leader who ignores institutions and their constraints on power also challenges their legitimacy.

The governor general agreed to Harper's request, and the coalition fell apart. The Liberal caucus, however, decided that something had to be done with its leader Stéphane Dion, who had lost to Harper in the October 2008 general election and also had lost the confidence of the parliamentary caucus. Liberal caucus members decided that it was imperative to replace Dion; they felt that he was hurting the party, and the polls suggested as much. Accordingly, personalism cuts both ways. Depending on the circumstances, it can strengthen or weaken the hand of individuals who have or aspire to power. Party strategists, the party's pollster, and Liberal MPs concluded that if a coalition was ever to be on the cards again, they did not think that Dion was up to the task. They managed to do away with a planned leadership convention and asked Michael Ignatieff to take over as leader.[28]

Harper, meanwhile, decided that party ideology or the party's policy preferences were less important than holding onto power. He and his minister of finance made it extremely difficult for the opposition parties to vote against the government by bringing down a carefully crafted budget that was highly interventionist and out of step with their party's philosophy. Within hours of the budget being tabled in the Commons, some high-profile Conservative commentators, who were out of reach of Harper's carrots and sticks, expressed their strong disenchantment with the budget. Tasha Kheiridin said, "It flies in the face of what the Conservative movement was hoping this government would achieve." Tom Flanagan, a former key Conservative campaign strategist, argued that the budget might "cause a number of party members to curtail donations," and Monty Solberg, a former Conservative cabinet minister, commented, "The Conservatives have easily escaped to fight another day, but what are they fighting for?"[29] Andrew Coyne wrote, "The Conservatives have not succeeded in replacing the Liberals. They have only succeeded in becoming them."[30]

To answer Solberg's question, the fight is about power, little else, and personalism trumps everything when it comes to acquiring and maintaining it. In less than three months, Canadians saw that the government was willing to go above the head of state to hold onto power and that the role of political parties had become virtually irrelevant on policy matters. The party leader and his or her court decides what the party's policies will be, and in the case of the Liberal Party, party members were even deprived of choosing their leader.

Canadians are increasingly coming to terms with the steady decline of political parties. Only 2 to 3 percent of Canadians belong to parties sitting in Parliament, and three well-known students of Canadian politics report that the average age of party membership is now over fifty years.[31]

The three-month period made the personification of politics complete, with political parties essentially left on the outside looking in, trying as best they could to figure out a role. It also brought to life once again the philosophy to governing encapsulated in "what matters is what works." Personalism now shapes what governments do, and as a result, governing is far more ad hoc than in the past. This has implications for the work of the media, in that ad hoc events offer them more to report on. In short, the pursuit of power in Canada has pushed political ideology, political parties, and policy debates to the background. What we are left with is partisan jockeying for position, with the media as the referee.

Partisanship today is not about ideology or even about debating policy options, it is about personalism. Political parties no longer get elected to make public policy; rather, a handful of individuals around party leaders craft political strategies and policy for the purpose of getting elected. In a political environment in which no one takes political parties seriously, there is little left to debate other than the personalities of party leaders and who has the sharper tongue to get the best ten-second clip on the evening television news.

The age-old debate among social scientists is whether institutions shape what individuals do or whether individuals shape how institutions decide. Institutions and organizations no longer determine much in real terms other than providing a setting for a handful of individuals to grab power and drive their agenda. When things really matter, prime ministers, their courtiers, and their policy tsars or champions have to take charge and drive initiatives through a process designed to make a mush of things. They are the only ones who can cut across organizations, establish support for their initiatives, and deal quickly with any political fallout from transparency requirements.

Fuzzy Boundaries Fuel Personalism

Don Kettl writes that the administrative orthodoxy of the twentieth century rested on establishing clear lines of responsibility and hierarchy.[32] We now have a fuzzy boundary problem, and hierarchy no longer works, certainly not to the extent that it did. Governments everywhere have been searching for ways to pull together resources, including people, money, and technology, to take on complex challenges. No government has been able to come up with the right formula to promote coordination and so, *faute de mieux*, we have relied on personalism to provide the necessary authority or power to push through to desired results.

We should never lose sight of the fact that Weber's work was essentially designed to answer the question, How best can we organize power? The traditional organizational model is today working under severe strain because activities are too complex to be delegated neatly into organizational boxes. Responsibilities now have to be shared to pursue any type of public policy objectives. Again, no government has been able to replace the traditional organizational model. Here, I can do no better than quote Kettl: "Public administration is built on the foundation of a theory of hierarchy and authority that is clear and straightforward, with a tradition that has continued for millennia. The actual work of public administration, however, has grown increasingly out of sync with the theory guiding it. As a result, public administration in theory and practice has sagged under the strain."[33] In the absence of a new theory, personalism has moved in to fill the void. When institutions, organizations, and formal processes lose relevance, power will find a home, and personalism is its new home.

But personalism is not without significant consequences for representative democracy. It is much more difficult to track power and influence under personalism than when it is housed in institutions and organizations. Personalism plays to the interests of the powerful by making the playing field even more uneven than in the past. Power is now mobile; it moves around among individuals, it can be traded, bought, and sold.

The economically powerful will connect with the politically powerful. But even if they are not able to connect directly, they can now hire lobbyists to do it for them. Well-funded interest groups can also gain or buy access or can finance a research project with a think tank or research institute to make their case before the politically connected or the media. Ordinary citizens, meanwhile, must rely on their MPs, but as this and other studies make clear, MPs have seen their role marginalized in recent years. Polls do matter to those in power, but they cannot replace political parties in their ability to shape public policy debates and decide how best to manage regional tensions or other cleavages in Canadian society. Political parties are or should be the "gatekeepers of civic life," and their role is or should be to organize political choices and coherence in a representative democracy.[34]

So Where Is Power and Who Has It?

Power today is more fluid and transient than at any time in the past. Personalism can never house power with the same degree of stability as institutions, organizations, and formal processes, and power in the hands of an individual can be fleeting. For generations, public servants in Ottawa or in provincial capitals could look to the Departments of Finance, External Affairs, or Industry when looking to locate power. They now have to look elsewhere. Some deputy ministers of finance can wield a great deal of power by virtue of who they are or because of their relations with the clerk of the privy council and their standing in the prime minister's court. However, some deputy ministers of finance or foreign affairs in recent years have had limited influence, less than their predecessors, because they do not enjoy much standing in government circles.

Those wishing to locate power now need to look beyond organizations, organizational charts, institutions, and formal processes. They need to look to networks, lobbyists, key personalities in the private sector and government, key actors in the global economy and in the media. In short, they need to look to personalism for answers.

Personalism favours the powerful and special interests with financial resources because it allows them to operate under different rules from everybody else. We have made our institutions and organizations so interdependent that key political, business, and bureaucratic leaders have decided that the only way to pursue their objectives successfully is to push them aside or, better yet, simply ignore formal processes and get on with the task at hand. No one else is able to do this. The powerful know who they are and, whenever the need arises, will engage in power swaps. They will connect directly or through hired hands to share information and pursue their agenda. In the process, institutions and organizations have been disempowered. They are trapped in a complex web of relations, transparency requirements, and developments in the global economy. In brief, they are unable to keep pace with the incessant pressure for change, with the need to react quickly to meet the demands of the day.[35]

In some sense, institutions and organizations have given up. One of Parliament's main responsibilities is to hold the government to account. It has essentially turned over this responsibility to a still growing number of officers of Parliament and to the media. But they can never perform the function as well as Parliament because they do not have the political legitimacy. We have somehow collectively lost sight of the fact that officers of Parliament are supposed to be there to support Parliament, not the other way around.

Cabinet is no longer performing its role of formulating the government's political and policy agenda, nor is it willing to assume collective responsibility for its development. It has largely abandoned its responsibilities to prime ministers and their courtiers. Political parties have, in turn, abandoned their policy-setting agenda, integrating diverse societal interests into a broad coalition to pollsters, professional political consultants, and other close advisers to party leaders.

The public service as an institution has been battered about by politicians, the media, and academe, with the result that its self-confidence has plummeted. It has not been able to take stock of its own weaknesses in order to work with political leaders to heal itself. The institution has lost confidence in its abilities, convinced that it has become misunderstood by everybody, starting with politicians, those it has the responsibility to support. There is plenty of evidence that it has lost a great deal of its policy-advisory role to partisan political advisers and outsiders. The well-known political commentator and pollster Allan Gregg insists that the government has "pushed the bureaucracy out of the decision-making loop and the bureaucracy is not coming forward unprompted with new ideas."[36] Those looking to locate influence and power need not look for very long to the public service as an institution. They should, however, still look to individual public servants, notably, clerks of the privy council and other members of the prime minister's court.

Institutions that are less political, however, have gained influence in recent years. The courts and officers of Parliament, unelected and largely unaccountable bodies, have been able to carve out an influential role, adapting better to changing circumstances and increasing their relevance. The courts can strike a decision without paying much attention to the interdependence of policy issues, policy networks, and oversight bodies. Their ability to establish a clear decision whenever they are asked is in sharp contrast to policy issues that are handled by the formal government policy- and decision-making processes.

But the courts and officers of Parliament have important limits. They lack political legitimacy, and when all is said and done, they are accountable to no one other than themselves. Officers of Parliament can bark all they want, but they have no bite. Good governance is about making difficult choices between competing demands, establishing an accountability regime that works, and having a process in place to arrive at a level of policy coherence that speaks to the interest of the wider community. This calls for political institutions, organizations, and formal decision-making processes that properly house power and influence and provide access for all citizens to see how decisions are taken and to be involved to the extent they want to be in shaping public policy. Personalism falls far short on this score. Our political institutions have come off their moorings, enabling personalism to take root.

Bertrand Russell maintains that governing has always involved inequalities of power.[37] The difference is that personalism gives those who have power still more opportunities to expand their reach. It also raises important issues of legitimate versus illegitimate kinds of power in a representative democracy.

11 THE SETTING OR
THE INDIVIDUAL?

Social scientists and students of government have been struggling with the question: When it comes to power, is it the setting or the individual that most matters? Traditional institutionalists have considered a country's constitution and its formal institutions to be the answer. But as far back as 1953, David Easton challenged this view, claiming that they had been largely superseded and that what truly counts now are such things as interest group activities and voting. The debate has intensified in recent years, with the rise of rational choice theory and new institutionalism.[1]

This study challenges the notion that the institution shapes the behaviour of individuals. We have seen the opposite in practice: powerful leaders and their close advisers have changed the behaviour of institutions. The Canadian Parliament, the Cabinet, and Ottawa's policy- and decision-making processes look vastly different today from forty years ago because powerful individuals took advantage of changing sociopolitical and economic circumstances to strengthen their own hands. As a result, scholars can now achieve greater analytic leverage by looking to individuals rather than institutions.[2]

Institutionalists speak to the traditional aspects of government: laws, the machinery of government, and formal processes designed to generate policy decisions.[3] In brief, they speak to what Americans call a "government of laws and not of men." Rational choice theorists, meanwhile, take a very different tack, arguing that individuals act essentially as autonomous actors, thus reducing collective behaviour to individual behaviour. The fundamental assumption of rational choice theorists is that individuals will inevitably seek to maximize their own self-interest.[4]

Where does personalism fit in this debate? To be sure, many of the findings of this study speak of the importance of individual behaviour. We have seen that political parties, organizations, and even formal processes are increasingly used by individuals to gain power and influence, not to promote collective decisions. Many now believe that formal institutions and processes serve no other purpose than to assist a handful of individuals to position their dots on the canvas of an abstract painting to gain power and influence. How the individual dots relate to institutions or organizations is now secondary.

Several forces have shifted the location of power in recent years. Bureaucracy bashing (some of it well justified), the acceptance that private-sector management is superior to that found in the public sector, the emphasis on transparency, the rise of oversight bodies, and the apparent inability to make horizontal government work have all contributed. Add to this list developments in the global economy, the decline of political parties, the work of the new media, and the decline of "loose power" available to national governments. These have shifted power away from organizations in favour of the individual.

A new unwritten bargain has emerged between political leaders and public servants and between government and the business community. This bargain has considerably strengthened the hand of the powerful and placed virtually everyone else on autopilot or on the receiving end of whatever the powerful are prepared to allow them. Institutions, organizations, and formal processes can no longer cope with what today's world throws at them. Only those with power and influence are able to manipulate institutions, organizations and processes to pursue their agenda or simply to get things done.

The new bargain relies on both formal and informal structures, depending on the circumstances. It is left to key individuals to decide; consequently, institutions, organizations, and processes affect individual behaviour only if it is in the interest of powerful individuals for them to do so. The mantra "what matters is what works" speaks to the above. But only the most powerful political and policy actors are in a position to decide what matters and pursue what works.

In this concluding chapter, we seek to cast the findings of this study in a broader context. The purpose is to explore whether personalism can add to our understanding of politics and our political and administrative institutions. It also seeks to shed light on the question: When it comes to power, is it the setting or the individual that matters?

The Setting

The setting in this study is broadly defined, no doubt overly so to the specialists. To be sure, there are important differences between institutions, organizations, and formal policy- and decision-making processes. There is an extensive literature that points to sharp differences in institutions and in how we define them. B. Guy Peters provides an excellent survey of institutions and institutional theories.[5] Suffice it to note that Peters writes that rational choice analysis alone offers four alternative views of institutions and that W.R. Scott insists that "institutions consist of cognitive, normative and regulative structure and activities that provide stability and meaning to social behaviour."[6] We also know that organizations are task-oriented and that formal policy- and decision-making processes are designed to produce decisions in an orderly, predictable, and collective manner. The public administration community, meanwhile, has produced a number of insightful studies on organizational change and on various policy- and decision-making processes.[7]

Institutions, organizations, and formal policy- and decision-making processes have some things in common. At a minimum, the three provide the setting and rules under which individuals decide what, when, and how information is aggregated into collective decisions and who participates in making the decisions. The setting also provides for a common language shared by a community of individuals.[8] In short, the purpose of organizations is to shape policies and make decisions. The more important question for our purpose, then, is how institutions, organizations, and formal policy- and decision-making processes and individuals interact.

Starting with Trudeau and continuing to this day, prime ministers and their courtiers have essentially redefined the role of Cabinet, the public service, political parties, government departments and agencies, and whatever formal policy- and decision-making processes stand in the way of their getting things done. Power today is mobile; it moves around among individuals rather than among institutions or organizations. It seems that only powerful individuals can cope with what the world serves up. Whenever they have a priority to pursue or an issue to deal with, they deliberately bypass institutions and organizations, tasking a close adviser, a responsive senior bureaucrat, a champion, a tsar, to look after things. Even the demands of the day, let alone bold attempts, are turned over to key individuals. Institutions and organizations can no longer play their traditional role, and in the process they have lost their capacity to generate traditional patterns of behaviour. Moreover, they are not able to generate patterns of behaviour outside the philosophy of "what matters is what works."

Powerful individuals have a wide variety of instruments with which to get their way, instruments that rely mostly on themselves and their ambitions. The result is that it is increasingly difficult to link the behaviour of individuals to their institutions or organizations; indeed, one can no longer explain their behaviour by looking at the structure in which they function.[9] As we saw, deputy ministers in Ottawa, for example, no longer identify with their department. For one thing, they are no longer a product of their department. For the most part, they made it to the top through working in the Privy Council Office, not in the department to which they were appointed. For another, their next promotion depends on how well they are perceived by the prime minister's court. For yet another, the rise of horizontal government has shifted attention away from their respective departments. This alone has shifted power away from departments and redefined the role of deputy ministers.

The setting has also assisted powerful individuals who want to accrue still more power. Emulating the private sector led political leaders to telescope as much of the loose power available in national governments into their own offices. Business leaders, from Jack Welch to Bill Gates, came to embody personally the success of their firms. The perception, if not the reality, is that they provided the leadership to build successful firms or drive change through many obstacles. Henry Mintzberg went to the heart of the issue when he argued that companies are not being managed, they are being "led, heroically no doubt." He added, "We have America's problem in a nutshell; the utter absence of collective introspection."[10]

As we have seen, political leaders concluded that what worked in the private sector could be made to work in the public sector. Certainly, the various attempts to reform government operations during the past thirty years in Anglo-American democracies have essentially been attempts to make the public sector look like the private sector.[11] Political leaders saw no reason why they should not emulate high-profile private-sector executives in their efforts to drive change.

While the private sector was in the ascendancy and leading business executives were gaining a high public profile, political leaders had to come to terms with the fact that there was less loose power available to national governments than in years past. We saw earlier that regional trade agreements and the courts stripped Ottawa of some of its powers, and that the Supreme Court is now both a "court of law *and* a political court."[12]

The setting has also exposed the inability of institutions and organizations to cope with today's political and economic circumstances. Globalization, complex financial markets, and the new media are forcing governments to react quickly – or be perceived as not in control. Institutions and organizations that cannot provide answers within hours – if not minutes, in some cases – are regarded as out of step with today's political and economic environment. Key political leaders and their courtiers, meanwhile, are able to come up with answers quickly if they so wish by moving organizations and processes to one side.

At the very time that we placed a premium on quick responses and on the perceived need to embrace change in all things, we saddled institutions and organizations with transparency requirements and elaborate consultative processes. Meanwhile, policy makers made government thicker by sponsoring numerous research institutes and think tanks, all clamouring to play a role in shaping government policies and decisions. Nevertheless, we expect government bureaucrats to be able to react as quickly as their private-sector counterparts. This is simply not possible, given the porous and consultative processes they must work in, thus shifting power to individuals with the power to act.

The machinery of government has been made so complex that even those inside government have difficulty in establishing who is responsible for what.[13] The same can be said about much of the economic world and many public policy issues. They, too, have become far too complex for national institutions and organizations to accommodate. Alan Greenspan went so far as to suggest in his memoirs that "markets have become too complex for effective human intervention."[14] This again plays to the interests of powerful individuals who, if they so decide, can take charge and, with their peers in other countries and in the private sector, and with close advisers, move things forward. National political leaders can, conversely, let matters meander through the elaborate decision-making process and have their courtiers keep an eye on things so that what comes out at the other end is acceptable to them if to no one else.

Permanent election campaigns have also had a profound impact on political institutions and public organizations. Election campaigns and governing have merged into one in Canada and in other Western democracies. As Hugh Heclo writes, "The more that campaigning infiltrates into governing, the more we may expect the values of a campaign perspective to overrule."[15] The goal is to promote and protect individual political careers by engaging in ongoing battles for public approval. The focus is on the individual, not on political parties, institutions, or organizations; political parties have been all but pushed aside by professional political consultants, pollsters, and image makers. The political interests of party leaders are what matter, and if they come in conflict with institutions and organizations, these are pushed aside.

The strategic use of individuals and institutions, organizations, and decision-making processes by powerful actors has given rise to democratic elitism.[16] Political leaders have borrowed a page from the private sector in believing that what matters is what works and in stressing output efficiency. Political leaders pursue their own policy agendas whether or not these were part of previous election campaigns or even were known to their own party (see, among many other examples, Chrétien's decision to introduce the millennium scholarship program or Harper's efforts to eliminate public subsidies to political parties).

Participative democracy, collaborative government, and government-sponsored research institutes, think tanks, and interest groups have not made representative democracy work better. The fundamental principle of representative democracy – political equality – has been tossed out of the window. Non-elected individuals are able to access a handful of individuals with the power to introduce change and make it stick. The dehierarchization of government organizations and other developments, including the rise of public-private partnerships, also have made it extremely difficult for non-elites to locate power and responsibility or to influence public policy and government decisions. All of this says that representative democracy is on a slippery slope or, in the words of British MP Tony Wright, may be "slowly coming to an end."[17] New and demanding transparency requirements and various other efforts to modernize public administration have not improved things; if anything, they have revealed how serious the problem is.

However, one thing is clear: supporters of traditional institutions and organizations are losing ground to actor-centred institutionalism.[18] The power of institutions, organizations, and formal decision-making processes has given way to powerful individuals. This development, among others, has made it virtually impossible for many elected representatives, let alone ordinary citizens, to play any meaningful role in shaping public policies and government decision making or holding government officials to account.

The setting has also changed the internal structures and processes of long-established organizations, resulting in a number of government actors becoming agents without principals.[19] Members of Parliament and the general public are overloaded with information that can be bewildering. The Internet has not solved the problem. If anything, it has made the situation worse. The media, meanwhile, should be uncovering power relations and hidden policy agendas, but far too many journalists are engaged in gotcha journalism, where personalities and uncovering gaffes dominate their work. As we have seen, the media have limited resources to undertake comprehensive or serious reviews of policy issues. Politics has become more personalized, and political personalities have become yet one more voice in the media market. Individual politicians have become part of a nation's soap opera. One only has to remember Bill Clinton and his relationship with Monica Lewinsky for evidence of that.[20]

In an earlier chapter, we reported on the principal-agency theory and made the point that the principal does not know as much as the agent, even on the most important issues, and that the interests of the principal and the agent are often in conflict. The argument is that principals need full access to information to see how agents behave to ensure accountability.

In this study we saw that resistance to transparency requirements increases as one goes up the power ladder. The setting has changed with right or access to information legislation, but as we saw, the practical impact has been modest in terms of opening up government, particularly at the highest level. It has, however, made government thicker and has encouraged partisan political advisers to intervene at many levels in the bureaucracy. Protecting the interests of political leaders matters more than either transparency requirements or organizations.

This study suggests that the principal-agency theory has broken down at many levels. This and other studies show that Parliament has lost the ability to hold government and bureaucracy to account.[21] As we saw earlier, the chair of the Public Accounts Committee summed up the problem well when he challenged the government's financial officers to include blank pages in their various reports to Parliament to see if any MPs would notice. His view was that neither MPs nor anyone else, for that matter, would notice that something was amiss.

This, then, is the setting in which institutions and organizations operate and individuals interact with them. At the risk of sounding repetitive, it plays to powerful individuals, enabling them to move things out of the way in the interest of what works and also to strike a new bargain with the bureaucracy. Many ambitious senior public servants wish to demonstrate that they can be responsive to the more powerful politicians and their courtiers, and there is plenty of evidence that this is in fact taking place.[22] Here, the principal-agency arrangement works to some extent because it is in the interests of both parties to make it work and because the principal gets what he or she is after. Powerful political leaders get a responsive bureaucracy at the most senior levels, with senior bureaucrats willing to pursue the leaders' objectives and also to protect their political interests. Responsive senior public servants can rise to the top of the bureaucracy by embracing with enthusiasm the political and policy agenda of their political masters.

It is no exaggeration to write that personalism and recent efforts to reshape political and administrative institutions have enabled powerful individuals to pursue partisan and personal interests in ways that do not advance the public interest, promote good government, or encourage Canadians to join political parties and participate in shaping public policy. It is also not too much of an exaggeration to write that representative democracy is slowly being replaced by public opinion surveys, focus groups, pressure groups, lobbyists, and powerful individuals pursuing their own economic self-interest. In a representative democracy, the key role is the citizen, but we have not been able to define a role for citizens in the political process, including political parties.[23] Rather, citizens are left on the outside watching a game called politics on television screens and seeing an "overmighty executive" restrained only by unelected judges appointed by the prime minister and journalists working in an increasingly fragmented and competitive media.[24]

The skills of senior bureaucrats, especially at the deputy minister level, are now more akin to the skills of politicians than those traditionally found in bureaucracy. As we have seen, those who become deputy ministers are rarely the product of the department or agency they are being asked to head. More often than not, they are officials from the Privy Council Office, where they became known and appreciated by the prime minister's court. They became powerful individuals because they served in the prime minister's court with distinction and not because of the knowledge they may have of the department or the relevant sectors.

Their expertise is tied to their ability to sense a looming political crisis, determine what works and what will not, and knowing how to navigate the policy-making process, how to make things happen, how to strike deals at the interdepartmental level, and how to deal with the private sector or with groups operating outside government. They know when to initiate a project and when to hold back. These are skills that traditionally belong to politicians, especially cabinet ministers. Now they are necessary skills for public servants who wish to make it to the top of their profession.[25] Senior public servants also have to deal with the realization that it is considerably easier to speak truth when buttressed by formal processes and structures than it is to confront powerful individuals, whether the prime minister or the clerk of the privy council, particularly when it is these two individuals who decide who makes it to the top of the public service.

The above may well explain the fault line that now exists between the most senior levels of the Canadian public service and the rest of the public service. Below the fault line is where the principal-agency theory breaks down. However, the breakdown is, again, in the interests of the powerful individual or the principal. In exchange for letting the public service grow, for tolerating public servants being kept busy by turning cranks not attached to anything of consequence, for tolerating non-performers, and for rich employee benefits (notably, an extremely generous indexed pension plan in which taxpayers contribute close to $2 for every $1 the employee contributes), the principal can count on the public service for the following tasks: ensuring that departments and agencies run on their tracks; managing departments and their ministers so as to avoid political gaffes as best they can; staying out of the media to the extent possible; and managing an elaborate, porous, and complex interdepartmental process that generates decisions only when the most powerful individuals desire it.[26] The principal gets a safe pair of hands to ensure that things do not go off the rails, while the agent is left essentially unchallenged when it comes to his or her self-interest.

The cost of maintaining such a system intact is very high, but it speaks to the self-interest of all involved. For example, the cost alone of social benefits to federal public servants – which includes pension benefits, dental care, pensioners' dental care, and life insurance premiums – amounted to nearly $5 billion in 2008.[27] Study after study has revealed that, leaving aside the most senior executive levels, workers in the public sector command a 5 to 20 percent wage premium over private-sector workers.[28]

One can easily speculate that the public service is too big and too expensive, but how is one to know? Public servants are not about to admit this, and only a handful of politicians and their advisers are in a position to ask penetrating questions about the overhead costs of government and the tendency to avoid dealing with non-performers. It is a rare occurrence indeed for a federal public servant to be let go. In any given year, only between 20 and 104 public servants out of about 275,000 are dismissed for "incompetence" or "incapacity."[29] It is in everyone's personal interest to leave well alone. It helps certain individuals to retain power and rank-and-file public servants to operate with a minimum of questions being asked about their salaries, the size of the bureaucracy, fringe benefits, and the competence or performance of individuals.

The above again speaks to "what matters is what works" and the ascendancy of powerful individuals in shaping policies and introducing change. Globalization, the growing importance of the private sector, the new media, transparency requirements, the arrival of political consultants and courtiers, the decline of political parties, and the complex nature of public policies have enabled powerful individuals to move things aside in the interest of getting things done. Decisions that must rely on collective decision-making are increasingly being put off. Institutions, organizations, and formal processes can no longer cope with a setting that has altered power relationships substantially and has also shifted where power is located.

The Individual

Power today centres on the individual. Powerful individuals will want to telescope still more power into their own hands or offices because it is in their interest to do so, but also because the setting now allows it. We have in Canada a personal or elite democracy where it is believed that change must be pursued outside institutions, organizations, and formal policy-making processes if they are to have any chance of success. The power to introduce or promote change in government is increasingly in the hands of a small number of individuals, from prime ministers and their hand-picked courtiers to lobbyists, political consultants, heads of research institutes and think tanks, some journalists, and leading private-sector executives.

Less and less of what powerful individuals do is formalized by law, by institutions, and by formal processes. Statutes are now so broadly defined that individuals are able to manoeuvre almost at will in the pursuit of "what matters is what works." Powerful policy actors are prepared to pursue initiatives even if statutes do not allow them to do so. In the introductory chapter, we reported that Bank of Canada officials may have violated the Bank Act when they decided to expand the types of securities they would purchase in open-market operations. We also saw earlier that Paul Volcker said that the decision in the United States to rescue Bear Stearns went to "the very edge of the Fed's lawful and implied powers."[30]

Stephen Harper made it clear that he wanted his 2009 stimulus budget approved by Parliament in record time, by 27 May 2009. In explaining why the budget had to get through Parliament at "lightning speed," a spokesperson for the government pointed out that there had been "a lot of pre-budget consultations."[31] Parliament was asked to take a back seat to pre-budget consultations in approving the budget. Put differently, for Harper and his spokespersons, pre-budget consultations were as important as Parliament's responsibility to review the government's budget, if not more so.

Powerful individuals are increasingly able to isolate themselves from the constraints of institutions and organizations, though they continue to require others to respect them. Indeed, constraints are even more restricting today than in years past for all those with no access to powerful individuals.

Individuals, depending on where they sit in the power structure, react to institutions and organizations in different ways. The few with the necessary power can isolate themselves from the constraints of institutions, while the great majority cannot. Institutions, organizations, and self-interest still structure their behaviour.[32] Thus, structures matter for many, but not for everyone.[33] Ambitious individuals will want to align themselves with more powerful individuals. Accordingly, if we want to understand politics and institutions, we need to understand where individuals now sit in society's power structure.[34]

It should come as no surprise that powerful individuals are, as noted above, on the lookout for still more power. This is true in both the private and the public sector. We saw earlier that CEOs at Canadian banks decided to "hard wire" most loan decisions, thereby stripping local bank managers of much of their power. The most senior government officials are no different, particularly when it comes to decisions designed to promote and manage change.

A new logic of appropriateness has set in for individuals. To the more powerful, institutions, organizations, and formal processes are there to be used to pursue their own agendas and to keep everything and everyone else under control. To everyone else in government, the objective is to manage complex, porous, and consultative processes as an end in itself; it is in their self-interest to avoid controversy and embarrassing their political leaders, and they will make every effort to do so in return for letting their departments or units run on autopilot.

Citizens, meanwhile, can take little comfort in the decline of institutions and organizations. Institutions should be key to constraining powerful individuals when necessary by shaping their behaviour, establishing what a good member should and should not do, and regularizing patterns of interaction between them and other organizations.[35] This has been lost, at least for the most powerful individuals. For other individuals, the principal-agency theory has broken down; this squares with the interest of all within government, but certainly not for Parliament or for citizens.

The political elite has discovered arrangements to gain power, manage power, and ensure that things that do not matter to them are put aside and handled so that the end result changes very little. We have seen the demobilization, deliberate or not, of institutions and organizations that are important to representative democracy, from political parties to traditional government departments, with their reliance on hierarchy.

If one is looking to locate power today, one should visualize an abstract painting on which unrelated spots represent powerful individuals who are able to bypass or, conversely, manipulate institutions, organizations, and formal processes, depending on the purpose at hand. Powerful individuals rely on one another in their pursuit of "what matters is what works," not on institutions, organizations, or processes. Political and economic elites know one another, and if they do not, lobbyists are able to establish the necessary network. Power now takes many forms, from soft power to hard power, with leaders still able to employ carrots and sticks to pursue their objectives. But what matters above all else is the individual, not institutions, not organizations, and not formal policy-making and decision-making processes.

INTRODUCTION

1 Bertrand Russell, *Power: A New Social Analysis* (London: Allen & Unwin, 1938; reprint, Unwin Books, 1960), 9.

2 From a conversation with a friend and colleague, Peter Aucoin, professor of political science and public administration at Dalhousie University, 27 September 2008.

3 Hans-Jurgen Bieling, "The Other Side of the Coin: Conceptualizing the Relationship between Business and the State in the Age of Globalisation," *Business and Politics* 9, no. 3 (2007): 2.

4 Benjamin Ginsberg and Martin Shefter made a similar point in their *Politics by Other Means* (New York: W.W. Norton, 1999), 172.

5 Donald J. Savoie, *Court Government and the Collapse of Accountability in Canada and the United Kingdom* (Toronto: University of Toronto Press, 2008), chapter 6.

6 See, for example, Fareed Zakaria, *The Future of Freedom: Liberal Democracy at Home and Abroad* (New York: W.W. Norton, 2007), 177.

7 Savoie, *Court Government.*

8 See, among others, Virginia Haufler, *A Public Role for the Private Sector* (Washington: Carnegie Endowment for International Peace, 2001).

9 Donald J. Savoie, *Governing from the Centre: The Concentration of Power in Canadian Politics* (Toronto: University of Toronto Press, 1999).

10 Quoted in "There's nothing like an RCMP raid to get the irony flowing," *Globe and Mail*, 17 April 2008, A15.

11 See, among others, ibid. and Charlie Savage, *Takeover: The Return of the Imperial Presidency and the Subversion of American Democracy* (Little, Brown, 2007).

12 Quoted in Louis W. Pauly and Edgar Grande, "Reconstituting Political Authority: Sovereignty, Effectiveness, and Legitimacy in a Transnational Order," in *Complex Sovereignty: Reconstituting Political Authority in the Twenty-first Century*, ed. Edgar Grande and Louis W. Pauly (Toronto: University of Toronto Press, 2005), 7.

13 I wish to thank one of the reviewers of the manuscript with McGill-Queen's University Press for bringing the distinction to my attention.

14 John Stuart Mill, *Considerations on Representative Government* (New York: Harper, 1869), 100.

15 See Savoie, *Court Government.*

16 Sir Andrew Turnbull's valedictory lecture, www.civilservice.gov.uk/publications/speeches/valedictory, 26 July 2005, 14.

17 Grande and Pauly, eds., *Complex Sovereignty.*

18 Susan Strange, *The Retreat of the State: The Diffusion of Power in the World Economy* (Cambridge: Cambridge University Press, 1996).

19 The Honourable Pierre S. Pettigrew, "Seattle: The Lessons for Future Governance," The 2000 John L. Manion Lecture (Ottawa: Canadian Centre for Management Development, 4 May 2000), 8–9.

20 Ibid., 12.

21 Quoted in "A realistic take on globalization," *Globe and Mail*, 17 October 2007, B2.

22 Thomas L. Friedman, *The Lexus and the Olive Tree: Understanding Globalization* (New York: Farrar, Straus and Giroux, 1999), 17.

23 See, among many others, "Credit gloom sends banks slipping and Rock sliding," *Guardian* (London), 22 November 2007, 20.

24 "Bear Stearns companies," *New York Times*, www.nytimes.com/top/news/business/companies, 28 April 2008.

25 John-Paul Koming, *What the Bank of Canada Act Needs Updating: A Lesson from the Sub-Prime-Crises – ebrief* (Toronto: C.D. Howe Institute, 4 December 2007).

26 Savoie, *Court Government.*

27 See, among others, Donald J. Savoie, *Breaking the Bargain: Public Servants, Ministers, and Parliament* (Toronto: University of Toronto Press, 2003).

28 There is now, for example, a National Council for Public-Private Partnerships that sponsors a multitude of activities. See www.ncppp.org/contactus.

29 See, among others, Neil Reynolds, "History 101: Have capitalism, will prosper," *Globe and Mail*, 10 October 2007, B2.

30 "International response needed to revive economic growth," www.number10.gov.uk, 30 January 2009, and interview with CNN on 1 February 2009 (*Edition*, www.cnn.com/2009).

31 Judith Maxwell, "Forget government, hire a business leader," *Globe and Mail*, 8 October 1997, B2.

32 Savoie, *Court Government*.

33 "Canada sends a message on foreign takeover," *Globe and Mail*, 8 December 2007, B1 and B4.

34 "Business gets a voice on Canadian delegation at Bali, www.theglobeandmail.com, 10 December 2007.

35 Consultations with two senior officials in the Department of Foreign Affairs, Ottawa, 25 January 2008.

36 Canada, *Budget 2009–2010* (Ottawa: Department of Finance, 2009).

37 Zakaria, *The Future of Freedom*, 167.

38 "The Chief Justice gives voice to unwritten principles," *Globe and Mail*, 15 May 2006, A13.

39 See, among others, "Supreme Court pick favours restraint," www.canada.com, *Network*, 28 February 2006.

40 "Contract specifies that consultant leave no paper trail in federal offices," www.macleans.ca, 10 October 2005.

41 Lord Wilson of Dinton, "The Mandarin Myth," fourth lecture in a series on Tomorrow's Government, Royal Society for the Encouragement of Arts, Manufacturers and Commerce, London, 1 March 2006, 1.

42 See, among others, Tom Resenstiel, *The Beat Goes On: President Clinton's First Year with the Media* (New York: Twentieth Century Fund Press, 1994), chapter 7.

43 John Lloyd, "The Media and Politics," in *Changing Times: Leading Perspectives on the Civil Service in the Twenty-first Century and Its Enduring Values*, ed. Baroness Usha Prashar (London: Office of the Civil Service Commissioners, 2005), 151–3.

44 Joseph S. Nye et al., eds., *Why People Don't Trust Government* (Cambridge: Harvard University Press, 1997).

45 Peter Hennessy, *Whitehall* (London: Secker and Warburg, 1989), 82.

46 Donald F. Kettl, *Reinventing Government: A Fifth-Year Report Card* (Washington, DC: Brookings Institution, September 1998), 36.

47 See R. Kenneth Carty, "The Shifting Place of Political Parties in Canadian Public Life," and William Cross and Lisa Young, "Are Canadian Political Parties Empty Vessels?" *Choices* 12, no. 4 (2006): 3–32.

48 Ibid., 21.

49 In light of the growing negative perception of public servants, Charles T. Goodsell decided to write a book in their defence, a polemic, as the author readily acknowledged, in response to widespread bureaucrat bashing. See Charles T. Goodsell, *The Case for Bureaucracy: A Public Administration Polemic* (Chatham, NJ: Chatham House, 1983).

50 Derek Bok, "A Daring and Complicated Strategy," *Harvard Magazine*, May–June 1989, 49.

51 See, among many others, Savoie, *Breaking the Bargain*, and Christopher D. Foster, *British Government in Crisis* (Oxford: Hart Publishing, 2005).

52 Lawrence Martin, "The unwritten bylaw of Bytown: Fall in line or fall out of favour," *Globe and Mail*, 9 August 2006, A1 and A6.

53 Jim Travers, "Branding Team Harper," www.thestar.com, 6 February 2007.

54 Quoted in "Foreign Affairs Department has no policy capacity and has become a roving travel agency and property management department," *Hill Times*, 29 October 2007, 28.

55 Even the Privy Council Office in the Canadian government made a similar observation in its publication on accountability. See Canada, *Accountable Government: A Guide for Ministers and Ministers of State* (Ottawa: Privy Council Office, 2008), 11.

56 "Ottawa should remove itself from its own fiscal forecasting: economist," *Globe and Mail*, 13 October 2004, B9.

57 Canada, *Federal Accountability Act and Action Plan*, www.faa.gc.ca.

58 Charles E. Lindblom, *Politics and Markets* (New York: Basic Books, 1977), 26.

59 John Kenneth Galbraith, *The Anatomy of Power* (Boston: Houghton Mifflin, 1983), 57.

60 Ibid., 57–8.

61 Ibid., 4.

CHAPTER ONE

1 Consultation with a New Brunswick entrepreneur, Moncton, New Brunswick, 29 December 2007.

2 See, among many others, "Janis Grantham on how to grow a business," *Globe and Mail*, 21 December 2007, B2.

3 "Toyota surpasses GM as sales leader," www.barons.com, 21 January 2009.

4 "Industry pleads for help to ease crisis," *Globe and Mail*, 4 November 2008, B1 and B9.

5 See, among others, Harvey Lazar et al., eds., *The Impact of Global and Regional Integration on Federal Systems* (Kingston: Institute of Intergovernmental Relations, 2003), and John H. Dunning, *Governments, Globalization, and International Business* (Toronto: Oxford University Press, 1997).

6 Lazar et al., *The Impact of Global and Regional Integration on Federal Systems*.

7 OECD stat extracts, *Central Government Debt* (Paris: OECD, 2007).

8 See, for example, "BMW hits out at aid distorting competition," *Financial Times*, 13 January 2009, 16.

9 See, among others, John H. Dunning, "Introduction," in *Governments, Globalization, and International Business*, ed. Dunning (Oxford: Oxford University Press, 1997).

10 Practitioners have made the same point. See, for example, Kevin Lynch, "Remarks by the Clerk of the Privy Council and Secretary to Cabinet," Richard Ivey School of Business, University of Western Ontario, 15 November 2007, 1.

11 Quoted in "Gift of Christmas a past warning for the future," *Globe and Mail*, 18 December 2007, B9.

12 Niall Ferguson, *The Ascent of Money: A Financial History of the World* (New York: Penguin, 2008), 329.

13 *World Investment Report, 2006* (New York: United Nations Conference on Trade and Development, 2006), 18.

14 "Hedge funds on hot seat," *Wall Street Journal*, www.wsj.com, 10 November 2008.

15 Some banks had to turn to outside sources to secure new equity to remain viable. See, for example, "Citigroup set to land cash infusion," *Globe and Mail*, 12 January 2008, B7.

16 "Financiers reap riches even as deals wobble," *Wall Street Journal*, 17 January 2008, A1 and A14.

17 Paul Krugman, "Innovating our way to financial crisis," www.economistsview.typepal.com, 3 December 2007.

18 "Bernanke takes aim at U.S. mortgage lenders," *Globe and Mail*, 19 December 2007, B10.

19 "Did Greenspan sell out investors?" *Globe and Mail*, 22 January 2008, B7.

20 "Greenspan denies blame for crisis, admits flaw," www.associatedpresswriters.com, 23 October 2008.

21 "How Government Intervention Caused the Credit Crisis," www.heritage.org/2008/10/16.

22 "Big Five prove inept at managing risk," *Globe and Mail*, 20 September 2008, A20.

23 "If everyone's finger-pointing, who's to blame?" www.nytimes.com, 22 January 2008.

24 See, among others, "Is Greenspan to blame for the housing crisis?" *U.S. News and World Report*, www.usnews.com/articles/business/economy, 22 September 2007.

25 See, for example, "Survey: CFOs place credit crisis blame on lenders and brokers," www.fei.org/financialexecutives.org, 16 October 2007.

26 "Buyer's remorse among pension funds," www.wsj.com, 27 August 2007.

27 Professor Alan Blinder, quoted in "Greenspan's legacy: Now the experts are hedging," *Globe and Mail*, 12 January 2008, B7.

28 George Soros, "The worst market crisis in sixty years," *Financial Times*, www.ft.com, 22 January 2008.

29 "Financiers reap riches even as deals wobble." See also "Two million foreclosures $100-billion in losses – 'You can see it coming,'" *Globe and Mail*, 19 January 2008, F1 and F6.

30 "Growing default fears unnerve U.S. markets," *Wall Street Journal*, 18 January 2008, A10.

31 "Grip on Freddie, Fannie may ease," *Wall Street Journal*, 17 January 2008, A3.

32 Henry Mintzberg, "Managing Government," *Harvard Business Review*, May–June 1996, 75.

33 Ibid., 83.

34 Ibid. See also Donald J. Savoie, *Breaking the Bargain: Public Servants, Ministers, and Parliament* (Toronto: University of Toronto Press, 2003).

35 Andrew Sheng, "Role of the Market Practices Committees in Foreign Exchange Market Development," Hong Kong Forex Association luncheon talk, Ritz-Carlton Hotel, Hong Kong, 4 November 1994, 2.

36 Ibid., 1.

37 www.newsvote.bbc.co.uk/onpapps, 21 January 2007.

38 Richard G. Lipsey, "Globalization and National Government Policies: An Economist's View," in Dunning, *Governments, Globalization, and International Business*, 92.

39 Donald J. Savoie, *Thatcher, Reagan, Mulroney: In Search of a New Bureaucracy* (Toronto: University of Toronto Press, 1994).

40 Galbraith, quoted in *Dimension*, Winter 1986, 13.

41 See, among others, "Comrades no more?" *BBC News*, www.news.bbc.co.uk, 15 March 2002.

42 Consultation with a former deputy minister with the Government of Canada, Ottawa, 13 December 2007.

43 See, among others, John R. Baldwin et al., *Changes in Foreign Control under Different Regulatory Climates: Multinationals in Canada* (Ottawa: Statistics Canada, March 2006), 1–6.

44 *World Investment Report, 2006*, 204.

45 Ibid., 4–8.

46 "Trends and Recent Developments in Foreign Direct Investment," in *International Investment Perspectives: Freedom of Investment in a Changing World* (Paris: OECD, 2007), 16–18.

47 Ibid.

48 Anne Golden and Hon. Jim Flaherty, quoted in "Hollowing is hardly a myth," *Toronto Star*, 30 January 2008, A4.

49 See, among others, J.A. Scholte, *Globalization: A Critical Introduction* (Basingstoke, UK: Palgrave, 2000).

50 Consultations with a senior Industry Canada official, Ottawa, 17 February 2009.

51 "Development agency seen as model for this province," *Telegraph Journal* (Saint John, NB), 11 January 2008, B1.

52 Ibid.

53 *World Investment Report, 2006*, 34.

54 Consultations with senior officials with the Atlantic Canada Opportunities Agency (ACOA), Ottawa and Moncton, various dates in 2007–08.
55 Based on a survey carried out by the United Nations Conference on Trade and Development, Survey of Trade Promotion Organizations (TPOs), January–March 2006.
56 Lester Thurow, "Globalization of Business Strategies in the 21st Century," www.epoch.org.tw/seminar, 2002, 4.
57 See, for example, *Cutting Red Tape: Comparing Administrative Burdens across Countries* (Paris: OECD, 2007).
58 Quoted in Savoie, *Thatcher, Reagan, Mulroney*, 124.
59 Christopher Redman, "Taming Ireland's Celtic Tiger," *Fortune*, 7 November 2006, quoted from www.cnnmoneyprintthis.com.
60 Constantin Gurdgiev, professor of economics at Trinity College, Dublin, made these observations in "The fall of the Celtic Tiger," *Globe and Mail*, www.reportonbusiness. com, 26 November 2008.
61 Arthur Laffer and Stephen Moore, *Rich States, Poor States* (Washington, DC: American Legislative Executive Council, 2007).
62 See, among others, *Insights on the Canadian Economy* (Ottawa: Statistics Canada, cat. 11-624-MIE, no. 013, 2006), 5–6.
63 Consultation with a New Brunswick entrepreneur, Moncton, NB, 29 December 2007.
64 See, for example, Donald J. Savoie, *Court Government and the Collapse of Accountability in Canada and the United Kingdom* (Toronto: University of Toronto Press, 2008).
65 Consultations with a senior Government of Canada official, Ottawa, 25 January 2008.
66 Donna Lee and David Hudson, "The Old and New Significance of Political Economy in Diplomacy," *Review of International Studies* 30, no. 3 (2004): 343–60.
67 Consultations with two senior officials with the Department of Foreign Affairs, Ottawa, 25 January 2008.
68 Ibid.
69 Ibid.
70 Ibid.
71 Ibid.
72 "Ontario's Premier threatens surcharge on Korean cars," *Globe and Mail*, 23 January 2009, A4.
73 Kevin Lynch, clerk of the privy council and secretary to the cabinet in the Government of Canada, made this point in his "Succeeding in a Globalized World: Canada's Challenge and Opportunity," remarks delivered to the Richard Ivey School of Business, University of Western Ontario, London, 15 November 2007, 2. Mr Lynch also served as executive director for the Canadian, Irish,

and Caribbean constituency at the International Monetary Fund in Washington between 2004 and 2006.

74 See, among many others, Ngaire Woods, *The Globalizers, the IMF, the World Bank, and their Borrowers* (New York: Cornell University Press, 2008).

75 A recent report revealed that $9 out of $10 in loans in India are "either squandered or stolen by corrupt officials and middlemen." See "World bank purge," *Wall Street Journal*, 18 January 2008, A12.

76 "U.K. PM calls for institutional change," *National Post*, 22 January 2008, A14.

77 See, among many others, Bernhard Boockmann and Axel Dreher, *The Contribution of the IMF and the World Bank to Economic Freedom*, Centre for European Economic Research, Discussion paper no. 02-18, undated, mimeo.

78 Lipsey, "Globalization and National Government Policies," 93.

79 Quoted in Peter Aucoin and Donald J. Savoie, "Launching and Organizing a Program Review Exercise," paper prepared for the Canadian Centre for Management Development, Ottawa, 1988, 2.

80 Ibid.

81 See, for example, Armelita Armit and Jacques Bourgault, eds., *Hard Choices or No Choices: Assessing Program Review* (Toronto: Institute of Public Administration, 1996).

82 See, among others, Donald J. Savoie, *Governing from the Centre: The Concentration of Power in Canadian Politics* (Toronto: University of Toronto Press, 1999).

83 Consultations with a senior forestry executive, Quebec City, on 14 September 2007.

84 "Auto projects at risk, Chrysler warns," *Globe and Mail*, 14 January 2008, B1.

85 Ibid.

86 VistaPrint Investor Relations, at www.vistaprint.com.

87 For detailed information on VistaPrint and its operations, consult Form 10K, *Annual Report Pursuant to Section 13 or 15(d) of the Securities Exchange Act of 1934: VistaPrint* (Washington: Securities and Exchange Commission, 2007), 1–99.

88 Form 10Q for VistaPrint Ltd., 31 January 2008, www.biz.yahoo.com.

89 See, among others, G. Jones, *Multinationals and Global Capitalism: From the Nineteenth to the Twenty-first Century* (Oxford: Oxford University Press, 2005), 7–8.

90 See, among many others, Christian Fuchs, *Internet and Society: Social Theory in the Information Age* (New York: Routledge, 2008), and Jan Van Dijk, *The Network Society* (London: Sage, 2006).

91 Manuel Castells, *The Information Age: Economy, Society and Culture – The Power of Industry* (Oxford: Blackwell, 1997), 359, 362.

92 See Catrin Pekari, "The Information Society and Its Policy Agenda: Towards a Human Rights-Based Approach," *Revue québécoise de droit international* 18, no. 1 (2005): 69.

93 Ibid., 70.

94 Bill Gates et al., *Gates: The Road Ahead* (New York: Penguin, 1996).

95 Ibid., 206–7.

96 Samuel Huntington, quoted in Laura Miller, "The Rise of the Superclass," salon.com books, 14 March 2008.

97 David Rothkopf, *Superclass: The Global Power Elite and the World They Are Making* (New York: Farrar, Straus and Giroux, 2008).

98 Ibid., xiv.

99 Quoted in Neil Reynolds, "Canada would benefit from a little laissez-faire," *Globe and Mail*, 16 January 2008, B2.

100 See, among others, David Held et al., *Global Transformations: Politics, Economics, and Culture* (Cambridge: Cambridge University Press, 1999).

101 Samuel Huntington, quoted in David Rothkopf, *Superclass: The Global Power Elite and the World They Are Making* (Toronto: Viking Canada, 2008), 275.

102 Stephen D. Krasner, "Globalization, Power, and Authority," paper presented at the America Political Science Association annual meeting, San Francisco, Department of Political Science, Stanford University, 29 August to 2 September 2001, 9, mimeo.

CHAPTER TWO

1 James Gillies in his preface to Carol Hansell, *What Directors Need to Know: Corporate Governance* (Toronto: Davis Ward Phillips and Vineberg, 2003), iii.

2 Bertrand Russell, *Power: A New Social Analysis* (London: Allen & Unwin, 1938; reprint, Unwin Books, 1960), 47.

3 See, among many others, *Governance* (Somerset, UK), March 2006, no. 149, and *Centre for Corporate Governance* at the London Business School.

4 *Where Were the Directors?* (Toronto: Toronto Stock Exchange Committee on Corporate Governance in Canada, December 1994), preface.

5 Ibid., summary, 1.

6 Ibid., 11.

7 See "Enron's Lay fights back," www.cnnmoney.com, 12 July 2004, and Donald J. Savoie, *Court Government and the Collapse of Accountability in Canada and the United Kingdom* (Toronto: University of Toronto Press, 2008).

8 *An Act to Protect Investors*, One Hundred Seventh Congress of the United States of America, 23 January 2002, Second Session, Washington, www.findlaw.com.

9 See Hansell, *What Directors Need to Know*, 2.

10 The Combined Code is a product of various reform measures, including *Report of the Committee on the Financial Aspects of Corporate Governance: The Code of Best Practice* (Cadbury Code, 1 December 1992), *Directors' Remuneration: Report of a Study Group Chaired by Sir Richard Greenbury* (Greenbury Committee Report, 17 July 1995), and *Committee on Corporate Governance: Final Report* (Hampel Committee Report, 28 January 1998), (London: Gee Publishing, various dates).

11 David Rothkopf, *Superclass: The Global Power Elite and the World They Are Making* (Toronto: Viking Canada, 2008), 80.

12 *Corporate Governance in Europe: Report of a CEPS Working Party* (Brussels: Centre for European Studies, CEPS Working Paper no. 12, 1995), and *Corporate Governance in Europe: Raising the Bar* (Paris: Heidricht Struggles, 2007).

13 *Corporate Governance in Europe*, 1–5.

14 Ibid., 3.

15 Ibid.

16 Ibid., 10.

17 One can access various governance charters and guidelines by going to a firm's website. See, for example, *VistaPrint Limited: Corporate Governance Guidelines*, www.vistaprint.com.

18 The authors presented their findings in Jiri Maly and David Anderson's "The metamorphosis of directors: From thinkers to doers," *Globe and Mail*, 28 January 2008, B5.

19 Consultations with a member of the board of directors of the Canadian National Railway, Moncton, NB, 2 February 2008.

20 Consultations with five members of different boards of directors of publicly traded companies in Toronto, 18 and 19 January 2008.

21 See, for example, "Good governance and tough times," and "Board reforms face crucial test," *Globe and Mail*, online at www.globeandmail.com, 10 November 2008.

22 See, among others, "The World's Best CEOs," www.online.barrons.com.

23 "Sarbanes-Oxley costs for wall compliance decline," *Wall Street Journal*, 1 May 2008, C3.

24 See, among others, "IIA Research Sox Looking at the Benefits," www.thesis.org/research/research-reports, and "Effect of International Control Deficiencies on Firm Risk and Cost of Capital," www.wbur.org/news.

25 Consultation with a board member of a large publicly traded Canadian company, Fox Harbour, NS, July 2008.

26 Ellen Engel, Rachel M. Hayes, and Xve Wang, "The Sarbanes-Oxley Act and Firms: Going-Private Decisions," *SSRN Electronic Paper Collection*, May 2004, 23.

27 Ehud Kamar et al., *Going-Private Decisions and the Sarbanes-Oxley Act of 2002: A Cross-Country Analysis* (Santa Monica, CA: RAND Corporation, April 2006).

28 "Going Private," *Business Week*, online at www.businessweek.com, 27 February 2006.

29 James Atwood of the Carlyle Group, quoted in "Media & Money: Is Going Private A Panacea?" www.paidcontent.org, 7 November 2007.

30 Mark Woodward, quoted in www.businessreviewonline.com/archives, 30 March 2006.

31 Michael Useem, quoted in *Going Private*.

32 "Does Sarbanes-Oxley hurt shareholders and hide poor management?" www.knowledge.wharton.upenn.edu/article, 1 November 2004.

33 Christian Leuz, Alexander Triantis, and Tracy Wang, "Why Do Firms Go Dark? Causes and Economic Consequences of Voluntary SEC Deregistrations," Social Science Research Network: Working Paper Series, March 2006, 25.

34 Consultation with a senior manager with the National Bank of Canada, Moncton, 11 December 2007. See also Equifax at www.econsumer.equifax.ca.

35 Ibid.

36 Consultation with a senior official with a Canadian bank, Barbados, 9 February 2008.

37 Ibid.

38 "Jamie Dimon: Lessons learned in Davos," *Globe and Mail*, 4 February 2008, B2.

39 See, among others, Thomas W. Malone, *The Future Work* (Cambridge: Harvard Business School Press, 2004).

40 See, for example, Jay R. Galbraith, *Designing Organizations: An Executive Guide to Strategy, Structure, and Process*, 2nd edn. (San Francisco: Jossey-Bass, 2002); K.A. Merchant, "The Control Function of Management," *Sloan Management Review* 23, no. 4 (1982): 43–55.

41 See "Is Empowerment Just a Fad? Control, Decision Making, and Information Technology," BT *Technology Journal* 17, no. 4 (1999): 141–4.

42 Wouter Dessein, "Authority and Communication in Organizations," *Review of Economic Studies* 69 (2002): 811–38.

43 See, among others, David Korten, *When Corporations Rule the World* (West Hartford: Kumaria Press, 1995), and Naomi Klein, *No Logo: Taking Aim at the Brand Bullies* (Toronto: Knopf, 2000).

44 See, for example, Caroline Thomas, *Global Governance, Development, and Human Security* (London: Pluto Press, 2000).

45 "Minister of Finance announces formation of economic advisory council," media release, Department of Finance, Ottawa, 18 December 2008.

46 John Kenneth Galbraith, *The Anatomy of Power* (Boston: Houghton Mifflin, 1983), 142.

47 Ralph Heintzman, "The Effects of Globalization on Management Practices: Should the Public Sector Operate on Different Parameters?" paper presented to the IPAC National Conference, Fredericton, NB, 30 August 1999, 7–9.

48 Quoted in "Speech by the Honourable Jim Flaherty, Minister of Finance, to the 15th Annual National Conference on Public-Private Partnerships hosted by the Canadian Council for Public-Private Partnerships," Department of Finance, Ottawa, 26 November 2007, 4.

49 Ibid., 7.

50 Joan Price Boose, "Beyond Government? The Appeal of Public-Private Partnerships," *Canadian Public Administration* 43, no. 1 (2000): 79.

51 Ibid.

52 See, among many others, Kenneth Kernaghan, "Partnership and Public Administration: Conceptual and Practical Considerations," *Canadian Public Administration* 36, no. 1, (1993): 57–76.

53 Ibid., 71.

54 Canadian Wildlife Service of Environment Canada (Toronto: IPAC submission,
January 1992), 9.

55 See Geert R. Teisman and Erik-Hans Klijn, "Partnership Arrangements: Governmental Rhetoric or Governance Scheme," *Public Administration Review* 62,
no. 2 (2002): 197–205.

56 See, among others, *Critical Choices: The Debate over Public-Private Partnerships and What It Means for America's Future* (Washington, DC: Council for
Public-Private Partnerships, 2003), 6.

57 Donald J. Savoie, "What Is Wrong with the New Public Management," *Canadian Public Administration* 38, no. 1 (1995): 112–21.

58 Ibid., 91.

59 Jennifer Berardi, "The Niagara Casino Partnership: Game of Chance?" in *Pro-
fessionalism and Public Service: Essays in Honour of Kenneth Kernaghan*, ed.
David Siegel and Ken Rasmussen (Toronto: University of Toronto Press, 2008),
229.

60 E.R. Yescombe, *Public-Private Partnerships: Principles of Policy and Finance*
(London: Elsevira, 2007), 25.

61 Jane Jacobs, *Systems of Survival* (New York: Random House, 1992).

62 Ibid.

CHAPTER THREE

1 Various consultations with the Right Honourable Roméo LeBlanc, various
dates between 1982 and 2004, Ottawa and Grande-Digue, NB.

2 See Donald J. Savoie, *Court Government and the Collapse of Accountability in
Canada and the United Kingdom* (Toronto: University of Toronto Press, 2008),
118.

3 Johan P. Olsen makes the same point in "Democratic Government, Institutional
Autonomy, and the Dynamics of Change," *West European Politics* 32, no. 3
(2009): 447.

4 Ronald Dworkin, *Law's Empire* (Cambridge, MA: Belknap Press of Harvard
University Press, 1986), 1.

5 Ibid., 357.

6 See, among others, Ian Greene, *The Courts* (Vancouver: UBC Press, 2006), and
Christopher P. Manfredi, *Judicial Power and the Charter: Canada and the Par-
adox of Liberal Constitutionalism* (Toronto: McClelland & Stewart, 1993).

7 www.constitution.org/fed/federa47.htm.

8 Adam Tomkins, *Public Law* (Oxford: Oxford University Press, 2003), 39, 40.

9 See, among others, Jeffrey Goldsworthy, *The Sovereignty of Parliament*
(Oxford: Oxford University Press, 1999), 26.

10 "Magna Carta," *Wikipedia*, undated.

11 L.G. Schwoerer, "The Contributions of the Declaration of Rights to Anglo-American Radicalism," in *The Origins of Anglo-American Radicalism*, ed. M.C. Jacob and J.R. Jacob (London: George Allen & Unwin, 1984), 112.

12 Tomkins, *Public Law*, 44.

13 W. Bagehot, *The English Constitution* (London: C.A. Watts, 1964), 220.

14 Quoted in Sir Norman Chester, *The English Administrative System, 1780–1870* (Oxford: Clarendon Press, 1981), 81.

15 C.D. Yonge, *The Life and Administration of Robert Banks, the Second Earl of Liverpool* (London, 1868), 3:340.

16 Quoted in Goldsworthy, *The Sovereignty of Parliament*, 227.

17 Ibid., 277.

18 Greene, *The Courts*, 154.

19 Europe, *Human Rights Act of 1998*, www.opsi.gov.uk/Acts/acts1998/1980042.htm.

20 "Canadian challenging authority, report says," *National Post*, 21 January 2002, A2. See also www.scc-csc.gc.ca/stat/sum-som.2009.

21 See, among others, Peter Russell, "The Effect of a Charter of Rights on the Policy-Making Role of Canadian Courts," *Canadian Public Administration* 25, no. 1 (1982): 1–34.

22 Remarks of the Right Honourable Beverley McLachlin, PC, Chief Justice of Canada, University of Western Ontario, Faculty of Law, London, Ontario, 6 November 2002, 4 and 5.

23 Tomkins, *Public Law*, 34.

24 James B. Kelly, *What Makes the Laws? The Struggle for Legislative Supremacy in Canada* (Ottawa: Seminar Series sponsored by the Canadian Federation for the Humanities and Social Sciences, 2 October 2003), 12.

25 Canada, Minister's speech at the Association for Canadian Studies conference, "Canadian Rights and Freedoms: Twenty Years under the Charter," Department of Justice, Ottawa, 18 April 2002, 3.

26 "NB holds more talks on early French immersion after losing court case," canadaeast.com, 11 June 2008.

27 www.gnb.ca/cab/news.

28 "Michel Bastarache reprend du service," *L'Acadie Nouvelle*, 23 August 2008, 3.

29 "Crown must justify adult sentences: ruling," *Globe and Mail*, 17 May 2008, A7.

30 See, among others, Tomkins, *Public Law*, 20.

31 Professor Allan Hutchinson on the judicial appointments process, *Lawyers Weekly* online, www.osgoode.yorku.ca/media, 23 September 2005.

32 Manfredi, *Judicial Power and the Charter*, 212.

33 Ibid., 212–15.

34 Donald R. Songer, *The Transformation of the Supreme Court of Canada: An Empirical Examination* (Toronto: University of Toronto Press, 2008), 253.

35 Greene, *The Courts*, 160.

36 Raymond Bazowski, "The Judicialization of Canadian Politics," in *Canadian Politics*, ed. James Bickerton and Alain G. Gagnon (Peterborough, ON: Broadview Press, 2004), 203.

37 See, among others, F.L. Morton and Rainer Knopff, *The Charter Revolution and the Court Party* (Peterborough, ON: Broadview Press, 2000).

38 See, among others, Joseph Fletcher and Paul Howe, "Public Opinion and the Courts," *Choice* 6, no. 3 (2000): 4–53.

39 Bazowski, "The Judicialization of Canadian Politics," 211.

40 "Judicial Appointments Commission: History," 2005, www.judicialappointments.gov. uk.

41 Baroness Usha Prashar, speech at the annual ILEX luncheon, Judicial Appointments Commission, Cloth Workers Hall, London, 17 May 2006, 2.

42 Jacob Ziegel, "Judicial Appointment – the real challenge for PM Harper," *Lawyers Weekly*, 14 November 2008, 2.

43 Canada, *Process for an Application for Appointment* (Ottawa: Office of the Commissioner for Federal Judicial Affairs, undated).

44 Songer, *The Transformation of the Supreme Court of Canada*, 109–11. See also, "Is there a women's view on top court?" www.theglobeandmail.com, 21 July 2009.

45 An excellent case in point is the parliamentary budget office established by the Harper government following commitments made in an election campaign. Harper dismissed out of hand advice from Parliament's budget officer as "dumb," and his government has launched efforts to restrict the scope of the officer's work. See, among others, "Harper rejects dumb budget advice," www.nationalpost.com, 11 July 2009.

46 See Sharon Sutherland, "Parliament's Unregulated Control Bureaucracy," *Briefing Notes* (Kingston: Queen's University School of Policy Studies, 2002), 9. It should be noted, however, that the Office of the Auditor General has statutory authority to launch comprehensive or value-for-money audits.

47 Ibid.

48 "The woman who enraged voters," *Ottawa Citizen*, 9 June 2004, B1.

49 Canada, *Annual Reports*, selected chapters (Ottawa: Office of the Auditor General, 22 November 2005, May 2007, and 30 October 2007).

50 Privacy Commissioner of Canada, "Privacy commissioner launches charter challenge," news release, Ottawa, 21 June 2002.

51 Ibid.

52 "First-ever Parliament budget officer now open for Hill business," *Hill Times*, 31 March 2008, 1, 31.

53 Quoted in ibid.

54 See, among many others, "Week of heavy job losses puts pressure on Flaherty to open stimulus taps wider," *Globe and Mail*, 6 February 2009, A1.

55 "Why Canada's budget watchdog is so good at dropping the gloves," *Globe and Mail*, 31 January 2009, F3.

56 "Put tether on budget watchdog, MPs urge," www.thestar.com, 17 June 2009.

57 "The role of the National Audit Office," www.nao.org.uk.

58 Paul G. Thomas, "The Past, Present, and Future of Officers of Parliament," *Canadian Public Administration* 46, no. 3 (2003): 311.

59 See www.gao.gov/cghome/index.html.

60 www.cbo.gov/aboutcbo/budgetrocess.

61 Jim Travers, "Challenges ahead for iconic force," www.thestar.com, 15 December 2007.

62 See, among others, "New scandals face RCMP," www.thestar.com, 29 May 2007.

63 *Rebuilding the Trust* (Ottawa: Report of the Task Force on Governance and Cultural Change in the RCMP; a report submitted to the Minister of Public Safety and President of the Treasury Board, 14 December 2007), 14.

64 Ibid., 27. See also "Dramatic restructuring of RCMP urged in report," www.thestar.com, 15 December 2007.

65 Savoie, *Court Government*, 232.

66 See Lord Lawson of Blaine, "Changing the Consensus," in *The Chancellors' Tales*, ed. Howard Davies (Cambridge: Polity Press, 2006), 120.

67 Tony Blair and Gordon Brown introduced the measure. Nigel Lawson, chancellor of the exchequer under Margaret Thatcher, applauded the decision. See ibid., 119.

68 "Former Fed insider sees Bear decision as mistake," *Globe and Mail*, 29 April 2008, B14.

69 "Ottawa should remove itself from own fiscal forecasting: Economists," *Globe and Mail*, 13 October 2004, B9.

70 Consultation with a senior member of the Chrétien government, Toronto, 8 June 2008.

71 Statement by the prime minister of Canada, 28 January 2008, www.pm.gc.ca/english.

72 See, for example, "Harper accepts broad terms of Manley report," 28 January 2008, www.ctv.ca/servlet/article/news.

73 "Jean's job will be to prove naysayers wrong," *Globe and Mail*, 4 August 2005, A4.

74 See Paul Light, *Thickening Government: Federal Hierarchy and the Diffusion of Accountability* (Washington, DC: Brookings Institution Press, 1995).

CHAPTER FOUR

1 Lord Wilson of Dinton, "The Mandarin Myth," fourth lecture in a series on Tomorrow's Government, Royal Society for the Encouragement of Arts, Manufacturers and Commerce, London, 1 March 2006, 17.

2 Steven Lukes, *Power, a Radical View* (London: Macmillan, 1974), 23.

3 See, among others, William Fox, "Belly-laugh funny video puts arts act on campaign radar," *Globe and Mail*, 8 October 2008, A7.

4 Jeffrey Simpson, "The brain of our existence: A lot of imitators but no equals," *Globe and Mail*, 16 May 2006, A13.

5 See, among others, Rom Resenstiel, *The Beat Goes On: President Clinton's First Year with the Media* (New York: Twentieth Century Fund Press, 1994), chapter 7.

6 See, among others, "And they're off," *Chronicle Herald* (Halifax), 9 April 2006, A6, and "Liberal Party run like an oligarchy: Grits," *National Post*, 2 March 2006, A7. See also Russell J. Dalton and Martin P. Wattenberg, eds., *Parties without Partisans: Political Change in Advanced Industrial Democracies* (New York: Oxford University Press, 2000), and various publications produced by the Institute for Research on Public Policy (Montreal) under its Strengthening Canadian Democracy series.

7 One could make the case that in Canada the *National Post* is sympathetic to the Conservative Party. But other newspapers, including the *Globe and Mail* and *Ottawa Citizen*, take pride in insisting that they do not favour any political party.

8 "CTV defends decision to air fumbled Dion interview," www.canadaeast.com, 10 October 2008.

9 Consultation with Edith Robb, a forty-year journalist with the Moncton *Times and Transcript*, various dates.

10 "Cameron and the sex clinic mystery," *Times*, 6 February 2006, 1.

11 John Major, *The Erosion of Parliamentary Government* (London: Centre for Policy Studies, 2003), 14.

12 Robin V. Sears, "Harper vs. the Press Gallery," *Policy Options* 27, no. 6 (2006): 5–8.

13 Ibid.

14 David Taras, *Power and Betrayal in the Canadian Media* (Toronto: University of Toronto Press, 2008), 1, 219.

15 I owe this insight to one of the reviewers of the manuscript.

16 Consultations with a journalist, Ottawa, 14 July 2009.

17 Consultations with Michel Cormier, Moncton, 31 July 2009. He had no objection in reporting my conversation with him for the purpose of this book.

18 See, among many others, Fox, "Belly-laugh funny video puts arts cuts on campaign radar."

19 Kathy English, "Why the Star does not unpublish," www.thestar.com, 31 January 2009.

20 "The National no more," *Newsweek*, 5 May 2008, 39.

21 Ibid.

22 Telephone conversation with Richard Foot, a journalist with Canada.com network, 27 October 2008.

23 William Cross, "Policy Study and Development in Canada's Political Parties," in *Policy Analysis in Canada*, ed. Laurent Dobuzinskis, Michael Howlett, and David Laycock (Toronto: University of Toronto Press, 2007), 425.

24 Quoted in "Volpé should quit Liberal race," *Toronto Star* online, www.thestar.com.

25 See, for example, M. Foley, *The British Presidency* (Manchester: Manchester University Press, 2000), 231, and Douglas Alexander and Stella Creasy, *We Can Be a Movement Capable of Making the Twenty-first Century the Era of Progressive Change* (London: Demos, 2006), 32.

26 "And they're off," *Chronicle Herald* (Halifax), 9 April 2006, A6. See also "Liberal Party run like an oligarchy: Grits," *National Post*, 2 March 2006, A7.

27 "Bonding, not policy, high on Tories' Winnipeg agenda," *Globe and Mail*, 10 November 2008, A5.

28 Janine Brodie and Jane Jenson, "Piercing the Smokescreen: Brokerage Parties and Class Politics," in *Canadian Parties in Transition*, ed. Alain Gagnon and A. Brian Tanguay, 52–72 (Scarborough, ON: Nelson, 1991).

29 Robert A. Young, "Effecting Change: Do We Have the Political System to Get Us Where We Want to Go?" in *Canada at Risk? Canadian Public Policy in the 1990s*, ed. G. Bruce Doern and B. Bryne Purchase (Toronto: C.D. Howe Institute, 1991), 77.

30 Christopher Foster, *British Government in Crisis* (Oxford: Hart Publishing, 2005), 280.

31 See, for example, Richard Johnson, André Blais, Henry Brady, and Jean Crête, *Letting the People Decide: Dynamics of a Canadian Election* (Montreal & Kingston: McGill-Queen's University Press, 1997).

32 Ibid.

33 Christopher Hood and Martin Lodge, *The Politics of Public Service Bargains: Reward, Competency, Loyalty, and Blame* (Oxford: Oxford University Press, 2006), viii.

34 Foster, *British Government in Crisis*, 280.

35 Jean Chrétien, *Straight from the Heart* (Toronto: Key Porter Books, 1985), 18.

36 The Honourable Reg Alcock made this observation when I was serving as the Simon Reisman Visiting Fellow at the Treasury Board Secretariat, Ottawa, in 2004.

37 Peter Van Onselen and Wayne Errington, "The Democratic State as a Marketing Tool: The Permanent Campaign in Australia," *Commonwealth and Comparative Politics* 45, no. 1 (2007): 78.

38 See, among many others, Sidney Blumenthal, *The Permanent Campaign: Inside the World of Elite Political Operations* (Boston: Beacon Press, 1980).

39 See, among others, James Travers, "Who do you trust: Politician or nerd?" *Toronto Star*, 20 September 2008.

40 "He learned from mistakes as Ontario premier, Rae says," *Globe and Mail*, 21 November 2008, A11.

41 See Donald J. Savoie, *Court Government and the Collapse of Accountability in Canada and the United Kingdom* (Toronto: University of Toronto Press, 2008), 296–300.

42 Veteran *Globe and Mail* columnist Hugh Winsor made this observation before Justice Gomery at the Toronto round table consultations, Commission of Inquiry into the Sponsorship Program and Advertising Activities, Ottawa, 5 October 2005, 18.

43 See Savoie, *Court Government*, 50.

44 Consultation with an official in the Library of Parliament, Ottawa, 17 November 2006.

45 Canada, Treasury Board Secretariat, "Canada's Performance Report and the Broader Issue of Reporting to Parliament: A Concept Paper," (Ottawa: Treasury Board Secretariat, 2005), 4.

46 Stephen K. Medvic and Silvo Lenart, "The Influence of Political Consultants in 1992 Congressional Elections," *Legislative Studies Quarterly* 22 (1997): 61–77.

47 See, among others, Douglas A. Lathrop, *The Campaign Continues: How Political Consultants and Campaign Tactics Affect Public Policy* (Westport, CT: Praeger, 2003).

48 See Pippa Norris, "The Battle for the Campaign Agenda," in *New Labour Triumps: Britain at the Polls*, ed. Anthony King et al. (Chatham, NJ: Chatham House Publishers, 1998), and James A. Thurber and Candice J. Nelson, eds., *Campaign Warriors: Political Consultants in Elections* (Washington, DC: Brookings Institution Press, 2000).

49 Martin Goldfarb, "The Art of the Pollster," in *Authority and Influence: Institutions, Issues, and Concepts in Canadian Politics*, ed. Carla Cassidy et al. (Oakside: Mosaic Press, 1985), 306.

50 See, among many others, Canada, *Renewal of Public Opinion Research in the Government of Canada: Annual Report 2006–2007*, www.tpsgc-pwgsc.gc.ca.

51 "Conservative spending on polls hits $31 million," *National Post*, 4 December 2007, 1.

52 "Feds conduct astounding number of opinion polls," *Ottawa Citizen*, 14 December 2007, 1.

53 Christopher Page, *The Roles of Public Opinion Research in Canadian Government* (Toronto: University of Toronto Press, 2006), 184.

54 Rand Dyck, *Canadian Politics: Critical Approaches* (Scarborough, ON: Nelson Lands, 1993).

55 See, among others, James Curran and Jean Seaton, eds., 6th edn., *Power without Responsibility: The Press, Broadcasting, and New Media in Britain* (London: Routledge, 2003), 346.

56 Ibid., 346–8.

57 Jean Seaton, "Broadcasting and the Theory of Public Service," in *Power without Responsibility*, 371.

58 Based on consultations with various Canadian journalists.

59 For a different perspective, see Stephen Bennett, "Video Malaise Revisited: Reconsidering the Relation between the Public's View of the Media and Trust

in Government," *Harvard International Journal of Press and Politics* 4, no. 4 (1999): 8–23.

60 Bill Fox, *Spinwars: Politics and the New Media* (Toronto: Key Porter Books, 1999), 244.

61 Seaton, "Broadcasting and the Theory of Public Service."

62 "Aide apologises for attacks memo," *BBC News*, 10 October 2005, www.bbc.co.uk.

63 See, among others, "Analysis: Confusing intimacy with leadership," www.canada.com, 15 October 2008.

64 UK Parliament, Select Committee on Public Administration, *Minutes of Evidence*, questions 352–9, 14 March 2002, 3.

65 See among others, "Number 10 machine overhauled," www.ft.com, 5 January 2009.

66 "Cronkite funeral held at Manhattan church," www.cnn.com, 23 July 2009.

67 Lord Winston of Dinton, "The Mandarin Myth," 9.

68 Quoted in UK Parliament, Select Committee on Public Administration, *Minutes of Evidence*, 2.

69 Ibid., 1.

70 I have had numerous discussions with several leading national and New Brunswick journalists in recent years about the power of the media.

CHAPTER FIVE

1 Consultation with a deputy minister, Ottawa, 2003.

2 Quoted in Kevin Theakston, *The Civil Service since 1945* (Oxford: Blackwell, 1995), 176.

3 See, among others, Edward Greenspon and Anthony Wilson-Smith, *Double Vision: The Inside Story of the Liberals in Power* (Toronto: Doubleday Canada, 1996).

4 Christopher Hood, "Transparency in Historical Perspective," in *Transparency: The Key to Better Governance?*, ed. Christopher Hood and David Heald (Oxford: Oxford University Press, 2006), 3.

5 Mel Cappe, "At the court of Her majesty's governments in Canada and the U.K.," *Policy Options*, December 2008–January 2009, 17.

6 Oscar Wilde, from the play *The Importance of Being Earnest*, 1895, Act 1.

7 Hood, "Transparency in Historical Perspective," 18.

8 Howard R. Wilson, "The Constantly Rising Ethics Bar," notes for a presentation to the Canadian Centre for Ethics and Public Policy, 7 November 2002.

9 Hood, "Transparency in Historical Perspective," 17.

10 "Obama to name Clinton secretary of state on Monday," *Wall Street Journal* online, www.wsj.com, 30 November 2008.

11 "How to Deal with Lies," welcome to Michael Moore.com, undated.

12 www.dwatch.ca.

13 See, for example, *Business Principles for Countering Bribery* (Berlin: Transparency International and Social Accountability International, June 2003).

14 Adrian Henriques, *Corporate Truth: The Limits of Transparency* (London: Earthscan, 2007), 3.

15 Gordon Pitts, "The Testing of Michael McCain," *Report on Business* (Toronto), December 2008, 60–6.

16 Ibid., 64.

17 Ibid.

18 "Maple Leaf CEO complains of inspection double standards," *Canada.com Canwest News Service* online, www.canada.com, 10 October 2008.

19 Canadian Food Inspection Agency, *Science and Regulations*, www.inspection.gc.ca.

20 "McCain takes aim at listeria oversight," www.theglobeandmail.com, 21 April 2009.

21 "Listeriosis outbreak was preventable incident report," www.ottawacitizen.com, 21 July 2009.

22 Henriques, *Corporate Truth*, 2–3.

23 Ibid., 103.

24 Ibid.

25 Canada, *Speech from the Throne*, www.pm.gc.ca, 4 April 2006.

26 See, among many others, Canice Prendergost, "A Theory of Yes Men," *American Economic Review* 83, no. 4 (1993): 757–70.

27 Russell B. Stevenson, Jr, *Corporations and Information: Secrecy, Access, and Disclosure* (Baltimore: Johns Hopkins University Press, 1980), 6.

28 This is the title of Andrea Pratt's chapter in Hood and Heald, *Transparency*, 91.

29 Canada, *Access to Information Act*, RSC 1985, c. A(1), 39.

30 Marcia P. Miceli and Janet P. Near, *Blowing the Whistle: The Organizational and Legal Implications for Companies and Employers* (Toronto: Maxwell Macmillan Canada, 1992), 45.

31 Paul Thomas, "Debating a Whistle-Blower Protection Act for Employees of the Government of Canada," *Canadian Public Administration* 48, no. 2 (2005): 153.

32 See, among others, Donald J. Savoie, *Court Government and the Collapse of Accountability in Canada and the United Kingdom* (Toronto: University of Toronto Press, 2008).

33 Kenneth Kernaghan, "Encouraging Rightdoing and Discouraging Wrongdoing: A Public Service Charter in Disclosure Legislation," in Canada, Commission of Inquiry into the Sponsorship Program and Advertising Activities, *Restoring Accountability: Research Studies*, vol. 2, *The Public Service and Transparency* (Ottawa, 2006), 76.

34 Canada, "Providing Real Protection for Whistleblowers," www.faa.1fi.gd.ca, 2005.

35 Kernaghan, "Encouraging Rightdoing and Discouraging Wrongdoing," 94.

36 Savoie, *Court Government*.

37 www.tbs-sct.gc.ca

38 Savoie, *Court Government*.

39 B. Holmström, "Moral Hazard and Observability," *Bell Journal of Economics* 10, no. 1 (1979): 74–91.

40 Consultation with the president-CEO of a publicly traded company listed on the Toronto Stock Exchange, Fox Harbour, NS, 18 August 2008.

41 John Crosbie, *No Holds Barred: My Life in Politics* (Toronto: McClelland & Stewart, 1997), 300.

42 J. Ashley, "Instead of a debate over war, there's been a national shrug," *Guardian* (Manchester), 23 December 2000.

43 "CBC still playing games with their numbers," *Times and Transcript* (Moncton), 29 November 2008, A7, and Canada, *A New Director: 2007–08 Annual Report* (Ottawa: Office of the Information Commissioner, 2008).

44 Andrea Mattozzi and Antonio Merlo, *The Transparency of Politics and the Quality of Politicians* (Pittsburgh: Penn Institute for Economic Research, PIER working paper 07-008, January 2007).

45 Quoted in Donald J. Savoie, *Breaking the Bargain: Public Servants, Ministers, and Parliament* (Toronto: University of Toronto Press, 2003), 50.

46 Ibid.

47 Consultations with four access to information coordinators, Ottawa and Gatineau, 4 February 2009.

48 Consultations with senior Government of Canada officials, Ottawa, 17 September 2008.

49 Ibid.

50 See, among others, Joseph S. Nye, Jr, Philip D. Zelikow, and David C. King, eds., *Why People Don't Trust Government* (Cambridge, MA: Harvard University Press, 1997).

51 Consultation with the Hon. Andy Scott, Sussex, NB, 9 September 2006.

52 Hugh Winsor made these observations at the Toronto round table, 5 October 2005, Commission of Inquiry into the Sponsorship Program and Advertising Activities.

53 Alasdair Roberts, "Administrative Discretion and the Access to Information Act: An Internal Law on Open Government?" *Canadian Public Administration* 45, no. 2 (2002): 175.

54 "Contract specifies that consultant leave no paper trail in federal offices," www.macleans.ca, 10 October 2005.

55 Consultations with a deputy minister, Ottawa, 11 June 2006.

56 "Ottawa's $2-billion hit list," *Globe and Mail*, 24 April 2006, A1.

57 John M. Reid made these observations in a letter to Justice Gomery that was made public in October 2005. Canada, Information Commission of Canada, Ottawa, 14 October 2005.

58 "Tories fail to take action on access to information," www.theglobeandmail.com, 26 February 2009.

59 Quoted in Lord Wilson of Dinton, "The Mandarin Myth," fourth lecture in series on Tomorrow's Government, Royal Society, London, 1 March 2006, 11.

60 "Big spending days over for Ottawa," *National Post*, 24 April 2004, RB1.

61 Canada, Commission of Inquiry into the Sponsorship Program and Advertising Activities, *Who Is Responsible?* (Ottawa: Public Works and Government Services Canada, 2005).

62 See, among others, Savoie, *Court Government*.

63 Ibid., 287.

64 Robert Marleau, quoted in "Tories fail to take action on access to information."

65 UK, Treasury, *Responsibilities of an Accounting Officer*, memorandum (London, undated), 6.

66 Christopher Hood, "Transparency in Historical Perspective," in Hood and Heald, *Transparency*, 20.

67 See, among others, Henriques, *Corporate Truth*, 163.

68 See Savoie, *Court Government*. See also Canada, Treasury Board Secretariat, "Canada's Performance Report and the Broader Issue of Reporting to Parliament: A Concept Paper" (Ottawa: Treasury Board Secretariat, 2005), 4.

69 Paul Thomas, "Who Is Getting the Message? Communications at the Centre of Government," independent background research study prepared for the Commission of Inquiry into Certain Allegations Respecting Business and Financial Dealings between Karlheinz Schreiber and the Right Honourable Brian Mulroney, Ottawa, March 2009, 48.

70 For an excellent review of access to information legislation from a comparative perspective, see Alasdair Roberts, "Dashed Expectations: Governmental Adaptation to Transparency Rules," in Hood and Heald, *Transparency*, 127–44.

71 Ibid., 141.

72 H.A. Gerth and C. Wright Mills, eds., *From Max Weber: Essays in Sociology* (London: Routledge, 1970), 233–4.

73 Peter Hennessy, *Whitehall* (London: Fontana Press, 1990), 345–6.

74 Lord Wilson of Dinton, "The Mandarin Myth," 26.

75 Consultation with a leading Canadian private-sector chief executive officer, Fox Harbour, NS, 28 July 2008.

CHAPTER SIX

1 Brian Laghi and Jeffrey Simpson, "Incremental plan," *Globe and Mail*, 4 October 2008, F1 and F7.

2 Jeffrey Simpson coined that phrase. See Jeffrey Simpson, *The Friendly Dictatorship* (Toronto: McClelland & Stewart, 2001).

3 Eddie Goldenberg, *The Way It Works* (Toronto: McClelland & Stewart, 2006), chapter 5.

4 Consultation with a former assistant to Prime Minister Jean Chrétien, Ottawa, 17 October 2002.

5 The round table was held in London at Canada House on 4 November 2002.

6 Quoted in Donald J. Savoie, *Thatcher, Reagan, Mulroney: In Search of a New Bureaucracy* (Toronto: University of Toronto Press, 1994), 114.

7 Donald J. Savoie, *Court Government and the Collapse of Accountability in Canada and the United Kingdom* (Toronto: University of Toronto Press, 2008), 144.

8 W.A. Matheson, *The Prime Minister and the Cabinet* (Agincourt: Methuen, 1975), and Denis Smith, "President and Parliament: The Transformation of Parliamentary Government in Canada," in *Apex of Power: The Prime Minister and Political Leadership in Canada*, 2nd edn., ed. Thomas A. Hockin (Scarborough, ON: Prentice-Hall, 1977).

9 See, for example, "All politics is local, or so we thought," www.ottawacitizen.com/story, 15 January 2009.

10 "Tories scrap proposal to end public subsidies for political parties," *Windsor Star* online, www.canada.com/windstar/news, 29 November 2008.

11 See, for example, Jeffrey Simpson, "Fighting for his career, Harper will use all weapons at his disposal," www.globeandmail.com, 2 December 2008.

12 Consultations with senior government officials, Ottawa, 4 and 5 December 2008. See also Jeffrey Simpson, "After the storm," www.globeandmail.com, 5 December 2008, A17.

13 Lawrence Martin, "The Canadian financier who wasn't," www.globeandmail.com, 15 December 2008.

14 "Harper's blunder deals blow to his credibility," *Globe and Mail*, 5 December 2008, A8.

15 Donald J. Savoie, *Governing from the Centre: The Concentration of Power in Canadian Politics* (Toronto: University of Toronto Press, 1999), 71.

16 Savoie, *Court Government*.

17 Charlie Savage, *Takeover: The Return of the Imperial Presidency and the Subversion of American Democracy* (New York: Little, Brown, 2007).

18 See, among others, Gerald F. Seile, "Obama's centralizing of power offers hints of how he'll operate," *Wall Street Journal*, 13 January 2009, 9.

19 *Federalist* (New York), 6 February 1788.

20 Ibid., chapter 13. See also Thomas E. Mann and Norman J. Ornstein, *The Broken Branch* (Oxford: Oxford University Press, 2006).

21 See, among others, Jan Crawford Greenburn, *Supreme Conflicts* (New York: Penguin, 2007).

22 Savoie, *Thatcher, Reagan, Mulroney*.

23 Jack Balkin, quoted in Jonathan Mahler, "After the imperial presidency," *New York Times* online, www.nytimes.com, 9 November 2008.

24 Eoin O'Malley, "The Power of Prime Ministers: Results of an Expert Survey," *International Political Science Review* 28, no. 1 (2007): 9.

25 Ibid., 17.
26 "Harper announces UNESCO deal with Quebec," www.ctv.ca, 5 May 2006.
27 See, among others, "Newfoundland, Ottawa sign immigration deal," and "B.C. signs new labour market deals with Ottawa," www.cbc.ca/canada/story, 1 September 1999 and 20 February 2008.
28 "Ottawa drafts new deal for provinces," www.globeandmail.com, 30 July 2008.
29 Donald J. Savoie, *Federal-Provincial Collaboration: The Canada/New Brunswick General Development Agreement* (Montreal & Kingston: McGill-Queen's University Press, 1981).
30 See Carl Dahlström et al., "Steering from the Centre: Central Government Offices and the Role in Governing," mimeo, University of Pittsburgh, August 2008, 5.
31 "Declaration of the Summit on Financial Markets and the World Economy," *White House News*, Office of the Press Secretary, Washington, 15 November 2008, 2. See also "G20 leaders vow to take action on economy," *Globe and Mail*, www.reportonbusiness.com, 15 November 2008.
32 Angelo Persichilli, "Political power is national, but economic power is global," www.thestar.com, 26 July 2009.
33 Quoted in Savoie, *Governing from the Centre*, 317.
34 "Inside story," *Globe and Mail*, 24 November 2006, A1 and A4.
35 "Nation plan costs Harper," *Globe and Mail*, 28 November 2006, A1.
36 Tom Kent, *A Public Purpose: An Experience of Liberal Opposition and Canadian Government* (Montreal & Kingston: McGill-Queen's University Press, 1988), 225.
37 Savoie, *Governing from the Centre*, 298.
38 Marc Lalonde, "The Changing Role of the Prime Minister's Office," *Canadian Public Administration* 14, no. 4 (1971): 513.
39 Quoted in Savoie, *Governing from the Centre*, 88.
40 George Radwanski, *Trudeau* (Toronto: Macmillan, 1978), 114.
41 Savoie, *Governing from the Centre*, 90.
42 Tom Axworthy, "Of Secretaries to Princes," *Canadian Public Administration* 31, no. 2 (1988): 260.
43 Christina McCall and Stephen Clarkson, *Trudeau and Our Times, The Heroic Delusion*, vol. 2 (Toronto: McClelland & Stewart, 1994).
44 James Douglas, "Review Article: The Overloaded Crown," *British Journal of Political Science* 6, no. 3 (1976): 492.
45 Consultations with a former senior official with the Department of Indian and Northern Affairs, Ottawa, 22 May 2003.
46 I am referring here to policy issues that have not grabbed the prime minister's interest or his or her court and not to the thousands of decisions made every day in government offices that flow from long-established government programs having prescribed criteria.

47 Gordon Robertson, "The Changing Role of the Privy Council Office," *Canadian Public Administration* 14, no. 4 (1971): 500.

48 Colin Campbell, *Governments under Stress: Political Executives and Key Bureaucrats in Washington, London, and Ottawa* (Toronto: University of Toronto Press, 1983), 17.

49 Patrice Dutil, "The Six Skills of Secretaries to Cabinet," *Public Sector Magazine* (Toronto), 19, no. 2 (2008): 20.

50 Paul Thomas, "Central Agencies: Making a Mush of Things," in *Canadian Politics: An Introduction to the Discipline*, ed. James Bickerton and Alain G. Gagnon (Toronto: Broadview Press, 1994), 288.

51 Patrick Weller, "A Comparison of the Budget Decision-Making Processes Used in Canada and Australia," paper published in mimeo form by the Canadian Centre for Management Development, Ottawa, August 1995, 6.

52 Savoie, *Governing from the Centre*, 326.

53 Quoted in Donald J. Savoie, *The Politics of Public Spending in Canada* (Toronto: University of Toronto Press, 1990), 114.

54 "Cat's Eyes: Intelligent Work versus Perverse Incentives – APEX Forums on Wicked Problems," *Optimum Online*, www.optimumonline.ca, 38, no. 3 (2008): 10 and 12.

55 See, for example, Paul Light, *Thickening Government: Federal Hierarchy and the Diffusion of Accountability* (Washington: Brookings Institution, 1995).

56 See, among others, Donald J. Savoie, *Breaking the Bargain: Public Servants, Ministers, and Parliament* (Toronto: University of Toronto Press, 2003).

57 Gordon Osbaldeston, *Keeping Deputy Ministers Accountable* (Toronto: McGraw-Hill Ryerson, 1989).

58 Canada, Treasury Board Secretariat, *Federal Institutional Governance Universe* (Ottawa, 2008). See also "Ottawa boasts over 453,000 people on payroll," *Hill Times* online, www.thehilltimes.ca, and Public Policy Forum, *Canada's Public Service in the Twenty-first Century: A Discussion Paper* (Ottawa, 2007), 6.

59 "New law puts green screen on government decisions," *Globe and Mail*, 21 July 2008, A4.

60 See www.canada.gc.ca/depts/.

61 Donald J. Savoie, *Visiting Grandchildren: Economic Development in the Maritimes* (Toronto: University of Toronto Press), 2006.

62 Ibid., 381–2.

63 Savoie, *The Politics of Public Spending in Canada*, 213.

64 Consultations with a senior Treasury Board Secretariat official, Ottawa, 14 November 2008.

65 See, among others, Savoie, *Court Government*.

66 Savoie, *Breaking the Bargain*, 224.

67 Savoie, *Court Government*.

68 Savoie, *Governing from the Centre*, 298.
69 www.tbs-sct.gc.ca/rpp/2008-2009/inst/TBD/TBD01.
70 Savoie, *Governing from the Centre*, 202.
71 "External Audit Advisory Committee Charter" (Ottawa: Environment Canada, 1 April 2006), 2.
72 Canada, *Speech from the Throne: Protecting Canada's Future*, www.pm.gc.ca, 19 November 2008.
73 Canada, *Annual Report* (Ottawa: Office of the Auditor General, December 2002), chapter 10.

CHAPTER SEVEN

1 See, among many others, Donald J. Savoie, *Thatcher, Reagan, Mulroney: In Search of a New Bureaucracy* (Toronto: University of Toronto Press, 1995).
2 Carol H. Weiss, "Efforts at Bureaucratic Reform," 10, and Stephen Michelson, "The Working Bureaucrat and the Working Bureaucracy," 175, in *Making Bureaucracy Work*, ed. Carol H. Weiss and Allen H. Barton (London: Sage, 1980); Herbert Kaufman, "Fear of Bureaucracy: A Raging Pandemic," *Public Administration Review* 49, no. 3 (1981), 1.
3 See, Savoie, *Thatcher, Reagan, Mulroney*, 90–2.
4 "Transcript: McCain announces Sarah Palin as his VP," www.npr.org/templates/story, 29 August 2008.
5 See, for example, Savoie, *Court Government and the Collapse of Accountability in Canada and the United Kingdom* (Toronto: University of Toronto Press, 2008), 320, and "Fired and muzzled officials," www.scandalpedia.ca, undated.
6 See, among others, S.H. Barnes et al., *Political Action: Mass Participation in Five Western Democracies* (London: Sage, 1979).
7 Richard Crossman, *The Diaries of a Cabinet Minister* (London: Hamish Hamilton and Jonathan Cape, 1975), 1:90.
8 David Lipsey, ed., *Making Government* (London: Fabian Society, 1982), 37.
9 See, among others, Savoie, *Thatcher, Reagan, Mulroney*, 82.
10 Prime Minister Margaret Thatcher in an interview with *Women's Own* magazine, London, 31 October 1987.
11 See, Savoie, *Thatcher, Reagan, Mulroney*.
12 Consultations with former senior officials in the British government. See also Geoffrey K. Fry, "The Thatcher Government, the Financial Management Initiative, and the New Civil Service," *Public Administration* 66, no. 2 (1988): 7.
13 Consultations with former senior British government officials, London and Oxford, various dates.
14 Savoie, *Thatcher, Reagan, Mulroney*, 119–49.
15 Derek Rayner, quoted in Les Metcalfe and Sue Richards, *Improving Public Management* (London: Sage, 1987), 16.

16 See, among others, Savoie, *Court Government.*

17 UK, *Modernising Government*, a document presented to Parliament by the prime minister and the minister for the Cabinet Office, 1999, 11.

18 See, among others, Paul Pierson, *Politics in Time: History, Institutions, and Social Analysis* (Princeton, NJ: Princeton University Press, 2004).

19 See, among many others, J. Wanna, L. Jensen, and J. DeVries, *Controlling Public Expenditure: The Changing Role of Central Budget Agencies, Better Guardians* (Cheltenham: Edward Elgar, 2003).

20 Herbert Kaufman, "Emerging Conflicts in the Doctrines of Public Administration," *American Political Science Review* 50 (1972): 1060.

21 See, among others, Peter Wilenski, *Public Power and Public Administration* (Sydney: Hale and Iremonger, 1986).

22 Canada, Privy Council Office, "Discussion Paper on Values and Ethics in the Public Service," Ottawa, December 1996.

23 Patrick Weller, "Introduction: The Institutions of Governance," in *Institutions on the Edge?*, ed. Michael Keating et al. (St Leonards, Australia: Allen and Unwin, 2000), 4.

24 Savoie, *Court Government*, 242.

25 Ken Beeson, "Advisory groups have fundamentally altered public policy-making in Ottawa," *Hill Times*, 24 March 2008, 10.

26 Ibid.

27 Christopher Pollitt, "Joined-up Government: A Survey," *Political Studies Review* 1 (2003): 46.

28 Canada, *Federal Accountability Act and Action Plan*, www.faa.gc.ca, 2004.

29 OECD, *Government of the Future* (Paris: OECD, 2000), 32.

30 See Alan C. Cairns, *Charter versus Federalism* (Montreal & Kingston: McGill-Queen's University Press, 1992), 172.

31 Tom Parklington, "Against Inflating Human Rights," *Windsor Yearbook of Access to Justice* (Windsor, ON: University of Windsor, 1982), 85.

32 Quoted in Donald J. Savoie, *Governing from the Centre: The Concentration of Power in Canadian Politics* (Toronto: University of Toronto Press, 1999), 517.

33 "Harper takes new swipe at nuclear watchdog," www.globeandmail.com, 11 January 2008, and "It only gets worse for Keen," www.nationalpost.com, 8 January 2009.

34 "Nuclear safety watchdog head fired for lack of leadership: ministers," www.cbc.ca, 16 January 2008.

35 Quoted in, "Nuclear fight a symbol of PS disintegration," www.canada.com, 12 January 2008.

36 K.C. Wheare, *Federalism: Origin, Operation, Significance* (Boston: Little Brown, 1964), 11.

37 A.H. Birch, *Federalism, Finance, and Social Legislation in Canada, Australia and the United States* (Oxford: Oxford University Press, 1955), 305.

38 Donald J. Savoie, *Federal-Provincial Collaboration: The Canada–New Brunswick General Development Agreement* (Montreal & Kingston: McGill-Queen's University Press, 1981).

39 Oliver James, *The Executive Agency Revolution in Whitehall* (London: Palgrave Macmillan, 2003), 1.

40 Savoie, *Court Government*.

41 Savoie, *Thatcher, Reagan, Mulroney*.

42 Nick Mulder, "Managing Special Operating Agencies: A Practitioner's Perspective," *Optimum* 22, no. 2 (1992): 19.

43 Ian Clark, "Special Operating Agencies: The Challenges of Innovation," *Optimum* 22, no. 2 (1992): 17.

44 Alti Rodal, "Special Operating Agencies: Issues for Parent Departments and Central Agencies" (Ottawa: CCMD, 1996), 5.

45 I put the question to senior officials at the Treasury Board Secretariat, and their answer was that no one has been able to demonstrate that programs are better managed in SOAs, and they expressed doubts whether such a question could actually be answered.

46 See David Roth, "Innovation in Government: The Case of Special Operating Agencies" (Ottawa: Minister of Supply and Services, Consulting and Audit Canada, September 1990), 2–3.

47 Michael Prince, "Banishing Bureaucracy or Hatching a Hybrid? The Canadian Food Inspection Agency and the Politics of Reinventing Government," *Governance* 13, no. 2 (2000): 217.

48 Peter Haas, "Addressing the Global Governance Deficit," *Global Environmental Politics* 4, no. 4 (2004): 1–15.

CHAPTER EIGHT

1 Joseph S. Nye, *Bound to Lead: The Changing Nature of American Power* (New York: Basic Books, 1990).

2 Joseph S. Nye, *Soft Power: The Means to Success in World Politics* (Cambridge: Perseus Books, 2004), 17.

3 Joseph S. Nye, *The Power to Lead* (New York: Oxford University Press, 2008), x.

4 This was sent to me by Doug Bland from Queen's University in July 2008. The documents include a discussion paper by Richard Shimooka, "Themes of the AJIP Study," for Canada's Department of National Defence and a series of memoranda in the form of e-mails from V. Rigby, M.P. Cessford, Lieutenant Colonel Eyre, and B.W. Gladmen, all employed by the Department of National Defence.

5 The quote, one of the most "widely emulated managers in business history," is borrowed from the jacket of Welch's book (written with John A. Byrne), *Straight from the Gut* (New York: Warner Books, 2001).

6 Among other measures, Welch fired about 10 percent of his least productive managers.

7 Even nurses saw merit in Jack Welch's ideas and in the Total Quality Management Movement. See, for example, A.J. Trofino, "Transformational Leadership: Moving Total Quality Management to World-Class Organizations," *International Nursing Review* 47, no. 4 (2001): 232–47.

8 See, for example, H. Rawlands, "Six Sigma: A New Philosophy or Repackaging of Old Ideas," *Engineering and Management Journal* 13, no. 2 (2003): 18–21.

9 David Osborne and Ted Gaebler, *Reinventing Government* (New York: Addison-Wesley, 1992).

10 Philippe Bezes and Patrick Le Lidec, "Steering from the Centre in France in the 2000s: Why Managerial and Organizational Tools for Steering Reinforce the Historical Politicization Pattern," paper prepared for the Steering from the Centre conference, University of Gothenburg, Sweden, 15–16 January 2009, 23–4.

11 Donald J. Savoie, *Pulling against Gravity: Economic Development in New Brunswick during the McKenna Years* (Montreal: Institute for Research on Public Policy, 2001).

12 "Government trimming provincial levies will be difficult without reforms, says report author" and "Former C.D. Howe president to launch flagship School of Policy Studies in Calgary," both available online at www.ucalgary.ca/news, undated.

13 See, among others, Leslie A. Pal, *Public Policy Analysis: An Introduction* (Toronto: Methuen, 1987); G. Bruce Doern and Richard Phidd, *Canadian Public Policy: Ideas, Structure, Process* (Scarborough, ON: Nelson Canada, 1992); and John W. Langford and K. Lorne Brownsey, eds., *Think Tanks and Governance in the Asia Pacific Region* (Halifax: Institute for Research on Public Policy, 1991).

14 Lord Wilson of Dinton, "The Mandarin Myth," fourth lecture in a series on Tomorrow's Government, Royal Society, London, 1 March 2006, 16.

15 See, among others, Lee Edwards, *The Power of Ideas: The Heritage Foundation* (New York: Jameson Books, 1997).

16 *The Fraser Institute, 1974–1999* (Vancouver: Fraser Institute, 2000), 74.

17 *Annual Report, 2006–2007* (Halifax: Atlantic Institute for Market Studies, 2007).

18 Ibid.

19 IRPP promotes its mission statement in all its publications. See, for example, Savoie, *Pulling against Gravity*, 1.

20 See, among others, Evert A. Lindquist, "Think Tanks or Clubs? Assessing the Influence and Roles of Canadian Policy Institutes," *Canadian Public Administration* 36, no. 4 (1993): 548.

21 The Hon. Paul Martin, *The Budget Speech 2001: Securing Progress in an Uncertain World* (Ottawa: Department of Finance, 10 December 2001).

22 G. Bruce Doern and R.W. Phidd, *Canadian Public Policy: Ideas, Structure, Process* (Toronto: Methuen, 1983).

23 Pal, *Public Policy Analysis*, 95.

24 Doern and Phidd, *Canadian Public Policy*, 542–3.

25 John W. Langford and K. Lorne Brownsey, "Think Tanks and Modern Governance," in *Think Tanks and Governance in the Asia Pacific Region*, ed. John W. Langford and K. Lorne Brownsey (Halifax: Institute for Research on Public Policy, 1991), 3.

26 Allan Tupper, "Think Tanks, Public Debt, and the Politics of Expertise in Canada," *Canadian Public Administration* 36, no. 4 (1994): 545.

27 Quoted in Peter C. Newman, *Titans* (Toronto: Penguin Canada, 1999). The Business Council on National Issues (BCNI), founded in 1976, changed its name to the Canadian Council of Chief Executives in January 2002.

28 Quoted in Donald E. Abelson, "Public Visibility and Policy Relevance: Assessing the Impact and Influence of Canadian Policy Institutes," *Canadian Public Administration* 42, no. 2 (1999): 241.

29 G. Bruce Doern and Brian W. Tomlin, *Faith and Fear: The Free Trade Story* (Toronto: Stoddart, 1991), 27.

30 See www.ppforum.com about history.

31 One example is the role that the forum played in the government's handling of a request for financial support of Canada's NHL hockey teams.

32 "Tories draft right-wing economist Brian Crowley to advise on finance policy," *Ottawa Citizen*, 9 November 2006, A1.

33 See www.policyresearch.gc.ca.

34 Ibid.

35 *Annual Review, 1999–2000* (Ottawa: Canadian Policy Research Networks, 2001), 29.

36 See, www.cprn.org.

37 See, for example, "Judy and Peter went to Ottawa," *Globe and Mail*, 11 February 1995, A4.

38 See, among others, "Peter Nicholson Appointed as First President of the Canadian Academies of Science," *Council of Canadian Academies*, www.scienceadvice.ca, 8 February 2006.

39 See R.S. Ritchie, *An Institute for Research on Public Policy: A Study and Recommendations* (Ottawa: Information Canada, 1971).

40 Leslie A. Pal, *Interests of State: The Politics of Language, Multiculturalism, and Feminism in Canada* (Montreal & Kingston: McGill-Queen's University Press, 1993).

41 Donald E. Abelson, "Public Visibility and Policy Relevance: Assessing the Impact and Influence of Canadian Policy Institutes," *Canadian Public Administration* 42, no. 2 (1999): 243–4.

42 Ibid., 258 and 264.

43 Justice Gomery was selected "Person of the Year" in 2004 by *Time* magazine.

44 James A. Smith, *The Idea Brokers: Think Tanks and the Rise of the New Policy Elite* (New York: Free Press, 1991), 231.

45 See, among others, Herman Bakvis, "Rebuilding Policy Capacity in the Era of the Fiscal Dividend," *Governance* 13, no. 1 (2000): 71–103.

46 Arthur Kroeger, "Reflections on Being a Deputy Minister," speech to the Canadian Club, Ottawa, 25 January 1991, 6.

47 Peter Aucoin, "New Public Management and the Quality of Government: Coping with the New Political Governance in Canada," paper prepared for the New Public Management and the Quality of Government conference, University of Gothenburg, Sweden, 13–15 November 2008.

48 "British firms top foreign spending on US lobbyists," *Times* (London), www.timesonline.co.uk, 20 January 2006.

49 See www.politicos.co.uk/category.jsp.

50 For an excellent review of the growth of the lobby industry in Canada, see John Sawatsky, *The Insiders: Government, Business and the Lobbyists* (Toronto: McClelland & Stewart, 1987).

51 Ibid., 140.

52 "The top 100 most influential people in government and politics in Ottawa," *Hill Times*, 22 December 2008, 1.

53 Canada, *Lobbying Act*, implementation notices 2, 3, 5, and booklet on the act (Ottawa: Office of the Registrar of Lobbyists, June 2008).

54 "New lobby rules mean more work for lawyers," *Globe and Mail*, 13 August 2008, B5.

55 "PM's former adviser accused of peddling access to corridors of power," www.theglobeandmail.com, 12 December 2008.

56 "Ian Brodie joins Hill and Knowlton Ottawa as senior counsel," news release, www.hillandknowlton.ca, 11 December 2008.

57 "The top 100 most influential people in government and politics in Ottawa," 1.

58 Kady O'Malley, "Luc Kily, the Federal Accountability Act doesn't apply to campaign co-chairs," blog.macleans.ca, 24 October 2008.

59 "Government of the people buys the people," *Globe and Mail*, 10 December 2007, A17.

60 Ibid.

61 Martin Linton, "Media: Are these six men the most influential journalists in Britain?" *Independent*, 5 January 1999, 1.

62 Consultation with one of Canada's print journalists, Ottawa, 3 February 2009.

63 Kathryn May, "Infrastructure gets new blood in PS shakeup," www.ottawacitizen.com, 18 June 2009.

64 Consultation with a deputy minister, Ottawa, 5 December, 2008.

65 The past three clerks have gone on to foreign appointments in London, Paris, and Rome.

66 Simon Reisman left government after Trudeau appointed Michael Pitfield clerk-secretary in 1975.

67 "When it came to achieving free trade, he was the right man for the job," *Globe and Mail*, 15 March 2008, S12.
68 See, for example, the Financial Administrative Act, the Public Service Employment Act, and the Official Languages Act.
69 See, among others, Savoie, *Court Government.*

CHAPTER NINE

1 See, among others, Martin Smith, "The Paradoxes of Britain's Strong Centre: Delegating Decisions and Re-Claiming Control," paper presented at the Steering from the Centre conference, University of Gothenburg, Sweden, 15–16 January 2009.
2 "The Global Elite," *Newsweek* online, www.newsweek.com, 5 January 2009, 12.
3 See, among others, David Rothkopf, *Superclass: The Global Power Elite and the World They Are Making* (New York: Farrar, Straus and Giroux, 2008).
4 Presentation given by Jan Landahl at the Steering from the Centre conference, Gothenburg.
5 "Sir Andrew Turnbull's Valedictory Lecture," London, 26 July 2005, mimeo, 14.
6 Philippe Bezes and Patrick Le Lidec, "Steering from the Centre in France in the 2000s: Why Managerial and Organizational Tools for Steering Reinforce the Historical Politicization Pattern," paper prepared for the Steering from the Centre conference, 23–4.
7 David Rieff, "The personalization of France's presidency is wearing thin," www.theglobeandmail.com, 7 April 2009.
8 See, among others, Donald J. Savoie, *Breaking the Bargain: Public Servants, Ministers, and Parliament* (Toronto: University of Toronto Press, 2003).
9 A report prepared under the direction of Carolyn Bennett, MP, Deborah Grey, MP, and Senator Yves Morin, *The Parliament We Want: Parliamentarians' Views on Parliamentary Reform* (Ottawa: Library of Parliament, December 2003), 6–7.
10 Adam Tomkins, *Public Law* (Oxford: Oxford University Press, 2003), 165.
11 Ibid.
12 C.E.S. Franks, *The Parliament of Canada* (Toronto: University of Toronto Press, 1987), 5.
13 John D. Huber and Charles R. Shipan make this very point in their *Deliberate Discretion? The Institutional Foundations of Bureaucratic Autonomy* (Cambridge: Cambridge University Press, 2002), 28.
14 Tomkins, *Public Law*, 165.
15 Jennifer Smith, "Democracy and the Canadian House of Commons at the Millennium," *Canadian Public Administration* 42, no. 4 (1999): 407.

16 C.E.S. Franks, "The Decline of the Canadian Parliament," *Hill Times*, 25 May 1998, 15.

17 Franks, *The Parliament of Canada*, 175.

18 "Rookie MPs say Parliament needs to change," *Telegraph Journal*, 23 June 2009, A8.

19 Quoted in D. Richards, "The Civil Service in Britain: A Case-Study in Path Dependency," in *Civil Service Systems in Anglo-American Countries*, ed. John Halligan (London: Edward Elgar, 2004), 37.

20 A senior deputy minister quoted in Donald J. Savoie, *Court Government and the Collapse of Accountability in Canada and the United Kingdom* (Toronto: University of Toronto Press), 320.

21 See, among others, Institute for Research on Public Policy, "Parliament's Performance in the Budget Process: A Case Study," *Policy Matters* 3, no. 5 (2002).

22 Consultations with Treasury Board Secretariat officials, Ottawa, 18–19 February 2009.

23 It was, for example, through an access to information request that *Globe and Mail* journalist Daniel LeBlanc was able to uncover the sponsorship scandal.

24 Robert Sibley, "Parliament's lost promise," *Ottawa Citizen*, 11 October 2008, A1.

25 John Turner, quoted in "The waning power of parliamentarians," www.ottawacitizen.com, 24 January, 2009.

26 Quoted in ibid.

27 Jocelyne Bourgon and Mel Cappe have both asked.

28 See, for example, Peter Hennessy, "Rulers and Servants of the State: Blair Style of Government, 1997–2004," *Parliamentary Affairs* 58, no. 1 (2005): 8.

29 Nevil Johnson, *Reshaping the British Constitution: Essays in Political Interpretation* (Basingstoke: Palgrave Macmillan, 2004), 84; Christopher Foster, *British Government in Crisis* (Oxford: Hart Publishing, 2005), and Christopher Hood, Oliver James, and B. Guy Peters, *Controlling Modern Government: Variety, Commonality, and Change* (Cheltenham: Edward Elgar, 2004), chapters 2, 2.1, and 3.9.

30 "The top 100 most influencial people in government and politics in Ottawa," *Hill Times*, 23 December 2008, 1.

31 Jean Chrétien, *Straight from the Heart* (Toronto: Key Porter Books, 1985), 85.

32 Canada, Commission of Inquiry into the Sponsorship Program and Advertising Activities, Ottawa, 25 January 2005, 62:11,045.

33 Consultation with senior government officials, Ottawa, various dates.

34 It is interesting to note that a similar observation was made in Britain in the Conservative Democracy Task Force's *An End to Sofa Government: Better Working of Prime Minister and Cabinet* (London: CDTF, 2007), 1.

35 Consultations with senior Foreign Affairs officials, Ottawa, various dates between March 2008 and February 2009.

36 Consultations with senior Foreign Affairs officials, Ottawa, various dates. See also www.speakers.ca, 2005, and "Interview with Jennifer Welsh," www.international.gc.ca, undated.

37 See, among others, "PM names Manley to head review of Afghan mission," www.cbc.ca, 12 October 2007.

38 See Savoie, *Court Government*, 135.

39 "Supplement to ex-deputy ministers on the rise," *Globe and Mail*, 2 July 2007, A4.

40 "Erosion of diplomatic corps will cost Canada, Clark says," www.ottawacitizen.com, 14 February 2009.

41 "Diplomats face communications crackdown," *Globe and Mail*, October 2007, A4.

42 See, among others, "Canadian bank economists see terrible start to 09," www.vancouversun.com, 7 January 2009.

43 Quoted in Guy A. Beaumier, *The Accountability Act and the Parliamentary Budget Officer* (Ottawa: Library of Parliament, 29 June 2006), 2.

44 "Parliamentary budget officer under fire from Commons and Senate speakers," Canwest News Service at www.canada.com, 3 November 2008.

45 See, for example, Paul G. Thomas, "The Past, Present, and Future of Officers of Parliament," *Canadian Public Administration* 46, no. 3 (2003): 311.

46 Gordon Robertson, "The Changing Role of the Privy Council Office," *Canadian Public Administration* 14, no. 4 (1971): 500, 505.

47 A.D.P. Heeney, "Mackenzie King and the Cabinet Secretariat," *Canadian Public Administration* 10 (September 1967): 373, and consultation with a senior PCO official, Ottawa, February 2008.

48 Consultations with a former senior federal government official, Ottawa, 3 February 2009.

49 Canada, *The Role and Structure of the Privy Council Office* (Ottawa: Privy Council Office, October 1987), 1.

50 Quoted in Donald J. Savoie, *Governing from the Centre: The Concentration of Power in Canadian Politics* (Toronto: University of Toronto Press, 1999), 114.

51 Jacques Bourgault, *Profile of Deputy Ministers in the Government of Canada* (Ottawa: Canada School of Public Service, 2005), 11.

52 Savoie, *Court Government*, 320.

53 I am thinking here of left-of-centre politicians such as Lloyd Axworthy. See ibid., 74.

54 Kevin G. Lynch, "Notes for Remarks on Public Service Removal and the Challenges of Misperceptions," Eighth National Managers Professional Development Forum, Vancouver, 21 April 2008, mimeo, 1.

55 See, among others, Donald J. Savoie, *Thatcher, Reagan, Mulroney: In Search of a New Bureaucracy* (Toronto: University of Toronto Press, 1994).

56 Consultations with senior Treasury Board Secretariat officials, Ottawa, 19 February 2009.

57 Consultation with a former deputy minister, Ottawa, 19 February 2009.

58 Paul G. Thomas, "The Changing Nature of Accountability," in *Taking Stock: Assessing Public Sector Reforms*, ed. B. Guy Peters and Donald J. Savoie (Montreal & Kingston: McGill-Queen's University Press, 1998), 361.

59 Lynch, "Notes for Remarks on Public Service Renewal and the Challenges of Misperceptions," 1.

60 See, for example, Peter Aucoin, "New Public Management and the Quality of Government: Coping with the New Political Governance in Canada," paper presented at the New Public Management and the Quality of Government conference, University of Gothenburg, Sweden, 13–15 November 2008, 15.

61 Ibid., 12.

62 Jean Chrétien, *My Years as Prime Minister* (Toronto: Knopf Canada, 2007), 39.

63 See, among others, Savoie, *Court Government*, 206.

64 Aucoin, "New Public Management and the Quality of Government," 10.

65 Savoie, *Court Government*.

66 Apart from my own *Breaking the Bargain*, see Christopher Hood and Martin Lodge, *The Politics of Public Service Bargains: Reward, Competency, Loyalty and Blame* (Oxford: Oxford University Press, 2006), 77.

67 See, for example, Hood and Lodge, *The Politics of Public Service Bargains*.

68 Savoie, *Court Government*.

69 Canada, *Annual Report of the Clerk of the Privy Council and Secretary to the Cabinet on the Public Service of Canada* (Ottawa: Privy Council Office, 1998), 14.

70 John Edwards, manager of PS 2000, "Revitalization of the Canadian Public Service," notes for a speaking engagement to the Association of Professional Executives, 11 March 1991, Ottawa, 13.

71 See, among others, Savoie, *Breaking the Bargain*.

72 Ibid., 278.

CHAPTER TEN

1 Charles E. Lindblom, *Politics and Markets: The World's Political-Economic Systems* (New York: Basic Books, 1977), 26.

2 "Volcker: Fed 'at Edge of Its Lawful and Implied Power,'" www.blogs.wsj.com/economics, 8 April 2008.

3 "Back on world stage, a larger-than-life Holbrooke," www.nytimes.com, 8 February 2009.

4 In the case of Canada, one can think, among others, of Don Drummond and Rick Hillier. One can also think of Paul Tellier, Derek Burney, and Ed Clark, who all left the Government of Canada to become president-CEOs of large Canadian corporations.

5 Consultations with a senior government official, Ottawa, 4 February 2009.

6 "Candour and Combat," www.cbc.ca/news/background/hillier, 15 April 2008.

7 Pankay Ghemawat, *Redefining Global Strategy: Crossing Borders in a World Where Differences Still Matter* (Cambridge: Harvard Business School Press, 2007).

8 See, among others, Stephen G. Brooks, *Producing Security: Multinational Corporations, Globalization, and the Changing Calculus of Conflict* (Princeton, NJ: Princeton University Press, 2005).

9 See, among others, Christopher K. Ansell and M. Stevens Fish, "The Art of Being Indispensable: Noncharismatic Personalism in Contemporary Political Parties," *Comparative Political Studies* 37, no. 3 (1999): 283–312.

10 "Henri-Paul Rousseau was the king," *Globe and Mail*, 31 January 2009, B1 and B4.

11 Aurel Braun, "Russia's leaders are beggaring the bear," *Globe and Mail*, 12 February 2009, A15.

12 See, among others, Donald J. Savoie, *Breaking the Bargain: Public Servants, Ministers, and Parliament* (Toronto: University of Toronto Press, 2003).

13 David Gergen made the point on CNN, "The Situation Power," www.cnn.com/cnn/programs/situation.room, 20 January 2009.

14 "Ain't misbehaviour," www.guardian.co.uk/education.2008, 23 September 2008.

15 See, among others, "Auto industry teeters as deadline looms," *Globe and Mail*, 16 February 2009, A1.

16 "Obama to create auto industry panel," www.cbsnews.com, 12 February 2009.

17 "Ottawa appoints P3 champion," *Globe and Mail*, 21 January 2009, B7.

18 UK, *Modernising Government*, a document presented to Parliament by the prime minister and the minister for the cabinet office, 1999, 11.

19 Donald J. Savoie, *Court Government and the Collapse of Accountability in Canada and the United Kingdom* (Toronto: University of Toronto Press, 2008), 258.

20 See ibid., among others.

21 Thomas L. Friedman, *The World Is Flat: A Brief History of the Twenty-first Century* (New York: Farrar, Straus and Giroux, 207).

22 Quoted in Guy Lodge and Ben Rogers, *Whitehall's Black Box: Accountability and Performance in the Senior Civil Service* (London: Institute for Public Policy Research, 2006), 48.

23 The Hon. Barbara McDougall, for example, made this observation in reviewing my *Breaking the Bargain*; see Barbara McDougall, "Life in Ottawa, Then and Now," *Literary Review of Canada* 12, no. 2 (2004): 6–7.

24 See, among others, Savoie, *Court Government*.

25 Ibid.

26 Quoted in "Harper avoids the axe," www.thestar.com, 5 December 2008.

27 Peter H. Russell makes this points very well in his "The Need for Agreement on Fundamental Conventions of Parliamentary Democracy," mimeo, Department of Political Science, University of Toronto, May 2009, 3.

28 James Travers, "A political makeover at full speed," www.thestar.com, 31 January 2009.

29 All three are quoted in "Some of the budget's biggest critics: Tories," www.theglobeandmail.com, 29 January 2009.

30 Andrew Coyne, "The Right in Full Retreat," *Maclean's*, 9 February 2009, 21.

31 P. Howe, R. Johnston, and A. Blais, *Strengthening Canadian Democracy* (Montreal: Institute for Research on Public Policy, 2005).

32 Donald F. Kettl, *The Transformation of Governance: Public Administration for Twenty-first Century America* (Baltimore: Johns Hopkins University Press, 2005), 59.

33 Ibid., ix.

34 Tony Wright, MP, made this point in his "Doing Politics Differently," *Political Quarterly* annual lectures, 4 March 2009, www.interscience.wiley.com/journal/poqu.

35 See, for example, John Wanna and Michael Keating, "Conclusion: Institutional Adaptability and Coherence," in *Institutions on the Edge? Capacity for Governance*, ed. Michael Keating, John Wanna, and Patricia Weller (St Leonards, Australia: Allen & Unwin, 2000), 230.

36 Quoted in "Federal public service not being consulted on new policies, say some experts, critics," *Hill Times* online, www.thehilltimes.ca, 9 June 2008.

37 Bertrand Russell, *Power: A New Social Analysis* (London: Routledge, 2004), chapter 13.

CHAPTER ELEVEN

1 See, among many others, M.D. McCubbins and T. Sullivan, *Congress: Structure and Policy* (Cambridge: Cambridge University Press, 1987), and P. Dunleavy, *Democracy, Bureaucracy, and Public Choice* (Englewood Cliffs, NJ: Prentice-Hall, 1991).

2 B. Guy Peters expressed a contrary view in his review of institutionalism in *Institutional Theory in Political Science: The New Institutionalism* (London: Continuum, 1999), 141.

3 The political science literature is rich in the study of institutions. I am thinking here of the work of Sam Finer and Carl Friedrich, among many others. See, for example, S.E. Finer, *The History of Government from the Earliest Times* (Oxford: Oxford University Press, 1997), and C.J. Friedrich, *Constitutional Government and Democracy: Theory and Practice in Europe and America* (Boston: Ginn, 1950). The reader will also want to consult the work of new institutionalists. See, among others, J.G. March and J.P. Olsen, *Rediscovering Institutions* (New York: Free Press, 1989).

4 See, among many others, Dunleavy, *Democracy, Bureaucracy, and Public Choice*.

5 Peters, *Institutional Theory in Political Science*, 53.

6 W.R. Scott, "Symbols and Organizations: From Bernard to the Institutionalists," in *Organization Theory*, ed. O.E. Williamson (Oxford: Oxford University Press, 1995), 33.

7 See, among many others, R.N. Johnson and G.D. Libecap, *The Federal Civil Service System and Problem of Bureaucracy* (Chicago: University of Chicago Press, 1994).

8 See, among others, L. Kiser and E. Ostrom, "The Three Worlds of Action: A Metatheoretical Synthesis of Institutional Approaches," in *Strategies of Political Inquiry*, ed. E. Ostrom (Beverly Hills, CA: Sage, 1982), 179.

9 There is a body of literature on this point. See, for example, A. Giddens, *The Constitution of Society: Outline of the Theory of Structuralism* (Cambridge: Cambridge University Press, 1984). Giddens insists that the relationship between agent and structure is dual.

10 Henry Mintzberg, "America's monumental failure of management," *Globe and Mail*, 16 March 2009, A13.

11 See, among many others, Donald J. Savoie, *Court Government and the Collapse of Accountability in Canada and the United Kingdom* (Toronto: University of Toronto Press, 2008).

12 Donald R. Songer, *The Transformation of the Supreme Court of Canada: An Empirical Examination* (Toronto: University of Toronto Press, 2008), 253.

13 Ibid.

14 Alan Greenspan, quoted in Neil Reynolds, "Poor devils and the lords of finance," www.theglobeandmail.com, 25 February 2009.

15 Hugh Heclo, "Campaigning and Governing: A Conspectus," in *The Permanent Campaign and Its Future*, ed. Norman J. Ornstein and Thomas E. Mann (Washington, DC: American Enterprise Institute, 2000), 15.

16 Peter Bachrach, *The Theory of Democratic Elitism: A Critique* (Boston: Little, Brown, 1967).

17 Tony Wright, MP, made this point in his "Doing Politics Differently," *Political Quarterly* annual lectures, 4 March 2009, www.interscience.wiley.com/journal/poqu.

18 See Fritz Scharpf, *Games Real Actors Play: Actor-Centered Institutionalism in Policy Research* (Boulder, CO: Westview, 1997).

19 Kjell Andersson, *Transparency and Accountability in Science and Politics: The Awareness Principle* (Basingstoke: Palgrave and Macmillan, 2008), 205.

20 Ibid.

21 C.E.S. Franks, *The Parliament of Canada* (Toronto: University of Toronto Press, 1987).

22 See, among others, Savoie, *Court Government*.

23 John P. Olsen, "Democratic Government, Institutional Autonomy and the Dynamics of Change," *West European Politics* 32, no. 3 (2009): 459.

24 Timothy Garton Ash, "Revolution at Westminster?" *Globe and Mail*, 9 July 2009, A13.

25 See, among others, Donald J. Savoie, *Breaking the Bargain: Public Servants, Ministers, and Parliament* (Toronto: University of Toronto Press, 2003).

26 On Ottawa's pension plan, see Canada, Treasury Board of Canada Secretariat Financial Statements (unaudited for the year ending 31 March 2008), (Ottawa: Treasury Board of Canada, undated), 15.

27 Ibid.

28 See Morley Gunderson, D. Hyatt, and C. Riddell, "Pay Differences between the Government and Private Sector: Labour Force Survey and Census Estimates," discussion paper, Canadian Policy Research Network, Ottawa, 2002. See also "Expenditure Review of Federal Public Sector: Overview," www.tbs.sct.gc.ca/ spsm-rqsp. The report is dated November 2006.

29 Data provided by the Government of Canada to the Commission of Inquiry into the Sponsorship Program and Advertising Activities, Ottawa, 31 May 2005. See also www.pwgsc.gc.ca/compensation/ppim/ppim-3-5-3-e.html, which provides for a general categorization of the reasons for Public Service of Canada employee departures.

30 "Volcker: Fed 'at Edge of Its Lawful and Implied Power,'" www.blogs.wsj.com/ economics, 8 April 2008.

31 See, among others, "Parliament to pass budget at lightning speed: MPs," *Hill Times* online, www.thehilltimes, 23 February 2009.

32 See, for example, R. Axelrod, *The Evolution of Cooperation* (New York: Basic Books, 1984).

33 I. Sened, "Contemporary Theory of Institutions in Perspective," *Journal of Theoretical Politics* 3, no. 4 (1991): 379–402.

34 Anthony Downs, *Inside Bureaucracy* (Boston: Little, Brown, 1967).

35 See, among many others, A. Etzioni, *A Comparative Analysis of Complex Organizations: On Power, Involvement, and their Correlates* (New York: Free Press, 1995).

Abelson, Donald, 180
access to information, 17–18, 106,
114–15; and audits, 122; and CBC, 119;
and communications, 124; and decision
making, 122, 127; and emphasis shift
to individuals, 127; financial resources
for, 121; and government operations,
120; Harper government and, 123–4;
media and, 118–19; and minister-
public servant relationship, 120; MPs
and, 97, 199; and "open" government,
125–6; and oral culture, 122; and
politician–public servant relationship,
119–20; and principal-agency theory,
236; and public sector, 118–23; and
public service, 209; and public service
anonymity, 107, 120, 164, 183; and
record keeping, 125; response to
requests, 124; sidestepping of, 12,
121–2, 123–4; and trust in
government, 126. *See also*
transparency
Access to Information Act, 107, 114–15,
122
accountability: business-management
model and, 157; citizens and, 14;
of courts, 229; of executive, 196–7;
federal government and, 150; of

government, 199, 228; Harper
government and, 16, 116–17, 123–4,
220; location of power and, 18; MPs
and, 199; of officers of Parliament, 77,
80–1, 229; Parliament and, 196–7, 199,
228, 236; political parties and, 196–7;
public-private partnerships and, 9, 65;
transparency and, 113, 236
accounting officers, 124, 220
Adelphia, 49
agents of Parliament. *See* officers of
Parliament
airports, 84
Alboim, Elly, 102
Alcock, Reg, 95–6
American Enterprise Association, 175
Amos, Sheldon, 71
Anderson Governance Group, 53
announcements: outside Parliament,
197–8; policy making by, 139
AOL, 20
appointment(s): of deputy ministers, 141,
210, 233; governors general and, 76; of
judges, 75–6; patronage, 142; power
of, 141
Armstrong, Robert, 104
Asia-Pacific Economic Cooperation
(APEC) summit, 129

Atlantic Institute for Market Studies
(AIMS), 176, 179
Atlantic provinces: globalization and,
31–2. *See also* New Brunswick
Attlee, Clement, 29, 106–7
Aucoin, Peter, 210
audit committees. *See* department and
agency audit committees (DAACs)
Auditor General, Office of, 77–8, 80
Australia: decision making in, 145–6;
financial crisis of 2008–09 and, 24;
"whole-of-government" in, 7
auto industry, 20, 21, 37, 40–1, 218
Axworthy, Lloyd, 155
Axworthy, Tom, 91, 143

Bagehot, Walter, 70–1, 120
Baird, John, 201, 202, 223
Balkin, Jack, 134
Bank of Canada, 8, 189, 215, 240
Bank of England, 8, 83
banks, 8; centralization of decision
making in, 58–9; chief economists at,
205; decision making in, 58–9; finan-
cial crisis of 2008–09 and, 21, 24–5,
26; investment bankers and, 58–9
Barrington, Nicholas, 122
Bausch & Lomb, 35
Bazowski, Raymond, 75
Bear Stearns, 8, 24, 83, 215, 240
Beeson, Ken, 161
Bennett, Carolyn, 79
Berardi, Jennifer, 65
Bernanke, Bernard, 24–5
Bezes, Philippe, 172
Bill of Rights (UK), 70
bin Laden, Osama, 215
Birch, A.H., 165
Bismarck, Otto von, 107–8
Blackburn, Lord, 71
Blair, Tony: and Bank of England, 83; and
centralization, 198; concentration of
power by, 130; modernization of gov-
ernment, 219; and private sector, 29;
and private-sector model for govern-
ment, 158; on time needed for action in
government, 200
Blinder, Alan, 25

bloggers, political, 90
BMW, 21
boards of directors, 47, 49, 50–1, 52–4,
56
Bok, Derek, 14–15
Bourgon, Jocelyne, 211
Braun, Aurel, 217
Bre-X, 49
Brodie, Ian, 185, 187
Brookings Institution, 175
Brown, Gordon, 9, 38, 103
Bryce, Bob, 202
Budd, Alan, 83
budgets, 5–16, 79, 81–2, 204, 206, 224–5,
240
bureaucrats/bureaucracy: and change,
222; and "conditioned instrument of
power," 17; cost of, 222–3; criticisms
of, 153–4, 155–6, 210, 214, 222; deal
making by, 35; and decision making,
14, 228; influence of, 14; and inter-
national/regional organizations, 168;
loss of credibility, 17; and policy, 14,
15, 156; politicians and, 15, 154, 156–7;
and power, 14, 15, 146, 153; and record
keeping, 126; and secrecy, 126; sharing responsibility with others, 159–62;
think tanks/research institutes and,
177; in UK, 154–5. *See also* public
servants/service
Bush, George W., 27, 134, 137
business schools, 47–8
Business Week, 56–7

Cabinet: Chrétien and, 140; and clerks
of privy council, 207; decision making
by, 200–2; as focus group, 193, 200–2;
Harper and, 140; and PCO, 208; power
of, 200; prime ministers and, 133, 134,
140, 193, 200, 228
Caesar, Julius, 3, 5
Caledon Institute for Social Policy, 176,
180
California, Proposition 13 in, 154
Cameron, David, 88–9
Campbell, Colin, 145
Canada Customs and Revenue Agency
(CCRA), 167

departments, 149; ministers' proposals and, 201; policy-making process and, 144; power and, 127; prime ministers and, 127, 143, 149; in public-private partnerships, 63; public servants and, 212; responsibility for, 7–8, 220; transparency and, 128; by Treasury Board, 149

Declaration of Rights (UK), 70

deference: decline of, 107, 214; media and, 13; and private sector, 11; toward public sector, 13–14; transparency and, 107

de Gaulle, Charles, 194

democracy. *See* representative democracy

Democracy Watch, 109

department and agency audit committees (DAACs), 116–17, 150

Department of Defence, 171

Department of External Affairs, 202, 208

Department of Finance, 16, 79, 191, 202, 203, 204–6

Department of Fisheries and Oceans, 15

Department of Foreign Affairs, 10, 36–7, 84, 203, 204, 206

Department of Foreign Affairs and International Trade, 78

Department of Indian Affairs and Northern Development, 12, 121

Department of Industry, 202, 206

Department of Justice, 199

Department of National Defence, 216

Department of Regional Economic Expansion (DREE), 31

departments: access to information and, 122; central agencies and, 202–3; communications specialists within, 103; and consultants, 182; decision making and, 149; deputy ministers and, 233; documentation sent to Parliament, 199; expansion of, 148; individuals and, 202; monitoring by central agencies, 116; and policy, 152, 160; and power, 202–8, 227; prime ministers and, 149; and public opinion surveys, 100; regional offices of, 148; senior civil servants and, 162; trust in, 15

deputy ministers: appointment of, 141, 210, 233; and departments, 233; influence of, 191–2; PCO and, 208; pension scheme, 204; power of, 227; prime ministers and, 210, 218, 233; resembling politicians, 237, 238; transparency and, 122–3. *See also* senior public servants

designated public office holders (DPOHs), 186–7

Dey Report, 50–1

Dimon, Jamie, 59

Dion, Stéphane, 88, 96, 202, 205, 224

disclosure: laws, 107; and private sector, 118; of wrongdoing, 116

Dodge, David, 39, 189

Doern, Bruce, 176–7

Douglas, James, 144

Douglas, T.C., 29

Drummond, Don, 205

Dworkin, Ronald, *Law's Empire*, 68

Easter, Wayne, 199–200

Easton, David, 230

Economic Advisory Council, 62

Economic Club of Canada, 205

economic development/growth: of Canada, 39; in Canadian North, 144; economics vs politics and, 31; globalization and, 43–5; government intervention and, 33; liberal regulatory climate and, 34–5; market forces and, 43–5; private sector and, 9; during 1970s, 29

economic nationalism, 29

efficiency: government reforms and, 153; of private vs public sector, 9, 62, 153; in public sector, 157

election campaigns/elections: candidate-centred, 98; gaffes in, 92, 94; Internet and, 90–1; lobbyists and, 185–6; media and, 89–90, 93–4; party leaders and, 94, 99, 221; as permanent, 87, 94, 95–9, 101, 234–5; and political consultants, 98; political parties and, 14, 91, 197; and power, 4; voter turnout, 4, 94. *See also* candidates

outside experts, 174; and parliamentary budget officer, 79, 206; and party leaders, 91–2, 94; and personalism, 221; and persuasion, 86; and political parties, 88; and politicians, 88–9, 95; pollsters and, 100; power of, 13, 86, 93–5, 104; and power within government, 103; presidents and, 102; prime ministers and, 102; professional codes of, 89; and public interest, 111, 112; and public service, 86, 104, 209; and RCMP, 82; in representative democracy, 101; and scandals, 102; single-issue movements and, 162; sovereignty and, 13; spin specialists and, 95, 102–3; tabloid, 89; and think tanks/research institutes, 175, 176, 180, 205; and transparency, 107, 118; and voters, 101; and war rooms, 88. *See also* journalism/journalists

Medvedev, Dmitry, 217

members of Parliament (MPs): and access to information legislation, 97, 199; and accountability of government, 199; ambitions of, 141; and citizens, 227; and constituencies, 97; courts and, 71; documents received by, 97–8; marginalization of, 227; as ombudsmen, 97; and Parliament, 195; and Supreme Court appointments, 76; visibility of, 97

Mexico, currency crisis in, 39

military, 16, 214, 216

Mill, John Stuart, *Representative Government*, 6

ministerial exempt staff, 209

ministerial responsibility, 152, 220

ministers: and communications specialists, 103; individual, 201; influence of, 201; and lobbyists, 184; offices of, 98, 103; and Parliament, 197; and partisan advisers, 210; and power, 130, 201; prime ministers and, 130, 201–2, 218; and public opinion surveys, 99; and public servants, 120, 208–9; skills of, 238

Mintz, Jack, 62, 173

Mintzberg, Henry, 27, 233

missteps. *See* gaffes/missteps

Mitterand, François, 194

Moncton, NB, business in, 19–20, 35

monetary policy, 34, 83

Moody's, 26

Moore, Michael, 109

Moore, Stephen, *Rich States, Poor States*, 34

Moores, Frank, 185

mortgages, 8, 24, 26, 27

Mulroney, Brian, 166; and access to information legislation, 114; and bureaucrats, 153, 155; and free trade agreement with US, 177; and growth of federal public service, 155; and Moores, 185; and Nielsen, 157; and PCO, 207

Murphy, Mike, 73

National Audit Office (UK), 80

National Bank of Canada, 58

National Council of Welfare, 180

National Energy Policy (NEP), 146, 185

nation-states: foreign direct investment and, 30; global economy and, 7, 20–1, 45–6; limiting of role, 45–6; market and, 10; and regional trade agreements, 39; and screening of foreign investment, 30–1. *See also* government(s)

neoliberalism, 9

networking: governing by, 163–4; hierarchy vs, 216–17; PCO and, 145; and public servants, 161

Neville, Bill, 185

New Brunswick: business in, 19–20; French immersion program in, 73; health-care services in, 73; jobs transferred from, 19–20; outside experts and government of, 172–3. *See also* Moncton, NB

New Public Management (NPM), 136–7, 150, 172

news management, 94, 95, 98, 103

Newsweek, 90, 193–4

New York Times, 25

Niagara Corporation, 57

Nicholson, Peter J., 179

Nicholson, Rob, 74

17, 134; sharing of power with one another, 138; US, 134, 137

Prime Minister's Office (PMO), 140, 142; and APEC summit, 129; and RCMP, 129; Trudeau and, 140

prime ministers (PMs): access to information and, 120; agendas of, 142–3; and Cabinet, 133, 134, 140, 193, 200, 228; chiefs of staff for, 190; clerks of privy council and, 190, 191, 203–4, 207–8, 220; and constituencies, 142; courts of, 201; and decision making, 127, 143, 149; and deputy ministers, 192, 210, 218, 233; duties of, 141–2; federal government and, 133; and foreign affairs, 203; governors general and, 131, 133; international gatherings and, 137, 138–9; and line departments, 149; and lobbyists, 184, 185; loose power of, 200–1; management responsibilities, 149; and media, 102; meetings of, 141–2; and ministers, 130, 201–2, 218; missteps by, 132; NPM and, 136–7; outside experts and, 179–80; overload problem, 144; and Parliament, 129, 197; and partisan advisers, 210, 222; and PCO, 140, 141, 142; personalism and, 217; pet projects of, 139; and PMO, 140; and policy, 136, 141, 144, 146; pollsters and, 99–100; power of, 5, 17, 129–30, 131–5, 136, 139–40, 214, 232; and power of appointment, 141; priorities of, 139–40, 141; proroguing of Parliament, 132; and public servants, 198; responsibilities of, 133; responsiveness to, 222; and Supreme Court appointments, 76; time and, 141–3, 222; and "what matters is what works," 194, 235

principal-agency theory, 113–14, 236–7, 238, 241

privacy: laws, 124–5; media and, 88–9; in private sector, 117; transparency and, 124–5

privacy commissioner, 78–9

private sector: and Bali climate-change conference, 10; citizens and, 11; and competitors, 118; deference towards, 11; democratic deficit and, 111; disclosure and, 118; and economic growth, 9; efficiency of, 9, 62; and foreign vs domestic governments, 35–6; government front-line managers and, 137, 172; hierarchy in, 66; influence of, 27; internationalization of operations, 35–6; IT in, 59–61; language of, 9–10; and lobbyists, 62, 184; management in, 9, 216, 219; media and, 118; middle managers in, 59–60; non-performers in, 223; partnerships with public sector (*see* public-private partnerships); personalism in, 215–16, 217; politicians and, 157; power of, 9–11, 29, 61–2, 66; principal-agency theory and, 114; privacy in, 117; public interest and, 111–12; public interest groups and, 112–13; public sector compared to, 9; public-sector emulation of, 62–3, 216, 219, 221–2, 233; relations with public sector, 61–2; responsibility in, 49; risk management in, 59; state corporations sold to, 157; transparency in, 56, 57, 108–13, 118, 127–8; values of, 66. *See also* corporate governance; firms; transnational corporations

privatization, 29, 215

Privy Council Office (PCO): and accounting officer model, 124; and Cabinet, 208; and deputy ministers, 208; economic units, 205; power of, 203, 206–8; prime ministers and, 141, 142; and public opinion surveys, 100; size of, 140–1, 145, 207. *See also* clerks of privy council

provincial governments: and Charter of Rights and Freedoms, 75; power of, 135–6; responsibilities of, 165

Public Accounts Committee (Canada), 77, 80, 124, 199, 236

Public Accounts Committee (UK), 80

public administration: hierarchy and, 226; media and, 13; non-governmental actors in, 159; organizational involvement and, 160; personalism in, 226;

prime ministers and, 133; and private sector terminology, 63

Public Interest Disclosure Act (PIDA) (UK), 116

public interest groups. *See* interest groups

public opinion surveys: departments and, 100; and election candidates, 99; federal government and, 100; and location of power, 99; and ministers, 99; and party leaders, 101; PCO and, 100; and permanence of election campaigns, 87; political leaders and, 93; and political parties, 101; and politicians, 198; on public servants, 14–15; and representative democracy, 12–13; and senior public servants, 100

Public Policy Forum (PPF), 177, 179, 180

public-private partnerships, 9, 11, 62–6, 215; accountability in, 9, 65; and blurring of public-private lines, 66; concerns with, 65; contribution of, 65; goals and, 65; and interest groups, 210; networks, 64; politicians and, 64; and power, 9, 64–5; and representative democracy, 235; and responsibility, 64–5; and services delivery, 11, 48, 158; and thickness of government, 65; values and, 66

public sector: access to information and, 118–23; business-management model in, 157–8; deference towards, 13–14; efficiency in, 157; emulation of private sector, 62–3, 216, 219, 221–2, 233; in France, 172; load shedding by, 64; loss of power by, 17; management in, 64, 158; non-performers in, 223; partnerships with private sector (*see* public-private partnerships); path dependency in, 158; personalism in, 217; principal-agency theory and, 113–14; private sector efficiency and, 9, 62; reforms to, 153–4; relations with private sector, 61–2; transparency in, 113–17, 128; trust in, 14; values of, 66

Public Sector Integrity Commission, 116

Public Servant Disclosure Protection Act, 116

Public Servant Disclosure Protection Tribunal, 116

public servants/service: access to information legislation and, 12, 120, 121–2, 164, 209; anonymity of, 107, 120, 163, 164, 189; and change, 198; concentration in Ottawa, 148; consultants and, 160, 182–3, 210; cost of, 238–9; criticism of, 208; cuts to, 156–7; and decision making, 145, 212; defensiveness of, 211; divided loyalties of, 212; and economic performance, 154; emulation of private sector, 62–3; fault line within, 238; in France, 194; and government's agenda for change, 210; growth of, 145, 155; horizontality and, 147–8, 161; individuals among, 198, 208, 211, 215, 228; and interest groups, 210; journalists and, 189; loss of confidence in, 68, 208; loss of self-confidence, 228; and management, 9, 157, 210; media and, 86, 209; ministerial offices and, 98; ministers and, 120, 208–9; morale of, 14, 211; networking by, 161, 163; neutral competence of, 159; new skills for, 161; and news management, 98; and oral culture, 121–2; and outside experts, 179; partisanship of, 210; and policy, 210, 228; and policy making, 153, 159, 160, 211, 212; politicians and, 86, 119–20, 126, 153, 155, 183, 208–9, 211, 228; and power, 150, 208–11, 227; prime ministers and, 198; public beliefs regarding, 14–15; and RCMP, 82; reform of, 211; responsive vs neutral competence of, 159–60; size of, 147, 239; and spin doctors, 95; strikes, 131; in UK, 156–7; unions, 222–3; visibility of, 209–10. *See also* bureaucrats/bureaucracy

Public Service Commission, 141

Public Service 2000 (PS 2000), 211

Public Service Staff Relations Act, 167

Putin, Vladimir, 217

Quebec: labour mobility agreement with France, 136; as nation, 140; seccession from Canada, 72; UNESCO and, 135

Question Period, 109, 197, 199

Rae, Bob, 96
RAND Corporation, 56
rating services, 26
rational choice theory, 230–1, 232
Rattner, Steven, 218
Rayner, Derek, 157
RCMP (Royal Canadian Mounted Police), 78–9, 82–3, 129
Reagan, Ronald, 29; and Grace, 157; and public sector, 153
regional economic development agencies, 206
Reisman, Simon, 191
representative democracy: courts and, 72; democratic deficit in, 111; and elites, 235; hierarchy and, 235; judicial activism and, 73; media in, 101; personalism and, 226, 237; political centre and, 94; and political equality, 235; political parties and, 93, 227; power and, 4; public opinion surveys and, 12–13; trust in, 113
Representative Government (Mill), 6
research institutes. *See* think tanks/ research institutes
responsibility: in banking, 58–9; of boards of directors, 51, 52–4; borders/ boundaries and, 6; communications technologies and, 48; and complexity of machinery of government, 234; corporate governance reform and, 50; for corporate scandals, 49; and decision making, 220; financial crisis of 2008–09 and, 25–6; globalization and, 7–8, 22; influence vs, 49; intergovernmental relations/agreements and, 165, 168; IT and, 59–61; ministerial, 152, 220; power and, 3, 5; private sector and, 9, 49; in publicly listed vs private companies, 58; and public-private partnerships,

63–5; shared, 8, 15, 226; sidestepping of, 16, 22; transparency and, 12
The Return of the Imperial Presidency, 134
Revenue Canada, 167
revenues, forecasting of, 84
Rich States, Poor States (Laffer, Moore), 34
rights movements, 161–2
right to know, 107
risk management: of banks, 25; DAAC and, 117; IT and, 60; in private sector, 59
Rivard, Michel, 89–90
Roberts, Alasdair, 125–6
Robertson, Gordon, 145, 207
Roman Catholic Church, 16–17
Roosevelt, Franklin D., 29, 89, 134
Rothkopf, David, 44, 45
Rousseau, Henri-Paul, 217
royal commissions, 181
Russell, Bertrand, 3, 4, 48, 229

Sarbanes-Oxley Act: avoidance by firms, 51; and CEOs, 54; and "command and control" management style, 127; cost of compliance with, 55, 56, 57; private equity firms and, 57; publicly traded companies and, 56, 57, 118; sidestepping, 195
Sarkozy, Nicholas, 194
Saucier Report, 51
Savoie, Donald, *Governing from the Centre,* 129–30, 194, 200, 205
Sawatsky, John, 185
scandals: corporate, 48, 49; media and, 102; RCMP, 82; sponsorship, 77–8, 123, 150; and transparency, 108. *See also* controversies
Scott, Andy, 121
Scott, W.R., 232
Sears, Robin, 89
Securities Exchange Commission, 57
Senate (Canada), 73
senior public servants: and departments, 162; emulation of private-sector

Times (London), 88–9
Tomkins, Adam, 69, 73, 195–6
Toronto Stock Exchange Committee on Corporate Governance, *Where Were the Directors?*, 50–1
Toyota, 20
trade: agreements, 5, 39, 138, 177; globalization of, 37
trade union movement, 16
transnational corporations: Internet and, 42; power and, 61, 138
transparency, 105; and accountability, 113, 236; and boards of directors, 56; CBC and, 119; CEOs and, 55; Chrétien and, 107; citizens and, 14; and "command and control" management style, 127–8; and decision making, 128; deference and, 107; and democratic deficit, 111; and deputy ministers, 122–3; disadvantages of, 107–8; financial costs of, 121; and firms "going private" or "dark," 57; and gaffes, 107; and government, 108–9; "idiot," 125; and individuals, 127; and influence, 164; interest groups and, 107, 109, 112; of judicial appointments, 76; in lobbying, 186–7; media and, 107; and "open" government, 128; opposition to, 106–7; and paper trail, 12, 120, 164; and politicians, 119; power and, 106, 109–10, 111, 123, 126–8, 164; and privacy laws, 124–5; in private sector, 56, 57, 108–13, 118, 127–8; of publicly traded firms, 111; in public sector, 113–17, 128; and regional tensions, 120; resistance to, 123; and responsibility, 12; scandals and, 108; and senior public servants, 119–20, 123; shareholders and, 108; sidestepping, 195; and trust, 112, 121; and truth, 107; unethical behaviour and, 111–12; and value of ignorance, 120–1. *See also* access to information
Transparency International, 109
Travers, Jim, 15, 82
Treasury Board, 149; Secretariat, 149, 167, 203, 209

Trudeau, Pierre: access to information legislation, 114; agenda of, 143; Chrétien and, 132; and constitution, 146; on declining role of Parliament, 96; and FIRA, 29–30; as *le boss*, 132, 133; and Lee, 185; meetings with senior officials, 141; on MPs, 96; and NEP, 146; and PCO, 207; and PMO, 140; and size of federal government, 147
trust: access to information legislation and, 126; by citizens for government, 113, 121; in government departments, 15; media and, 102; in power, 109; in private vs public sector, 68; and public sector, 14; in representative democracy, 113; transparency and, 112, 121
Turner, John, 199

United Kingdom: accounting officers in, 124; banks in, 24; Bill of Rights, 70; bureaucracy in, 154–5; Civil Service Code, 116; civil service in, 156–7; Committee of Public Accounts, 80; corporate governance in, 51; Declaration of Rights, 70; economy of, 33, 43; European Convention of Human Rights and, 71–2; executive agencies in, 166, 167; FDI in, 30; Freedom of Information Act, 122; House of Commons, 70–1; Human Rights Act, 12, 71–2; and IMF, 33; "joined-up" government in, 6–7, 152; Judicial Appointments Commission, 75–6; lobbying in, 184; media in, 118–19; modernization of government in, 219; monarchy in, 69–71; National Audit Office, 80; officers of Parliament in, 80; Parliament, 69–71; power in, 69–70; privatization in, 29; Public Interest Disclosure Act (PIDA), 116; public-private partnerships in, 63; public service oral culture in, 122; Reform Acts, 196; spending of, 21; Thatcher reforms and, 33; tsars in, 218
United Nations, 38; on capital controls, 30; climate-change conference, Nusa